Microeconomic Effects
of Monetary Policy
THE FALLOUT OF SEVERE MONETARY RESTRAINT

Microeconomic Effects of Monetary Policy

THE FALLOUT OF SEVERE MONETARY RESTRAINT

Ervin Miller

with *Alasdair Lonie*

ST MARTIN'S PRESS
New York

Library of Congress Cataloging in Publication Data

Miller, Ervin, 1918–
  Microeconomic effects of monetary policy.
  Includes bibliographical references and index.
  1. Monetary policy. 2. Monetary policy—Great Britain. I.
Title.
HG221.M645   332.4'9   77–17980
ISBN 0–312–53173–7

Fryed. 18.50/16.65/9/18/81

Contents

Tables

Figures

To

C. R. WHITTLESEY

Teacher, Colleague, Friend

Early Dissenter from Monetary Orthodoxy

Preface

The US economy has been engulfed in a difficult ordeal since 1965. In an environment already filled with fears of inflation (not because of significantly rising prices, but mainly because of the failure of prices to fall in recessions after that of 1948–9), a significant inflation developed during the escalation of US involvement in the Vietnam War. A braking of the rate of inflation in late 1966 and early 1967 (by monetary stringency) proved temporary and prices soon resumed their upward march, leading to the use of extraordinarily severe monetary restraint in 1968–70 with resulting recession in 1970–1. Then followed price controls, agricultural shortages, world-wide boom, price decontrol, formation of OPEC and great rises in oil prices, the severest monetary squeeze in US history, and finally, mass unemployment as inflation ground on inexorably.

In the context of these matters, this book addresses itself to the adverse consequences and indeed futility of the use of severe monetary restraint to control an inflation whose causes are not generally demand oriented. Society has magnified the problem by allowing fear of inflation to create fear of full employment. In turn society has become a victim of its own fears, creating a psychological straitjacket which has paralyzed the creative and logical instincts of large numbers of sophisticated people. This point was illustrated in a press account of a speech made several years ago by the chairman of the Federal Reserve Board in which he was reported as saying that while a looser monetary policy could logically be used to combat unemployment, it was not desirable since public awareness of rising rates of growth of the money supply would accelerate inflationary expectations and so possibly lead to inflationary business behavior.

It is my view that society, aside from setting unreasonably optimistic goals, has been unable to cope more successfully with its recent economic difficulties partly because of an excessive reverence for central bankers and economists. Central bankers, operating in an aura of relative mystery, seem to have regarded themselves (at

least since World War II), as sent from heaven to protect an un-
enlightened citizenry from the sin of creating inflation. Most modern
economists have sought rigor in economic analysis and have found
it typically by building models of economic performance resting on
assumptions very often remote from the real world. Nevertheless,
many of these economists somehow confidently manage to apply
the findings of their model worlds to the real world. All too frequently those findings have led in recent years to fears of full
employment.

Central bankers, economists and the governmental authorities
whom economists advise, are in a significant sense 'trigger happy'.
Unemployment is the first medicine that seems to come to mind
in their efforts to contain inflation. Always, however, this is done
from a position of economic security by the policy makers. I am
reminded of a brilliant piece of satire by Russell Baker in the *New
York Times* of 6 October 1970. In this piece – an imaginary tele-
vision interview – Mr Baker pictures an involuntarily unemployed
worker as an inflation fighter, a sort of economic infantryman in
the front lines of the war against inflation. This worker revels in
the performance of his patriotic duty of fighting inflation by being
unemployed. He achieves his highest happiness by looking for work
all day and not finding any, since he knows he 'won't be generating
any of those ugly inflationary pressures'.

It is a familiar maxim that war is too important to be left to the
generals. Analogously monetary policy is too important to be left
to central bankers and their economist advisors. Monetary policy
is in fact partly employment policy and additionally acts as a major
force on fiscal policy at all levels of government. In all-embracing
matters that profoundly affect the welfare of the entire population,
as do these, the opinions of an enlightened, intelligent citizenry
should prevail, for subjective values lie behind the priorities established. This book is addressed to such a group and not merely to
economists.

It is customary at this point to thank all who have helped the
writer. I am very grateful to several economists who have read and
criticized an earlier draft of this study. I refrain from identifying
them to spare them captive association with unorthodox and possibly
unpopular views.

Philadelphia, June 1977   *Ervin Miller*

Introduction

1.1 The Ideological Framework

In the United States and most western European countries, worship of a free market, at least in the sense of lip service, is a distinguishing feature of economic life. A free market is assumed to be a prerequisite for freedom of consumer choice. Philosophically, this is presumed to embody economic democracy, which to some is a corollary of political democracy. Free market worship (which in practice tends to mean private market worship) is widespread, embracing in varying degree conservatives and liberals, economists and non-economists, capital and labor. True, there are exceptions and variations, with liberals, for example, tending to (1) want ground rules for insuring that free markets are fair markets and (2) permit a wider state sector than would conservatives. Overall, however, this seems a fair characterization of the situation.

Conceivably, one may attempt to challenge the foregoing characterization in terms of the Keynesian revolution. One might argue that, with the Great Depression of the 1930s as a backdrop, Keynesian non *laissez-faire* thinking emerged, gradually conquering most of the non-socialist world. Macro-demand management became respectable and, indeed, the normal state of affairs, with fiscal policy generally accorded a major role. Arguments persisted concerning the optimum methods of demand management (including their relative importance) and the levels at which to maintain aggregate demand. However, given the levels of aggregate demand set, there was a fairly wide consensus that market forces should determine the responses of the factors of production (subject, of course, to constraints involving maintenance of minimum standards in areas such as health, welfare and competitive conditions, constraints whose rigor was also a source of controversy).

Keynes, it will be recalled, was trying to save capitalism, not supplant it.

In the post-Keynesian world, the very methodology of mainstream economics was one of the key forces insuring the dominance of a basically free market ideology. Post-Keynesian mainstream economists generally sought quantification of economic relations and rigor in analysis (implying, for many, existence of, and search for, 'laws'). They generally sought to rid the subject of a backbone of verbal analysis that had limited capabilities for manipulation of numerous simultaneous variables. They sought to emulate the physical sciences in precision of analysis, to convert economics to 'economic science.' This necessarily involved a search for regularities in human motivation and responses both at any given moment of time and to some extent over time.

Reputations were – and are – made by the discovery of abstract mathematical–economic relationships and by their statistical testing. Reputations were far less likely to be made by focusing on difficulties of institutional origin and finding solutions for them. Thus, young economists seeking success and recognition for the most part stayed within the paths of finding new, or refining old, *a priori* mathematical–economic relationships or testing hypotheses statistically.[1] Conservatism reigned, with no significant challenge to existing institutional arrangements. Indeed, if anything, the kingdom of conservatism was probably strengthened. In business finance, for example, mathematical economists conquered the field, extending the reign of alleged economic law farther and sharply reducing major concern of economists with institutional problems.

These fundamental tendencies seem to have been strongest in the United States, but they have persisted in varying degrees in other developed countries. Canada, not surprisingly, resembles the United States very closely. Australia, too, is similar. The United Kingdom, on the other hand, has been subject to greater interference with market forces and perhaps to less worship of them. However, the economic failures and difficulties of Britain have been seized upon by critics as evidence of the folly of 'contradicting' economic law. The importance of government guidance in the successes of the Japanese and French economies, meanwhile, tends conveniently to be overlooked.

Ultimately one runs into the fact that the field of economics is international. Scientific methodology has penetrated the world and made prisoners of its priests. Demand management has become the basic function of macroeconomic policy-makers, with the fallout or micro-consequences left to the social worker, the politicians, the harsh punishment of the market place, and if necessary the bankruptcy courts.[2]

Institutional economics as a school or force has virtually been extinguished in developed countries. Except for a scattering of generally uninfluential economists, the institutional field has been left to a handful of socialist economists, labor union economists (who have little intellectual influence in professional economic circles), governmental agencies, social welfare specialists and an occasional prominent economist dissenter (e.g. John K. Galbraith and Kenneth Boulding in the United States). Institutional economics by definition tried to examine the *real* world, where it could find unhappy economic conditions related to institutional situations and not to economic 'laws,' thus calling for non-*laissez-faire* solutions beyond demand management. In the latter twentieth century, principal interest in institutional economics has been in less developed countries.

1.2 The Anti-Micro-Policy Environment

The anti-micro-policy environment is defined here as one in which concern for the overall welfare of individuals is largely subordinated to macroeconomic considerations in attempts to control business cycle and price movements in the short run. Concern for the individual extends not much beyond assuring funds for subsistence. Policy focuses on broad devices such as tax rates, government expenditure levels and monetary management. The following paragraphs illustrate the implications of such an environment.

Here *aggregate* unemployment rates are placed on center stage. High unemployment rates in specific sectors are viewed by the policy-maker as having relatively low importance, while low rates in other sectors are viewed as of high importance and used in part to justify the necessity of *aggregate* unemployment rates as high as, e.g. 5 or $5\frac{1}{2}$ per cent as a goal.

With a free market orientation within a demand-management framework, adverse fallout affecting individuals can be attributed to structural conditions. A full-employment definition embodying a fairly high unemployment content can be justified on the grounds that the structure of the economy tends to produce inflation if virtually all who are seeking jobs can in fact find them. The policy-makers argue that a satisfactory unemployment rate, say 5 per cent, is really better than appears on the surface because for married males over, e.g. twenty-five years of age, the rate tends to be much less, say $2\frac{1}{2}$ per cent. The policy-makers conveniently ignore the alternative interpretation, namely that 5 per cent is worse than appears on the surface, because it embodies a 10 per cent unemployment rate for some groups. Strangely, also, $2\frac{1}{2}$ per cent for the favored group is not viewed as a disturbingly inflationary rate, but somehow it would be inflationary if those having 10 per cent unemployment were able to establish a similar $2\frac{1}{2}$ per cent category for themselves.

A condition of fairly high unemployment can also be viewed as embodying satisfactory levels of aggregate demand (and in turn can be viewed with equanimity) if there is evidence of large numbers of unfilled jobs. The unemployment is then regarded as structural and presumably shows the need for retraining of workers. In turn, want-ad (classified advertisement) data are developed as indicators of macroeconomic conditions and money is poured into manpower training programs. All of this fits neatly, of course, into a macroeconomic system mathematically expressed and controlled.

In this approach no real appraisal is made of society's needs and of the sector (private or public) best suited to fill those needs. In turn, no specifications are drawn of the job requirements to fill the needs and no analysis made of the availability of unemployed to meet the job requirements. (The closest approximation to tailoring production to meet society's real needs, in turn to tailoring the job requirements to the character of the potential labor force, was in World War II, with near-miraculous results.) In the United States, at least, there is no public evidence of governmental studies to produce an overall view of society's needs and resources and to develop a comprehensive plan to meet those needs with an appropriate distribution of tasks to the private and public sectors of the economy.

All of this is in the face of obvious starvation of the needs of the public sector in the United States. Cities are dirty and under-maintained generally; city parks are insufficient in number, in-adequate in facilities and often poorly maintained; museums are only partly open for lack of funds to pay guards and other per-sonnel. Here are a myriad of needs calling for the employment of the unskilled. Meanwhile, the unskilled are largely ignored because they are unskilled. Want-ads are often ubiquitous in the frivolous, socially less important private sectors where applicants are in short supply, while such advertisements are very limited in important public sectors where unemployment among potential applicants is heavy.

That elsewhere throughout the economic system there are large numbers of business firms and individuals who may be victims of macroeconomic policy is seemingly of little concern to policy-makers. One is reminded here of the old 'sin' theory of depression and its prescription of 'healthy' bankruptcies to facilitate recovery; i.e. a depression was viewed as a consequence of economic mis-conduct and a vehicle for secular change, allowing obsolete and non-viable industries to die. A healthy recovery required such in-dustries to vanish and economic miscreants to be purged from the system by failure.

In this macro-dominant approach to economic policy, aggregate statistics receive the focus of attention, but not all receive equal billing. Movements in the numbers of families living at or below presumed poverty levels (defined in terms of minimum levels of in-come needed for subsistence) are noted with interest occasionally. Unemployment rates are quoted with great frequency (partly, per-haps, for the political and fiscal significance they embody and partly, no doubt, for their market implications to the business world). Move-ment in aggregate numbers on relief rolls draws intermittent atten-tion, probably mainly because of the budgetary implications for state and local governments (and in the case of New York City, one suspects, as an indicator of the alleged absence of a 'work ethic' in large numbers of people).

Only occasionally is there a burst of journalistic coverage of the meaning of poverty, the personal consequences of living on relief. This is likely to occur when unemployment and distress are rising rapidly, and the stories are likely to be of the 'human interest' variety. Worse than lack of continuing journalistic attention,[3] probably, is the rarity of official studies of such conditions. The rarity of the exceptions to journalistic and official neglect lends dramatic qualities to the distressing conditions that may be found, e.g. in the congressional surveys of hunger in the South (in the 1960s) prompted by private medical surveys of malnutrition.

Ultimately then, aside from providing funds for subsistence, policy-makers and advisors tend to show only nominal concern for individuals *per se*. Economists and economic policy-makers take on the character of social engineers, while human beings are analogous to pieces of machinery. Dials are set on the controls and levels of employment result – for machines, persons and business firms, with machines and persons having seemingly equal emotional significance for policy-makers.[4]

1.3 Objectives of This Study

The principal objective of this study is to appraise the use of severely restrictive general monetary policy, a key form of demand management, as a tool to fight inflation. The focus is on those consequences of severe monetary restraint that tend to be overlooked or swept under the rug in the ideological framework and anti-micro-policy environment that have pervaded the world of economics in the post World War II era. The period since 1966 is singled out for study since it is the period in which restriction has been most severe and some of those consequences most serious. The analysis is in terms of the United States, but is applicable to most other developed capitalist economies in varying degrees.

What follows is essentially an institutional study of a world in which impediments to competitive conditions are large-scale and routine. Thoroughgoing use of demand management would pose only modest problems if those multitudinous barriers to competition were absent. A restriction of demand would then not have to be of disastrous proportions to end an inflation, and indeed, could cease at a full-employment level. A restriction of demand would not be accompanied by perverse increases in prices by semi-monopolistic units. Incomes policies would have no meaning in such a world, and economic planning would have far less reason to exist. Most of the unhappy situations that are the subject of this study also would not exist.

In the pages that follow there is concern with both economic and non-economic consequences of monetary policy. In the economic area we deal with impacts on the financial and real sectors. In the financial sector we are concerned with impacts on interest rates and capital values and implications of those impacts for individuals, business firms and non-profit organizations. We are also concerned with the stability of financial markets.

In the real sector we are concerned with impacts on costs, prices and allocation of resources. To be considered are implications for growth, domestically and internationally. We are very concerned with unemployment and its economic and social implications.

Other concerns include the character of the inflation engulfing the world since 1966 and the relevance of monetary policy to deal with that inflation. We also examine the implications of persistent use of restrictive monetary policy for the effectiveness and character of future uses of restrictive monetary policy.

Finally, we consider alternatives to the use of restrictive demand management as a primary vehicle for the containment of non-demand-pull inflation. This leads to broadening of the discussion and consideration of what has come to be called indicative economic planning and the role of incomes policies in such planning.

FOOTNOTES

1. Cf. Wassily Leontief, 'Theoretical Assumptions and Nonobserved Facts,' *American Economic Review*, March 1971, p. 3.
2. The challenge of the Monetarists does not alter these conclusions. They, too, are demand-managers, albeit with a different emphasis on tools and different judgements as to causal linkages in macroeconomic relationships. Their free market ideology, of course, tends to be much stronger than that of most Keynesian economists, at the limit calling for a strict monetary rule (i.e. a fixed rate of growth of the money supply) in terms of which aggregate demand is to operate.
3. It would be startling indeed to find a social welfare section in a major newspaper along with its regular sections such as business, theatre, real estate and automobiles.
4. Obviously, all establishment economic policy-makers and their advisors do not fall in this mold, nor does all federal domestic economic policy in the United

States reflect the picture given here. Typically, programs designed to reach people at a personal level (e.g. job-retraining and health care) are of a longer-run nature and aim at structural problems. It is in the management of cyclical problems and inflation that one sees relative indifference to human problems created beyond those of physical subsistence.

2 Impacts of Severe General Monetary Restraints on Prices and Financial Markets

2.1 Direct Inflationary Consequences of Rising Interest Rates – General Considerations

In earlier discussions of tight money, reference was occasionally made to interest rates as a cost of production, hence to rising interest rates as a force tending to increase prices. However, since interest rates were typically a small item in business costs except in such areas as real estate, public utilities and finance companies, the price-increasing aspects of tight money tended to be viewed as of generally minor consequence. Moreover, whatever cost impact existed was presumed a desirable deterrent to business expenditures, while efforts to prevent interest rate increases implied an increased supply of money which was viewed as undesirable since it presumably increased aggregate demand.

The matter attained new dimensions with the levels of interest rates and magnitudes of changes in them that appeared in the United States in 1965 and subsequent years. Table 2.1 shows for a number of recent years the growth of monetary interest paid, the growth of net interest originating in non-financial corporate business, the behavior of various interest rates, and selected relationships to key aggregates. Monetary interest paid, for example, rose about 250 per cent from 1965 to 1974, while net public and private debt rose about 100 per cent. As a proportion of national income, monetary interest paid rose from about $12\frac{1}{2}$ to about 22 per cent. At the interest rate levels existing in much of the decade beginning with 1965, most businesses no longer viewed interest as a nominal item; instead it was viewed as something to be managed very carefully as net interest originating in non-financial corporate businesses rose to levels not too far from profits tax liability, e.g. about 68 per cent in 1974 (see Table 2.1). Where interest was a major factor

Table 2.1 Debt and Interest in Relation to Selected US Income Accounts, and Sele

Year	Monetary interest paid (net of monetary interest received by government)[a]	National income	Monetary interest as per cent of national income	Net public and private debt (end of year)	Treasury bills 3-month new issue[b]	Conventiona home first mortgage contract rat (new homes
	(1)	(2)	(3)	(4)	(5)	(6)
1960	42.8	412.0	10.3	874.2	2.93	—
1965	70.3	566.0	12.5	1245.0	3.95	5.74
1966	79.7	622.2	12.8	1339.9	4.88	6.14
1967	87.9	655.8	13.4	1439.6	4.32	6.33
1968	99.3	714.4	13.9	1583.4	5.34	6.83
1969	116.4	767.9	15.2	1737.6	6.68	7.66
1970	133.1	798.4	16.7	1869.6	6.46	8.27
1971	140.9	858.1	16.4	2050.7	4.35	7.60
1972	154.5	951.9	16.2	2275.9	4.07	7.45
1973	196.5	1064.6	18.5	2532.1	7.04	7.78
1974	246.3	1135.7	21.7	2768.6	7.89	8.71

[a] Gross values, except for government.
[b] Averages.

Sources: *Survey of Current Business*, July 1969, p. 45; July 1972, p. 45; July 1973, p.
Federal Reserve Bulletin, December 1968, p. A32; January 1972, pp. A3
Economic Report of the President, January 1977, p. 265;
US Department of Commerce, *The National Income and Product Accounts of*

rest Rates, 1960, 1965–74 (dollar amounts in billions)

	State and local govt bonds^b	Corporate bonds (composite)^b	Gross domestic product of non-financial corporate business			Net interest as per cent of:	
Govt g-term ds^b			Total	Net interest originating	Profits tax liability	GDP	Profits tax liability
(8)	(9)	(10)	(11)	(12)		(13) $=\dfrac{(11)}{(10)}$	(14) $=\dfrac{(11)}{(12)}$
1	3.69	4.73	277.3	3.5	19.2	1.3	18.2
1	3.34	4.64	392.1	6.1	27.2	1.6	22.4
6	3.90	5.34	430.7	7.4	29.5	1.7	25.1
5	3.99	5.82	452.9	8.7	27.7	1.9	31.4
5	4.48	6.51	498.4	10.1	33.6	2.0	30.1
0	5.73	7.36	541.8	13.1	33.3	2.4	39.3
9	6.42	8.51	560.6	17.0	27.3	3.0	62.3
4	5.62	7.94	602.5	17.9	29.9	3.0	59.9
3	5.30	7.63	671.0	19.1	33.5	2.8	57.0
0	5.22	7.80	752.0	23.1	39.6	3.1	58.3
9	6.19	8.98	810.0	29.0	42.6	3.6	68.1

uary 1976, Part 2, pp. 8, 9, 24, 25; July 1976, pp. 27, 30, 64;
ril 1976, pp. A27, 28, 45;

ited States, 1929–1965: Statistical Tables, Washington, DC, 1966, pp. 151–2.

in costs, large changes were viewed as apprehensively as changes in labor costs or raw material costs.

It is also possible for severe monetary restraint to contribute to inflation by reducing aggregate supply to a greater extent than aggregate demand through the mechanism of unemployment. The unemployed, to the extent that personal savings are available, draw on them to buy goods and services. Unemployment insurance helps finance expenditures by those who are covered, but for limited periods of time. Finally, in the absence of personal resources, welfare payments finance spending by those without unemployment insurance coverage and by those who have exhausted their unemployment insurance benefits. Each of these means of meeting the needs of the unemployed sustains aggregate demand, preventing it from falling as much as earned income, while aggregate supply falls as a result of their unemployment with virtually no offset.[1] One rough measure of such a decrease in aggregate supply is possible with the familiar (US) rule that an increase of 1 percentage point in the unemployment rate gives rise roughly to a 3 per cent decline in GNP. In relation to a 4.0 per cent unemployment rate (one often viewed as desirable), there was thus loss of perhaps $65 billion in US output at the average 5.6 per cent unemployment rate of 1974 (about $4\frac{1}{2}$ per cent lost output). On the same basis, with an average unemployment rate of $8\frac{1}{2}$ per cent in 1975, there was a loss of some $200 billion in output (measured in current dollars in each case). The final folly of the unemployment approach to containing inflation is a *reductio ad absurdum* in which everyone is unemployed, thus living on relief, unemployment compensation and/or past savings (plus some property income). This is not deflationary. Quite the contrary, it is inflationary!

2.2   Direct Inflationary Consequences of Rising Interest Rates – Sectoral Impacts

Let us turn now from general inflationary implications of severe monetary restraint to the consequences in some specific sectors of the economy. The basic elements involved in sectoral impacts are probably four: the capital intensity of an industry, its degree of reliance on external finance, the degree of elasticity of demand it faces, and the durability of its capital goods. Capital intensity is measured in terms of a capital–output ratio. Given two industries of equivalent capital investment but large differences in sales generated at capacity, the industry with the lower sales is more capital-intensive. Ordinarily, greater capital intensity also implies longer life of capital goods. The higher the capital intensity of an industry and the longer the life of its capital goods, the greater is its tendency to rely upon external financing. The mixture of these ingredients basically determines the degree of inflationary impact of rising interest rates: the higher the capital intensity, the more durable the capital, the greater the reliance on external financing, and the more inelastic the demand for the product of an industry, the greater is the likely price pressure attributable to rising interest rates.

2.2.1 Housing

In the housing area the forces just cited may be seen most clearly in multiple-unit rental properties. As a financial venture the developer has a calculus involving cost versus value of a proposed unit with a high capital–output ratio. His value is a stream of anticipated receipts, with the more remote ones depressed in magnitude by the uncertainties associated with time, discounted at an appropriate market rate of interest to find the present value. Rising interest rates automatically depress the value of the investment. The likely response of the market is to raise rentals and thus anticipated future returns, in turn to reduce construction to a degree determined by the elasticity of demand for new multiple-unit housing, and to transmit the higher rental values to existing housing, where overall demand tends to be quite inelastic. Moreover, since developers rely overwhelmingly on external, borrowed funds, they face the full wrath of the financial markets, having no way of giving themselves preferential treatment via the medium of internally available funds. In addition, given the inelasticity of demand of the overall housing market and the well-known impediments to the supply of housing finance (in the United States, at least) in periods of financial stringency, a further inflationary fillip may possibly be generated by a significant decline in new construction, with a consequent declining vacancy rate and rising rents.

In the single-family, owner-occupied dwelling units, which domi-
nate the housing scene in the United States, the same forces are at
work and the same type of analysis is applicable, with an owner-
occupant viewed as renting to himself. In practice, the train of
events is viewed in more simplified terms by the prospective purchaser of a house. With low down-payment and long maturity loans,
the interest component is a large proportion of cost to a typical
home-buyer. Mortgage rates rising from, say, 5 to 9 per cent build
sharply higher long-run costs into home ownership. For example,
on a twenty-five-year, $25,000 mortgage the difference is about 44
per cent (about $768 annually) in the interest and principal costs.
Whether the unit be owner-occupied or rented to another party, the
results are the same: higher expenditures for implicit or explicit
rent.[2]

2.2.2   Other Construction

The analysis suggested above basically extends also to commercial
rental construction such as office buildings, stores, shopping centers, industrial parks and specialized construction financed by sale–
leaseback arrangements. All of these meet the tests of high capital–
output ratios, durability and the use of long-term, external financing. Institutional and legal forces are far less likely to constitute impediments to the supply of finance in commercial construction,
giving a clearer picture of pure interest rate impact. As with housing, the escalation of interest rates on commercial construction
presses on into the area of existing rental properties, raising costs
of tenants generally and tending to elevate prices of the goods and
services sold by them.

2.2.3   Utility Rates

The area embraced by utilities includes electric power, gas piped
into users' premises, telephone service and water service, combined frequently with sewer service. One can find occasional additional utilities, e.g. centrally distributed heat, but these are of little
overall importance. We exclude transportation, treating it
separately.

With privately owned public utilities (which are dominant in the United States), the story is much the same as with residential housing, particularly large-scale, multi-unit rental housing. Utilities (along with railroads) are historically the most capital-intensive, large-scale economic units. Capital–output ratios for electric generating and distributing firms, for example, are likely to be of the order of, say, 3 or 4 (or higher): 1, i.e. 3 or 4 units of capital investment required to produce 1 unit of output or sales.[3] Admittedly, such ratios are in part arbitrary, since controlled monopoly pricing of output is customary and valuation of capital in a going enterprise is arbitrary. Nevertheless, there is no ground for disputing the basic conclusion concerning capital intensity, rough estimates of which may be gleaned from Table 2.2. This is combined with exceedingly long life of capital goods, with hydroelectric facilities representing something of an ultimate in durability – again, like housing. The heavy use of external funds, mainly borrowed (via bonds), but partly preference shares (which behave much like bonds) and common or ordinary shares (which historically have constituted stable, conservative investments still behaving somewhat like bonds), again prevails. Overall costs of capital funds constitute a major share of charges to customers, e.g. perhaps 15 to 20 per cent or more in an electric power company.[4] Inelasticity of demand in the utility area is almost complete, given the fundamental necessity of the services, with perhaps a significant degree of elasticity entering only when there is a choice between two or more forms of utility service, for example, gas v. electricity or public service v. generation of one's own energy.

Here, then, are virtually optimum conditions for rising interest rates to reinforce an inflationary maelstrom. A sharp rise in costs of fixed-return capital, e.g. a doubling of levels combined with expectations that very high costs will persist indefinitely, could lead gradually to a rise in electricity charges of, say, 10 to 12 per cent. Moreover, given the close correspondence of the behavior of ordinary or common shares to fixed-return securities (in public utilities), the consequences of rising interest rates are rising costs of equity funds which feed into the inflationary situation much as do fixed charges. The inflationary impact may be either lagged or fairly immediate. If electricity-producing capacity generally had comfortable margins over demand, there would presumably be only a slow, gradual impact on the price of electric power, since rising

Table 2.2 Selected Aggregates and Interest Paid in Relation to Net Income (less Deficit), Depreciation and Federal Income Tax: Large Firms in Selected Industries, 1962, 1965, 1970, 1971 (assets exceeding $250,000,000)

Industry	$ thousand				Ratios of interest to (per cent)			
	1962	1965	1970	1971	1962	1965	1970	1971
Metal mining								
Interest	25,597	8,372	33,478	51,254				
Income	−12,358*	189,609	256,795	−35,978*	−207.1	4.4	13.0	−142.5
Depreciation	60,436	69,969	119,625	138,450	42.4	12.0	28.0	37.0
Tax	43,186	76,159	111,454	29,570	59.3	11.0	30.0	173.3
Cost of sales	290,888	706,311	1,230,642	1,520,676	8.8	1.2	2.7	3.4
Business receipts	614,102	1,097,189	1,919,640	2,058,515				
Assets[a]	1,143,892	767,566	1,535,611	2,025,778				
Food and kindred manufacturing								
Interest	34,311	86,721	599,433	645,021				
Income	546,634	1,110,668	1,736,209	2,007,236	6.3	7.8	34.5	32.1
Depreciation	207,012	365,645	822,648	989,258	16.6	23.7	72.9	65.2
Tax	281,066	516,940	879,518	981,937	12.2	16.8	68.2	65.7
Cost of sales	9,012,437	13,914,713	24,248,263	28,014,649	0.3	0.6	2.5	2.3
Business receipts	11,282,072	18,384,354	34,074,772	40,087,362				
Assets[a]	2,767,043	5,391,808	11,777,228	13,651,559				
Tobacco manufacturing								
Interest	25,620	21,045	183,331	193,320[b]				
Income	520,758	599,134	852,109	951,631[b]	4.9	3.5	21.5	20.3
Depreciation	36,368	43,886	136,112	152,647[b]	70.4	48.0	134.7	126.6
Tax	270,311	285,021	414,566	439,130[b]	9.5	7.4	44.2	44.0
Cost of sales	2,480,429	2,716,616	3,967,012	4,586,467[b]	1.0	0.8	4.6	4.2
Business receipts	4,249,186	4,946,856	7,002,633	7,866,841[b]				

services

Interest	1,107,278ᶜ	1,248,703	3,503,716	40.7	35.2	103.1	117.3
Income	2,718,346ᶜ	3,548,092	2,986,933	52.2	48.1	69.9	70.6
Depreciation	2,121,743ᶜ	2,595,544	4,962,907	77.5	74.5	205.6	246.1
Tax	1,430,181ᶜ	1,676,497	1,423,480	14.5	12.6	17.7	17.5
Cost of sales	7,629,861ᶜ	9,903,521	20,068,939				
Business receiptsᵃ	16,501,557ᶜ	20,334,027	38,434,628				
Assetsᵃ	50,202,415ᶜ	58,542,367	109,084,530				
Retail trade, general merchandise							
Interest	57,434	210,437	769,903	10.8	33.5	58.0	48.1
Income	531,312	628,714	1,601,930	40.4	78.8	164.5	130.6
Depreciation	142,051	267,018	589,640	21.9	49.8	127.9	100.3
Tax	262,369	422,357	767,900	0.8	1.8	4.0	3.4
Cost of sales	6,874,484	11,382,555	22,892,653				
Business receiptsᵃ	11,125,529	18,652,479	37,733,385				
Assetsᵃ	2,645,337	5,167,900	11,962,492				
Contract constructionᵈ							
Interest	230,717	321,679	790,632	37.4	25.6	46.2	41.1
Income	617,156	1,257,632	1,925,178	31.4	33.1	42.2	44.4
Depreciation	734,138	972,906	1,782,559	62.9	62.0	91.1	87.0
Tax	366,800	519,126	908,429	0.7	0.7	1.0	1.0
Cost of sales	33,857,740	46,611,664	78,412,715				
Business receiptsᵃ	40,311,096	55,696,213	88,945,385				
Assetsᵃ	5,698,841	8,095,460	12,995,880				

* Deficit.
ᵃ Depreciable assets (at depreciated value) plus inventories.
ᵇ Assets exceeding $100,000,000.
ᶜ Excludes water supply and other sanitary services in 1962.
ᵈ All firms.

Source: US Treasury Dept, *Statistics of Income – Corporation Income Tax Returns*, Washington, DC, 1962, Table 2; 1965, Table 5; 1970, Table 6; 1971, Table 6.

costs of capital funds would be felt only slowly. On the other hand, if as in 1973–4 reserve capacity was almost non-existent at high levels of demand, the impact on prices would be rapid, delayed only by the necessity of getting permission from typically sympathetic public utility commissions. Quick, substantial rate increases would be essential if utilities were to be able to raise the capital for expansion. Inability to obtain quick rate increases or fears of such would lead to postponements or cancellations of expansion plans, with further implications for future inflationary impacts. Such postponements and cancellations (noted later in Chapter 4) were, in fact, widespread in the United States in mid-1974 in the electric power industry.

The inflationary impact of rising costs of capital would affect publicly owned utilities similarly. Given the assumption that a government-owned electric power company is to be self-sustaining at the minimum and possibly return some yield to government on its investment, rising costs of capital must be transmitted to the users in the same fashion as with the private electric company. Governments, of course, can subsidize utility operations, in which case rising capital costs need not be put on the bills of the users. The subsidy must be met in some way, however, presumably by some form of direct or indirect tax, or by borrowing. However, indirect taxes enter price indexes and additional government borrowing tends to push all interest rates higher.

As for differences between types of utilities, they are matters of degree, but the principles are the same. Telephone operations are basically similar, as are water and sewer, although capital intensities and longevity of capital may vary. In the case of water and sewer, government operation is customary, although private water companies are found occasionally.

2.2.4 Rail Transportation

This is the area of transportation closest in character to public utilities in terms of capital intensity, capital longevity and necessity for external financing. In terms of elasticity of demand for its services, there is usually, in the United States at least, a competitive element to worry about: trucks, buses and airplanes.

We shall not dwell here on railroads. Passenger service in the

United States is nationalized and beset with political and other difficulties which overshadow cost of capital by far. Freight haulage comes close to the utilities theoretically, but in one respect is less vulnerable to rising costs of capital because of the non-growth character of the industry. On the other hand, in the United States there is need for vast sums of capital to rehabilitate seemingly endless thousands of miles of deteriorated tracks and to modernize equipment. Complicating the picture is the future of major portions of the nation's railroads removed from bankruptcy to governmentally financed and sponsored reorganization.

In other industrialized countries the railroads may be viewed as sharing the key financial characteristics of nationalized utilities. Their exposure to extreme monetary stringency and the consequences thereof are, in turn, similar.

2.2.5 Federal Debt Costs

Soaring interest rates can add to inflation as a result of their impact on national debt service. A rapidly expanding debt will build in rising interest costs rapidly. A debt that is heavily short-term in character will have fairly rapid conversion to expensive costs. In effect, current costs of national debt service embody roughly a moving average of interest rates. Overall, the speed and extent to which rising interest rates affect government expenditures are determined by the rate of expansion of the debt, the current rate of change in interest rates, the maturity structure of the debt and interest rates on components of the existing debt. It should be noted that even a once-for-all rise in current market interest rates to a plateau higher than any previous rates will create a lagged rise in interest costs, continuing until all the existing debt is converted.

The fact is that in recent years circumstances in the United States have caused rising interest rates to exert an inflationary impact. Between year-end 1964 and year-end 1974 net federal public debt securities in the hands of the public (Federal Reserve holdings are excluded) rose from $222.5 billion to $271.0 billion, or 17.6 per cent. In fiscal 1965 estimated net interest was $8.5 billion, while in fiscal 1975 it was about $19.8 billion, an increase of 114.1 per cent.[5] Meanwhile, the overall privately held marketable federal debt was falling in average maturity: in December 1965, 1970 and 1974, 31.1, 16.2 and 14.6 per cent, respectively, of marketable US debt had a maturity of five years or more.[6] For all marketable, interest-bearing federal public debt, the average maturity was 5⅓, 3⅔ and 3 years, respectively, at fiscal year-end 1965, 1970 and 1974.[7] Thus, interest costs on a shortening debt rose far more rapidly than the debt itself, beginning in 1966. Under such conditions, one can no longer slough off the inflationary aspect of rising interest rates paid by the Treasury as of minor consequence.

Not only is there inflationary impact from an expenditure standpoint, but there may be such an impact from a cost point of view. This is obvious if excise taxes are levied to finance the rise in interest expense, but it is also true to the extent that corporate income taxes help to finance the costs, since businesses often treat the corporate income tax as a quasi-cost item in pricing policies.[8] In practice, this inflationary impact is obscured by the fact that a specific tax is not tied to debt service.

2.2.6   Inventory Holdings

Inventory is, of course, simply a type of capital good. As with fixed capital, industries vary widely in the relative importance of inventory. If two firms – or industries – were identical in all economic characteristics except that one had to carry twice as large an inventory as a second firm (say, because of a greater variety of sizes of products), then in the first firm sales would have to cover twice as large a cost of financing inventory. Thus, the larger the inventory–sales ratio, other things being equal, the greater the inflationary impact of rapidly rising interest rates. The cost of financing the produce merchant should have an inconsequential effect on the price of fresh fruits and vegetables at retail. The effect should be quite different for stocks of whisky aged for some years, for raw materials that are bought long in advance of use, for crops that are held in storage for long periods before utilization (e.g. grains, cotton, tobacco), for canned fruits and vegetables and for items whose production period is prolonged, thus embodying much work-in-process inventory (e.g. airplanes, ships).

As noted earlier, the relative degree of use of external financing affects the outcome. This results from the probably lower cost as-

signed to internally generated funds and from the fact that external finance sets up a cash flow requirement that *must be met*.
In the retail automobile business, for example, virtually all inventory is externally financed. If interest rates were 15 per cent for such
financing, and if dealers on the average hold a sixty-day supply of
cars, $2\frac{1}{2}$ per cent of the wholesale value of a car is added to the
retail price at the minimum, a *not* inconsequential sum. A clue to
the potential importance of this item in selected business areas can
be gleaned from Table 2.2. In retail trade, where financing of inventories is very important, interest as a percentage of cost of sales
in general merchandise establishments rose from 0.8 per cent in
1962 to 4.0 per cent in 1970.

Proponents of very tight money usually regard high interest rates
as a deterrent to inventory speculation by virtue of thc cost effect
and would probably suggest that tight money also inhibits inventory speculation by reducing anticipation of price rises. While
doubtlessly true for some groups in the economic world, high interest rates may also produce quite different results for other
groups. For the latter, borrowing for inventory acquisition may
be accelerated in fear of higher rates or lack of availability of funds
later, tending to drive up further both interest rates and prices.[9]
With forces operating in both directions, the net outcome would
be unpredictable.

2.2.7   Other Non-Financial Business

Further consideration of individual industries or sectors will be
avoided. There are hundreds of thousands of firms in a multitude
of industries with vastly varying characteristics. At or near one extreme is a hydroelectric-based electric power company. At or near
another extreme is the fresh fruit and vegetable retail market. In
between there is essentially a continuum. In turn, there is a continuum in impacts of severe monetary restraint upon prices. For
aggregate impacts, rough gleanings may be found in interest relationships shown in Tables 2.1 and 2.2. Thus, interest as a percentage of cost of sales rose over the period 1962–71 from 14.5 to
17.6 in utilities, from 0.3 to 2.3 in food and kindred manufacturing,
from 1.0 to 4.2 in tobacco manufacturing, but only from 0.7 to
1.0 in contract construction. To conclude, rising interest costs stem-

ming from central bank actions are cost-push factors in the same sense as rising wages stemming from union wage demands or monopolistic price actions of business firms.[10] Indeed, if as argued in the next chapter extremely high interest charges have contributed to financial difficulties of business firms, clearly they have also been of real significance as costs in such firms.

2.3   Consequences in the Financial Sector

2.3.1   Capital Values

Just as in an earlier day economists focused on the cost-deterrent impact of restrictive monetary policy and dismissed the cost-push element, so economists then paid little attention to its impact on capital values. A generation or so ago attention began to be paid to the real balance effect with respect to money, but this was in relation to prices of goods and services and spending on them. In 1951, during the debates over fixed v. flexible interest rate policies (part of the financial aftermath of World War II, when fixed, low-interest rates were the pattern in war finance), the notion of 'locking-in' particular holders of government securities via rising interest rates and falling capital values became fashionable, but large increases in interest rates were not then in the scheme of things. Manipulation of capital values also was envisaged as a device to generate uncertainties generally, to create fears of future changes in capital values, thus to be a device to influence the financing timetables and plans of the business world.[11] But in the United States, at least, where discussions and debate along these lines flourished for the most part, relatively little concern was evident concerning possible adverse consequences of falling capital values, or of the aggregate magnitudes that might be involved. Of course, postwar rises in interest rates in the United States did not lead in that earlier day to levels out of touch with ordinary historical precedent, or to collapsing capital values, and so perhaps a lack of concern was understandable. In the United Kingdom, on the other hand, consuls issued at 2 per cent, precariously sensitive to rising interest rates, saw market values of 60 to 50 per cent of par in the 1950s, reflecting yields that generally exceeded 4 per cent and at times exceeded 5 per cent. Still, little professional concern was evident.

With the increasingly severe credit squeezes of 1966, 1969–70 and 1973–4 finally bringing interest rates higher than any in the recorded history of the United States, capital values were in a state of collapse. Now, in addition to the financial press, which is always concerned about the fate of financial markets, evidence of increased professional concern in this area at long last appeared.[12]

The relative lack of professional (including governmental) attention to the consequences of falling capital values is a serious matter, in the opinion of this writer. Falling capital values have consequences somewhat comparable to those of inflation, the disease for whose cure falling capital values are a sacrificial lamb. While inflation erodes the purchasing power of savings denominated in fixed terms, severe monetary restraint does the same in the short run to (1) savings in marketable form with fixed maturity values, (2) savings in marketable form with very stable incomes but without fixed maturity values, and (3) ultimately all capital values of marketable assets. Although the erosion in capital values relates only to the short run and not, as with inflation, both to the long and short run, the short-run 'thievery' of severely restrictive monetary policy cannot easily be written off as of minor significance vis-à-vis the 'thievery' of inflation.

Let us turn now to the losses in capital values of financial assets most directly involved in three periods of credit restraint in the United States in the decade beginning 1965. The first period was characterized by slowly developing restraint in early 1966, followed by an intense credit squeeze later in the year, which was relaxed in late 1966 as the authorities saw a 'mini-recession' appearing. The relaxation, however, was of but modest proportions and gave way to an intense, prolonged squeeze beginning in late 1968, which relaxed in mid-1970 with the Penn-Central Railroad failure and accompanying credit crisis. The relaxation was followed in 1973 by a gradually intensifying restraint reaching unprecedented severity by mid-1974. In Table 2.3 are estimates of some of the capital losses in this last and most severe case. In 1973–4, which covers fairly well the movement from relaxation to peak of vigor, US government long-term bonds fell from an

Table 2.3 Estimated Losses in Capital Values of Long-Term Financial Instruments (dollar amounts in billions)

Item	Price or yield (year-end)[a] 1972	1974	Estimated 1972 amount outstanding (year-end) Face value 1972	Market value 1972	1974	Estimated loss in market value 1972–4 Dollars	Per cent
(1) US Government	69.87	58.96	13.983[b]	9.770	8.244	1.53	15.6
(2) State and local govt bonds	87.1	68.6	165.693[c]	144.319	113.665	30.65	21.2
(3) Corporate bonds[d]	—	—	103.417	94.487	79.303	15.18	16.1
(4) Preferred stocks	6.7	10.2	—	20.522	15.745	4.78	23.3
(5) Public utility common stocks (NY Stock Exchange listed)	—	—	—	101.000	69.859	31.141	30.8
(6) Corporate stock[e]	—	—	—	1136.9	638.0	498.9	43.9
(7) Mortgages (residential, commercial, farm)	—	—	564.825	—	—	81.0[f]	16.0
(8) Total securities ((1)+(2)+(3)+(6))	—	—	—	1385.476	839.212	546.26	39.4

[a] Coverage of price indices is not identical to securities embodied in amount outstanding.
[b] Marketable, ten years and over, held by private investors.
[c] Average of fiscal year-end 1972 and 1973.
[d] New York Stock Exchange listed, including foreign governments.
[e] Includes listed, over-the-counter and closely held stock; excludes intercorporate holdings. New stock issued in 1973–4 is not removed from 1974 market value.
[f] Loss assumed equal to that on corporate bonds, about 16 per cent. Market value at year-end 1972 is assumed 90 per cent of face value.

Sources: *Survey of Current Business*, March 1973, pp. S20, S21; May 1975, pp. S20, S21, S22; *Federal Reserve Bulletin*, June 1975, pp. A35, A42; New York Stock Exchange, *1973 Fact Book*, pp. 29, 79; *1975 Fact Book*, pp. 32, 76; SEC *Statistical Bulletin*, May 1975, p. 437; US Bureau of the Census, *Governmental Finances in 1972–73*, Washington, DC, 1974.

estimated 70 per cent of par to about 60 per cent of par with a
loss of perhaps $1.5 billion to holders in the private sector.[13] State
and local government bonds fell about 21 per cent or about $30
billion. Corporate bonds declined about 16 per cent giving a loss of
perhaps $15 billion for all corporate bonds listed on the New York
Stock Exchange (including foreign bonds and assuming a loss for all
bonds similar to that on high grade bonds). Median yields on dividend-
paying preferred stocks rose from 6.7 per cent in December 1972
to 10.2 per cent in December 1974, or $3\frac{1}{2}$ percentage points. If yields
on preferreds as a whole rose similarly, the loss in capital value
was perhaps $5 billion, or close to 23 per cent. Public utility
common shares dropped about 31 per cent during this period –
perhaps $31 billion. For all shares listed on exchanges, sold over-
the-counter or closely held (excluding intercorporate holdings),
there was a decline from the December 1972 value of $1,137 billion
to a 1974 year-end figure of about $638 billion or a loss of
about $500 billion (without taking account of new issues during
the period) or roughly 44 per cent.[14] If one now considers mortgage
credit, the $565 billion outstanding at year-end 1972 (with a market
value of, say, $500 billion) declined, conservatively estimated, per-
haps $80 billion, assuming a decline in mortgage values comparable
to that on high-grade corporate bonds (i.e. about 16 per cent).[15]

Summing up these losses in capital values in 1973–4, one finds
a fall in the neighborhood of $165 billion in interest-bearing debt
and related securities (preferred shares and public utility common)
and about $465 billion in other stocks, or well over $600 billion. Moreover, these loss estimates are not complete, ignoring as
they do billions in privately placed bonds.

A similar set of estimates of capital losses in the 1966 and
1968–70 credit squeezes does not appear in Table 2.3. However,
they were of comparable relative magnitudes. For example, US
government long-term bonds lost about $10 billion in market value
between 1965 and mid-1970 as they dropped from about 84 to
61 per cent of par. At the same time, state and local government long-term issues lost about 35 per cent in market value as
they dropped from about 111 per cent of par to about 63 per
cent.[16] Between year-ends 1965 and 1969, non-convertible preferred
shares fell about 30 per cent, while common shares of public
utilities fell about a third from their 1965 average to mid-1970. In
the 1968–70 stock market collapse over $150 billion, about 21

per cent, was lost by the New York Stock Exchange's listed shares alone.[17]

One cannot attribute all of the above losses to restriction of the money supply, since the demand for money is also involved, a point that is stressed later. However, monetary stringency is a prime causal element. Yields on non-convertible, marketable, interest-bearing obligations are most directly affected. Preferred shares (non-convertible) are closely comparable to bonds in this respect. Much like preferred shares are common shares in public utilities. Existing mortgages tend to respond much as do bonds to the extent that they are traded in secondary markets, although with differences in lags. (In the United States great efforts have been made to stimulate trading in mortgages through the development of institutions in the secondary mortgage markets.) With respect to the great bulk of common stocks, the links to severe monetary restraint are much less close and much less direct. Too many other forces enter the picture. However, in the great bear market of November 1968 to May 1970, and the even worse collapse of 1973–4, one found little doubt among analysts concerning the heavy responsibility of the Federal Reserve authorities, including their role in creating anticipation of recession.

We leave the subject of losses in capital values temporarily, having established that the magnitudes involved are great and having noted that there may be adverse consequences. We return to these later in this chapter and again in Chapter 3.

2.3.2   Instability of Financial Markets

Here we are concerned with the nature, incidence and consequences of instability in the financial markets resulting from monetary restraint. Instability is viewed as a condition in which change appears or threatens to appear and tends to provoke cumulative anticipatory or defensive actions, possibly involving financial positions that are weak or endangered and subject to much damage quickly.

Capital Markets

There are various aspects and components of instability in capital markets; one aspect that in the United States at least, receives

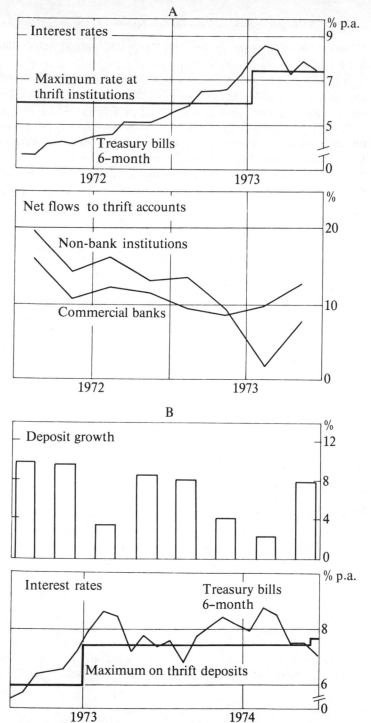

A

Interest rates   % p.a.
                                                    9

Maximum rate at
thrift institutions   7

                                                    5

Treasury bills
6-month
                                                    0
        1972   1973

Net flows to thrift accounts   %

                                                    20
    Non-bank institutions

Commercial banks   10

                                                    0
        1972   1973

B

Deposit growth   %
                                                    12

                                                    8

                                                    4

                                                    0

Interest rates   Treasury bills   % p.a.
                        6-month

                                                    8

Maximum on thrift deposits

                                                    6

                                                    0
        1973   1974

Figure 2.1   Selected Interest Rates and Thrift Deposit, 1972–3 and 1973–4

great attention is disintermediation. Not only does it include shifts by individuals from asset holdings in financial institutions to holdings in direct financial market instruments; but more generally, it involves a reduction in the number of tiers in the layering of claims, and thus it also includes a shift from deposit claims in non-bank institutions to deposits in commercial banks. Disintermediation in the US scene in recent years was mainly a consequence of monetary policy grinding down against a legal, regulatory or institutional framework which sets up inducements to shift asset holdings from one form to another (see Figure 2.1). For example,

In April the nation's savings banks reported a net outflow of $650 million – larger than in any other month in history, including the worst months of the 1966 and 1969 credit crunches. And in the same month, federally insured savings and loan associations had a net outflow of $335 million, the first outflow since last September and the first April outflow since 1969.

Investors are drawing their funds from the mortgage-making thrift institutions to invest elsewhere in the money market where rates have become more attractive.[18]

Interest rates in the thrift institutions were unable to rise to money market levels, partly because of regulatory restrictions on maximum rates and partly because such institutions held asset portfolios accumulated over preceding years at lower interest rates which were not yielding sufficient average returns to pay current open market interest rates without threats of insolvency.

This type of instability is obviously a threat to the liquidity and solvency of thrift institutions. In the United States it reached a new high in intensity in July 1974, when the aggressive and innovative Citicorp, holding company for the giant First National City Bank (now Citibank), issued $650 million in floating rate notes, with interest set at 1 percentage point above the Treasury bill rate, which in turn had been above maximum rates allowable on savings accounts. This constituted a direct threat to thrift institutions.[19]

Closely related to the disintermediation situation was the instability introduced into the mortgage markets in which thrift institutions play so large a role. In 1974 thrift institutions largely dried up as a source of residential mortgage funds, while other lenders had preferred areas of lending elsewhere, reflecting in some measure legal restraints on residential mortgage rates. Mortgage bankers then found their operations turning chaotic as they made commitments to carry mortgages which they later could sell to permanent holders only in a falling market (i.e. at rising interest rates). Meanwhile, they had to carry the mortgages in inventory by bank financing at interest rates rising rapidly above the rates earned on their inventories (see Figure 2.2 for a comparison of the volatility of key long and short rates).[20] In effect, the liquidity of the residential mortgage markets, which the government for years had been trying to develop, vanished, leaving government and quasi-government agencies as virtually sole sources of liquidity.[21] With ensuing losses

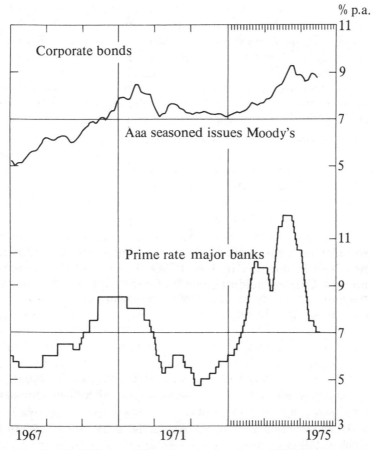

Figure 2.2   Basic Long-Term and Short-Term Interest Rates, 1967–75

of the mortgage bankers, the future strength of their industry – and of the mortgage markets – was threatened.

Compounding the threats to the stability of the mortgage markets were the liquidity troubles of a relatively new type of maker of construction loans (not permanent mortgages), the real estate investment trust (REIT). Faced with inability to sell new stock, with soaring interest rates on floating interest rate bank loans (e.g. 17 per cent)[22] and on their commercial paper – rates exceeding those on existing construction loans made by them – and with rapidly rising customer delinquencies, the REITs fell into a state of chaos in 1974.[23] In short, a complicated mortgage market largely sponsored and nurtured by the government was hit by an avalanche of hammer blows by that same government in the form of fiercely restrictive monetary policies of the central bank, which was simultaneously striking blows on the principal savings conduits of the mortgage market, the thrift institutions.

We turn next to instability in the bond markets. What needs indelible emphasizing in interest rate determination is that there is no simple, firm relationship between a given demand schedule for money and a given supply of money, even for very short periods. The demand schedule is volatile in response, among other things, to change in the supply schedule and to lack of change in the supply schedule. Investors are constantly speculating over the future course of central bank policy. Any given money supply is therefore consistent with a host of different levels of interest rates depending on the financial community's expectations concerning the future course of monetary policy and its likely consequences. Instability in this sector, in turn, represents a condition in which there are substantial cumulative shifts in the demand for money (or near-monies) and opposite shifts in the demand for non-short-term, interest-bearing financial assets, e.g. a cumulative unloading of bonds in response to fears of higher interest rates in the future, or vice versa. (In practice, instability tends to be associated in the public mind with falling bond prices, not with rising bond prices, but this is technically incorrect.) Instability may also be thought of as involving unusually wide fluctuations, rather than cumulative unidirectional movement, and it may be regarded as indicative of unusual uncertainty, coupled with great sensitivity to presumed clues to future events.

Instability poses problems both for suppliers and demanders of securities, with resulting interaction between the two sides. In falling markets in which investors previously participated, they cease buying, causing prices to fall even further. If existing holders of securities suspect a likely fall in bond prices, they will compound the difficulties by selling. Such instability and its implications for suppliers and demanders of securities in turn pose problems for society generally.

Three times in the eight years between spring 1966, and autumn 1974, the US monetary authorities visited instability on the US capital markets: in the short credit crunch of spring to autumn 1966, in the prolonged crunch of November 1968–May 1970, and in most of 1973–4. Each of these crunches led to the vast declines in capital values previously described, and the market instability that concerns us here persisted during the movement of interest rates to their eventual peaks or, oppositely, of bond prices to their ultimate troughs. Figures 2.3 and 2.4 portray the course of selected security prices during these periods, but they cannot convey the feeling of instability prevailing during them. The newspapers and financial press must be consulted to glean this.[24]

Instability in the security markets, just as in the mortgage markets, poses threats to the market-makers and their market mechanisms, jeopardizing the future viability of the market and posing the threat of future instability. In the securities markets, dealers (like mortgage bankers) typically hold their inventories with borrowed funds and, in the case of US government securities, have enormous inventories.[25] Thus, the industry is subject to heavy potential losses in the event of even small declines in prices. Heavy losses have from time to time been realized, driving some dealers out of business. In 1966, and again in late 1968, unprecedentedly strong, arbitrary forces of this type appeared in the bond markets as a whole and helped shake the securities industry to its foundations by 1970. Obviously, the stock market collapse which commenced in 1968, along with administrative difficulties beginning in preceding boom years and continuing during the collapse, were the primary forces sealing the fates of many a securities firm. Nevertheless, losses accruing to securities firms from underwriting and market-making added to the difficulties and, in some cases, were probably decisive.[26]

The year 1973 and the earlier part of 1974 saw more of the same, including plunging of the stock market to a twelve-year

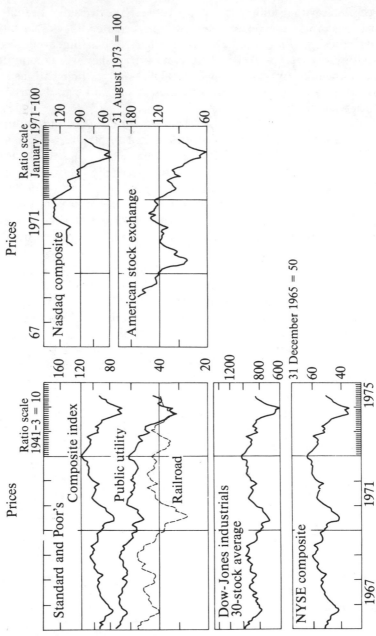

Figure 2.3   Stock Price Indices, 1966–75

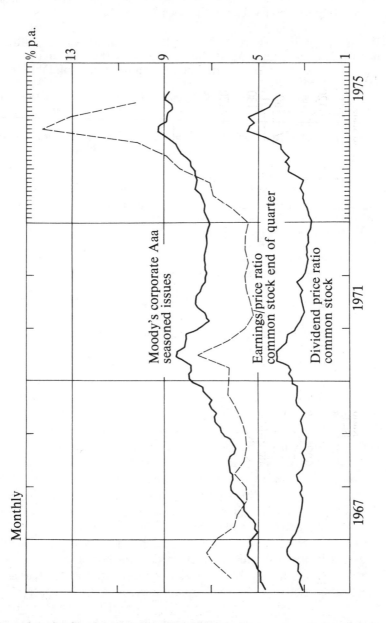

Figure 2.4 Stock and Bond Yields, 1966–75

low in money terms and considerably lower in real terms,[27] with devastating consequences for the securities industry.

Prices of bonds ... have plummeted ... to three-year lows. Bond dealers ... who loaded up at the beginning of the year in anticipation of rising prices have been caught with huge piles of debt issues in their inventories.
... losses have been tremendous. Street sources estimate that the combined losses during March of some two dozen major dealers ... was $150 million ...
According to New York Stock Exchange figures, the composite net worth of member firms shrank 13% in 1973 to $3.65 billion from $4.20 billion at the end of 1972. Only $49 million of the $550 million decline was attributable to operating losses: the rest was accounted for by shrinkage in the market value of capital (some of which was in the form of marketable securities) and by the flight of capital as investors switched stakes to ventures that seemed less risky....
During the week ended Feb. 13, according to Federal Reserve Bank of New York figures, optimistic dealers built their bond holdings by 36% to $5.01 billion. By April 3 those holdings had been reduced to $3.59 billion as dealers sold in despair.[28]

By July 1974 the situation reported in April had deteriorated much more, reaching near-panic proportions. Almost daily, announcements appeared in the press of large losses and mergers of troubled firms.[29] Between January 1973 and July 1974, forty-three New York Stock Exchange firms (about 8 per cent) disappeared and 221 members (34 per cent) of the National Association of Security Dealers (firms handling unlisted securities) similarly were merged or liquidated.[30]

The securities industry – and the general public – were in fact suffering through a self-generating downward spiral launched by the Federal Reserve. Once the downward spiral in security prices was in motion, it triggered reinforcing elements just as in the 1929 stock market crash. Speculative selling took place. Margin calls went out as collateral values fell and inevitably some collateral was sold.[31] Collateral trust bonds threatened by the falls in value of the securities behind them doubtless caused liquidity difficulties for issuers. Disintermediation at thrift institutions, as noted above, led to sales of securities by them at losses to meet withdrawals, reducing the lending potentials of such institutions still further. Losses in trading departments in commercial banks also reduced the credit-granting potential of commercial banks.[32] Casualty insurance companies, concerned about capital adequacy, were reported to be selling in a falling market apparently in fears of further falls in prices.[33] This, in turn, put additional pressure on security values and again lowered the credit-granting potential of the affected institutions.

Instability of security markets had many effects beyond its impact on the financial market machinery. Repercussions were felt obviously in non-financial sectors of the economy where there were interrelationships. Some of these will be noted on future pages.

Money Markets

Perhaps the most common connotation of instability in money markets involves fears of creditors concerning the safety of short-term claims on depository institutions or other financial and non-financial businesses. In an earlier day, such fear concerned mainly note and deposit claims on banks, and, to a lesser extent, certain other bank liabilities such as bankers' acceptances. It came also to relate to open-market commercial paper of non-banking firms. In an earlier day, too, it related to bills of exchange drawn on well-known firms to finance trade, especially international, but for years in the United Kingdom the domestic bill of exchange was also involved significantly.

The consequences – or manifestations – of such instability in money markets have taken several forms over the centuries. The old classic form was the bank run on notes and deposits, i.e. shifts from notes to specie and from deposits to notes or specie. It has taken also the form of avoiding or minimizing holdings of credit instruments of non-financial and financial business, viz. trade acceptances, bankers' acceptances, open-market commercial paper, etc. It has involved minimizing or even refusing creditor positions in inter-bank relationships – domestically and internationally. The extreme form of such instability is the general liquidity crisis. One consequence of all such instability was rising interest rates.

Another form of money market instability is interest rate instability relating to rapid or sudden changes in the demand for money *vis-à-vis* the demand for short-term, interest-bearing claims. This form of instability may be independent of, and even unaccompanied by, fears concerning the safety of short-term debt. On the other hand, both may arise together; indeed, interest rate instability may precede and lead the way to the more serious form of money-market instability. This type of instability relates to changes in the character of expectations with respect to the future of short-term interest rates and availability of credit. In recent years it has been largely a product of reactions to current central bank policies, to their statements and to consequent estimation of the future course of central bank policy. Since, in practice, central banks are not able to meet short-run targets with precision, recorded current data concerning central bank and commercial banking system monetary positions may lead to public misinterpretation of actual central bank intentions, hence to reactions of the financial community that are shown later to be inappropriate and that may increase instability. In addition, since the future behavior of business and government demand for bank credit cannot always be predicted accurately – especially in periods of great strain in the system – the possibility of further overshooting and undershooting short-run interest rate targets of the central bank becomes stronger and stronger. To some extent, a cobweb situation is likely to develop in periods of monetary stress, i.e. shifts into and out of money reflecting the 'undershooting' and 'overshooting' of short-run central bank interest rate targets.

The sensitivity of an economy to these forms of instability is determined in part by the importance of financial intermediation and paper claims in it, and this in turn is related to the degree of financial development. In the United States and United Kingdom in the 1970s the degree of financial intermediation was exceedingly high compared with that in less developed countries of the world and compared with the situation in the same two countries in earlier phases of their development.[34] This implies a vast 'layering of claims,' a multiplication of creditor–debtor relationships. This has involved in the United States and the United Kingdom the creation of more and more 'near-monies' relative to money narrowly defined. The decade beginning in 1965, especially, saw an explosion in the volume of very liquid credit instruments and claims in the United States, e.g. federal funds (inter-bank funds), commercial paper (including paper floated by bank holding companies), bank acceptances, Eurodollars, the sale of bank loans (with and without repurchase agreements) to the non-bank public and to banks' own affiliates, negotiable certificates of deposit, bank-guaranteed open-market paper, variable interest rate capital note issues of banks and other businesses. Similar developments also occurred in the United Kingdom.

It is in periods of prolonged, intense monetary stringency such as 1968–70 or 1973–4 that the layering of claims is most stimulated; there is a constant incentive to the financial world to build temporary pyramids, i.e. intermediation devices which are inherently fragile. Proliferation of liquid asset (money market) substitutes facilitates shifts of suppliers of funds out of one market into another with shifting interest rates, and with the internationalization of the money markets the shifts do not stop at national boundaries. Meanwhile, users of credit can shift from market to market in response to changing interest and availability patterns.[35]

At the same time, severe monetary restraint tends to increase the demand for short-term credit. Business firms with bonds maturing or with a need for new long-term credit are induced to substitute short-term credit for long-term obligations.[36] Thus, pressures tend to become even more intense on short-term markets and interest rates. Indeed, if any substantial industry is known to rely heavily on borrowed funds, and if doubts arise concerning its ability to generate the cash flow needed to absorb very high interest rates, that industry's short-term obligations (e.g. commercial paper) may be shunned by the market place, with resulting mounting pressures on banks and liquidity positions generally. Gyrating interest rates and liquidity fears then tend to merge as manifestations of money market instability.[37] Rumors, too, tend to appear, founded or unfounded, concerning weaknesses at individual firms. Ultimately, the shaking of confidence in an area of intermediation or market credit instruments may lead to a 'run' on it by its creditors (suppliers of funds).[38] With tightness in the system as a whole, needy borrowers in the affected area may be unable to find alternative sources of funds and a general liquidity crisis could be on. In short, prolonged severe monetary restraint is a destabilizer of money markets.[39]

Worth noting with respect to the period beginning in 1966 are two differences from earlier periods. First, responding to monetarist pressures, central banks placed greater emphasis on the money supply as a target, with decreased emphasis on interest rates and much less concern for their stability. Secondly, central banks increasingly *made* the wind rather than just lean against it.[40] Thus, the character of the interest rate instability changed in terms of its originating force.

Meanwhile, psychological forces were sharply escalated: there was, in effect, a fierce 'battle' between the central bankers aggressively enforcing severe restraint and the financial world struggling to obtain liquidity. Tension was the dominant motif in the several periods of stringency and it was evident most vividly in the daily financial reports in the press. In the United States, moreover, the rapid, record-breaking upward movements in short-term interest rates often under-represented the degree of tension. The Federal Reserve Open Market Committee set a permissible range of fluctuation for its key money market interest rate (the federal funds rate),[41] and presumably intervened in the market to insure success. It was then to the press that one had to turn to get the full 'feel' of the underlying strain. Tension accelerated during most of 1973, quieted down in late 1973 and early 1974, then promptly accelerated upwards to reach, by midsummer, heights probably unprecedented since 1920–1. The daily issues of the *Wall Street Journal*, the *Financial Times* (London), the *New York Times*, and the *American Banker* all bear witness to this state of affairs. By midsummer, interest rate instability had been joined with liquidity fears and, more or less continuously, forecasts appeared of bankruptcies to come, sacrificial lambs of the extraordinarily tight money.[42] Indeed, in the next chapter we shall deal with bankruptcy and related problems.

FOOTNOTES

1. There may be non-market offsets in the form of 'do-it-yourself' activities at home, e.g. house painting and other maintenance.
2. Further discussion of housing problems appears later in this study.
3. The Philadelphia Electric Company, e.g. had utility plant of $3.0 billion (original cost less depreciation) on 31 December 1973 and operating revenues for 1973 of $767 million (*Annual Report 1973*, pp. 26, 31). Reproduction cost presumably would have been much higher even after allowance for improvement in technology in replacement units.
4. Interest on borrowed funds and dividends on preferred shares at Philadelphia Electric Company were $196 million or 25.6 per cent of operating revenues in 1973. In 1963 the percentage was 18.9 per cent (*Annual Report 1973*, p. 31). The total cost of capital, of course, also includes that related to common stock.
5. *Economic Report of the President*, February 1975, Washington, DC, pp. 333 and 329.
6. *Federal Reserve Bulletin*, January 1969, p. A41; March 1972, p. A45; and April 1975, p. A35.
7. *Economic Report of the President*, op. cit., p. 334.

8. State and local government debt in the United States do not fit into the same framework as federal debt. While state and local government gross debt is huge ($188.5 billion at fiscal year-end 1973 – US Bureau of the Census, *Governmental Finances in 1972–73*, Washington, DC, 1974, p. 40) and has been growing rapidly, the net debt is nominal. Holdings of state and local government insurance trust funds, pension systems etc. have been virtually equal to the gross debt (e.g. $185.6 billion at fiscal year-end 1973 – see ibid.).

9. If interest rates have been rising, the case may be viewed as one in the elasticity of interest expectations. See J. R. Hicks, *Value and Capital*, 2nd edition, London, Oxford University Press, 1948, pp. 205, 280–1.

10. In contrast to the views of most economists, businessmen participating in a series of conferences on inflation convened by the White House reportedly shared the view expressed here that persistent, very high interest rates raise prices (*New York Times*, 22 September 1974, Section 3, pp. 1, 11).

On the other hand, in a recent econometric study (S. A. Seelig, 'Rising Interest Rates and Cost Push Inflation,' *Journal of Finance*, September 1974, pp. 1049–61), it was concluded that the 'impact of changes in interest rates on price changes is fairly negligible' (p. 1060). This study (covering 1955–69) is inadequate, from our point of view, in not focusing on the magnitudes of levels reached, and changes in levels of interest rates, in 1973–4, or on their overall rise from 1965 to 1974. Moreover, the total inflationary effect of severe monetary restraint goes beyond costs in a group of products and services sold. It includes the direct effects on federal government expenditures for interest and the subsequent impacts on levels of taxes. It involves the effects of administered unemployed on aggregate supply and on budgetary difficulties (expenditures and tax receipts) at all levels of government. It includes the effects on mortgage costs and on housing rents.

11. See R. V. Roosa, 'Interest Rates and the Central Bank,' in *Money, Trade and Economic Growth* (prepared in honor of John H. Williams), New York, Macmillan, 1951, pp. 270–95.

12. Cf. Barry Bosworth, 'The Stock Market and the Economy' (with 'Comments and Discussion') in *Brookings Papers on Economic Activity*, Vol. 2, 1975, pp. 257–300; A. M. Okun, 'Rules and Roles for Fiscal and Monetary Policy,' in J. J. Diamond (ed.), *Issues in Fiscal and Monetary Policy: The Eclectic Economist Views the Controversy*, Chicago, DePaul University, 1971, pp. 55–7.

13. Most interesting, the relative modesty of the loss reflected the average very short-term character of the public debt.

14. Bosworth calculated a 'loss of stockholder wealth in market prices ... [of] ... $525 billion, or 43 percent' (*Bosworth*, op. cit., p. 257).

15. Yields of conventional first mortgages on new homes rose from 7.66 to 9.37 per cent. High-grade (Moody's AAA) corporate bonds rose in yield from 7.08 to 8.89 per cent during this period (*Federal Reserve Bulletin*, November 1975, pp. A28, A43; and March 1973, pp. A36, A55).

16. Ervin Miller, 'The Pains of Monetary Restraint,' *Lloyds Bank Review*, July 1973, p. 40.

17. *ibid.*, p. 41. Real financial household wealth *per capita* was estimated to have fallen by about one-quarter in the period 1968–70 and by about one-third in the period 1972–4, when it 'reached its lowest point since 1958.' (See 'Recent Changes in the Liquidity of Major Sectors of the US Economy,' *Federal Reserve Bulletin*, June 1976, pp. 464–5).

18. *Wall Street Journal*, 12 June 1974, p. 42. The situation became even worse in July 1974. See, e.g., *New York Times*, 14 September 1974, p. 35, and 25 September 1974, pp. 57, 65. Comparable problems were reported in the United

Kingdom. See, e.g., *Financial Times* (London), 22 July 1974, pp. 9, 46; *Bank of England Quarterly Bulletin*, June 1974, p. 139.

19. In the storm set up by Citicorp's action (actually a toned-down affair compared with its original intentions), it was proposed in Congress that the Government subsidize thrift institutions to enable them to compete with such commercial bank actions and safeguard their liquidity. Specifically,

> The Treasury Department told a Senate panel Wednesday that the savings and loan industry might need a $30 million to $100 million interest rate subsidy in coming weeks to help replace deposits lost to higher-yielding securities, such as those sold Wednesday by ... Citicorp.
> ... funds ... would be used to give thrift institutions a below-market interest rate on advances from the Federal Home Loan Bank System.
> Currently, Federal S&Ls are paying 8.92% for money raised for them by FHLBB borrowings from capital markets. Under the proposed plan, they would get a 2% to 4% interest rate break on the cost of borrowings, it was suggested. S&Ls would be expected to use the funds for mortgages. [*American Banker*, 25 July 1974, p. 1]

For a general review of the difficulties besetting the thrift institutions of the United States in 1974, see 'Nonbank Thrift Institutions in 1974,' *Federal Reserve Bulletin*, February 1975, pp. 55–9.

A completely different aspect of disintermediation was its use as a tool of monetary policy to force an outflow of funds from large banks in late 1968 as part of a policy of severe restraint. This episode is well known and was a subject of great controversy.

Disintermediation may also initiate or intensify instability in the securities markets. The New York Bank for Savings, for example, liquidated large amounts of federal, state and municipal obligations at losses in order to meet withdrawals in the first half of 1974, according to its preliminary prospectus covering a proposed note issue shortly thereafter.

20. The speed with which short-term interest rates were driven up in the credit squeeze of 1973–4 was of crucial importance in the difficulties of the makers of mortgage markets (and, indeed, of makers of security markets). Had the authorities at least allowed rates to rise gradually, the market-makers would probably not have been caught holding substantial mortgage inventories whose interest yields (which were inherently less volatile than short-term yields by virtue of their long-term character) were being overtaken by rising short rates. Indeed, sharp change in the term structure of interest rates is one of the by-products of rapid change in the intensity of monetary pressures. Adjusting to a rapidly changing term structure may then be too much for enterprises whose operations consist of borrowing in one sector of the market to lend in another sector. Cf. A. D. Bain, 'Monetary Control Methods in the United Kingdom,' in G. Clayton, J. C. Gilbert and R. Sedgwick (eds), *Sheffield Seminar on Monetary Theory and Monetary Policy in the 1970's*, London, Oxford University Press, 1971, p. 162.

21. See *Wall Street Journal*, 1 July 1974, p. 22. See also 'Nonbank Thrift Institutions in 1974,' op. cit.

22. See *New York Times*, 29 June 1974, p. 35.

23. ibid; see also *Wall Street Journal*, 27 June 1974, p. 8 and 24 May 1974, p. 7. The troubles extended to the second- and third-largest real estate investment trusts in the country.

24. See, e.g. *New York Times*, 7 July 1974, Section 3, pp. 1, 5; *American Banker*, 25 July 1974, p. 23 (concerning state and local government bonds); *Wall Street Journal*, 8 July 1974, p. 15; 11 July 1974, p. 19; 30 July 1974, p. 24.

25. In 1974 daily average dealer inventories varied widely; for example, $3.653 billion (par value) in January, a low point of $263 million in June and a high of $4.831 billion in December (*Federal Reserve Bulletin*, February 1975, p. A38).
26. For a picture of the shaky condition of the securities industry in this period, see 'Year of the Bloodbath,' *Finance*, March 1970, pp. 6–10; *Wall Street Journal*, 1 October 1970, pp. 1–7.
27. *New York Times*, 14 September 1974, pp. 35, 41. Meanwhile, under similar pressures (and other complications), prices on the London Stock Exchange plunged to a twenty-year low (*Wall Street Journal*, 12 December 1974, p. 14). Similar situations prevailed in Amsterdam, Tokyo, Paris, Johannesburg, Sydney, Hong Kong, Germany and Milan (*Financial Times* (London), 16 August 1974, p. 13).
28. *Wall Street Journal*, 11 April 1974, p. 1.
29. For samples of the situation, see *New York Times*, 26 July 1974, pp. 43, 49; 3 July 1974, p. 44; *Wall Street Journal*, 15 July 1974, p. 4; 2 July 1974, p. 7; 24 May 1974, p. 5; 1 August 1974, p. 23.
30. *New York Times*, 12 August 1974, p. 35.
31. Cf. *New York Times*, 14 September 1974, p. 36. The most spectacular case involving collateral was that of Burmah Oil Company, which was rescued by the Bank of England when British Petroleum Company shares owned by Burmah Oil collapsed in value while pledged as backing for huge loans. See *New York Times*, 24 January 1975, p. 39.
32. *Wall Street Journal*, 14 January 1975, p. 14.
33. *New York Times*, 23 December 1974, pp. 43, 45.
34. Cf. R. W. Goldsmith, *Financial Structure and Development*, New Haven, Yale University Press, 1969, pp. 43–6, 321, 332–3, 340, 373–8.
35. Further discussion of the layering of claims is found in Chapter 4.
36. See, for example, *Bank of England Quarterly Bulletin*, June 1974, p. 137.
37. Increasingly, under such conditions in 1974 news stories appeared warning of possible bankruptcies, and presumably generating further fears. For examples, see *Financial Times* (London), 20 July 1974, p. 2; *Wall Street Journal*, 29 July 1974, p. 1 (in 'The Outlook').
38. An example of sectoral money market near-collapse follows:

    The $11.7 billion bankers acceptance market has come almost to a halt in the past two weeks, leaving hundreds of banks around the country unable to use these instruments for liquidity they had intended.
       The decision to terminate the operation of M&T Discount Corp., announced last week, capped difficulties experienced in this sector by all but the very largest and best regarded banks. M&T Discount was the largest of a handful of dealers specializing in acceptances and it was willing to deal with a great number of regional banks which now have no outlet through other dealers.
       As a result, many of these banks may be forced to retain their acceptances until maturity, a period of less than 270 days, when the trade transaction underlying the acceptance is paid off.
       And so these regional banks, already strapped for liquidity, have had another path to money closed off to them in the current market atmosphere. [*American Banker*, 10 July 1974, p. 1]

39. As noted earlier, destabilization of capital markets is linked to destabilization of money markets.
40. James Tobin, 'Inflation, Interest Rates, and Stock Values,' *Morgan Guaranty Survey*, July 1974, pp. 6–7.
41. See, for example, 'Numerical Specifications of Financial Variables and Their Role in Monetary Policy,' *Federal Reserve Bulletin*, May 1974, p. 333.

42. For an interesting theoretical analysis of the nature and causes of financial instability, see H. P. Minsky, 'Financial Instability Revisited: The Economics of Disaster,' in Board of Governors of the Federal Reserve System, *Reappraisal of the Federal Reserve Discount Mechanism*, Washington, DC, 1972, pp. 97–136.

3 Impacts of Severe General Monetary Restraint on Non-Depository Establishments and Households

3.1 Non-Depository Business and Non-Profit Institutions

In this section we continue the analysis of impacts of severe restraint. The items of concern now are the problems created for non-depository businesses and for non-profit institutions. These problems range widely, from bankruptcy to perhaps only inconvenience in having to search harder for sources of funds. While such problems are being treated here as consequences of monetary action, other factors, particularly those at which the monetary restraint is directed, in practice tend to be involved in varying degrees (in some cases, indeed, to a great degree – e.g., inflation, as in the financial squeeze of electric utility firms in 1974, which related primarily – probably – to rapidly rising prices, which in turn intensified the impact of the restraint by increasing borrowing requirements). Of course, income levels in the economy may also be crucial and are a by-product, in part, of the degree of monetary restraint employed.

3.1.1 Some Aggregative Measures

Definitive or fully persuasive statistical data showing the consequences of severe general monetary restraint for the wellbeing of non-depository businesses are not easily produced. In some cases, there may be no apparent impact, for example well-financed firms with much market power, which simply pass on added costs of capital – both explicit and implicit – to customers, with little impact on sales because of highly inelastic demand for its goods. At the other end of the spectrum are firms driven into bankruptcy courts by inability to refinance maturing debts or by rates of interest so high as to create cash flow problems compounded by falling sales owing to the impact of severe restraint on the economy generally. Such firms show up in the business failure statistics. Other firms with similar problems, but not at a level acute enough to produce bankruptcy, may have their difficulties reflected in falling profits, or falling liquidity ratios. Still other firms may simply liquidate without default. Problems may also show up in overdue trade credit and lengthening periods of payments for trade credit.

Whatever measures one uses, however, there will still be doubt generally concerning the relative contributions of monetary restraint and other forces. Recessions may occur without intense monetary restraint, although presumably with different timing. Business failures and financial difficulties would then follow. The period of increasing monetary restraint beginning in 1973 is particularly difficult to evaluate since it was accompanied by an accelerating rate of inflation and shortages, which put a cushion under the wellbeing of some business firms while hurting others. We will never know the extent to which data of the types suggested here were prevented from reaching grimmer levels by the inflation whose eventual stopping was the goal of the unprecedented monetary restraint. In short, inflation obscures the measurable impact of severe restraint by intensifying the impact of any given degree of restriction of monetary aggregates, by cushioning profit positions of many businesses and by eroding the profit positions of still others.

Given the limitations of such data, let us nevertheless examine them briefly to see what light, if any, they shed on the problem under consideration. It is clear that businesses were defaulting increasingly on debts owed. One measure of this was the loss experience of banks:

The banking industry's loss experience on commercial loans worsened sharply last year, according to Robert Morris Associates.
The findings from a survey of 473 banks across the country showed the banks wrote off as net losses an average of $26 for each $10,000 of business loans in their portfolios. That was up 24% from $21 per $10,000 in 1972.[1]

For all loans at member banks, net loan losses to average loans outstanding 'increased moderately from 0.23 per cent in 1972 to 0.25 per cent in 1973;' in 1974, however, the ratio rose sharply to 0.39 per cent.[2] It was reported, too, that for US non-financial cor-

porations 'the so-called "cash" ratio, i.e., cash plus liquid US
government securities to current liabilities, now is at its lowest point
since World War II, and possibly since the Depression of the
1930's.'[3] Weakness was also obvious in the current ratio (current
assets to current liabilities) for a number of manufacturing industries[4] and in the ratio of liquid assets to short-term debt for
non-financial corporations (see Figure 3.1).[5]

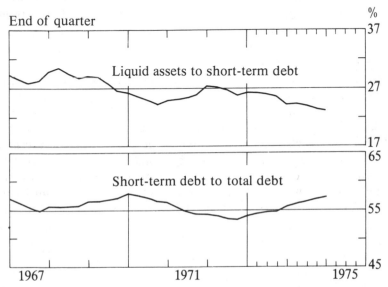

Figure 3.1   Liquidity Ratios of Non-Financial Corporations

Measures of business failure (which is a broader category than
bankruptcy[6] give inconclusive results, given the vast complexities
and changing forces in the economy (see Tables 3.1, 3.2 and 3.3).
In 1966 and 1967 the failure rate fell despite the intense credit
squeeze of 1966. Presumably the squeeze was too short to create
severe difficulties for the business world. In the next intense squeeze
beginning in late 1968 the failure rate fell sharply through 1969. It
rose sharply, however, in 1970, the peak year of the restraint and
the beginning of recession. In the next period of restraint the failure
rate at first fell (1973), then rose somewhat in 1974 as restraint was
most severe, and soared in 1975 with severe recession and easing
monetary conditions. Overall one senses a good deal of business

failure responding to severe monetary stringency through the latter's role in creating recession. Thus a lag may be expected in the business failure rate in response to severe credit restraint and, further, such a rise in the failure rate appears to require a period of restraint long enough to produce recession. Current liabilities in business failures behave directionally much as do failure rates, but when prices are

Table 3.1 Industrial and Commercial Failures – Number and Current Liabilities: 1950–75[a]

Year	Total concerns in business ('000)	Number	Failures[b] Rate per 10,000 concerns	Current liabilities[c] ($ million)	Average liability ($ thousand)
1950	2,687	9,162	34	248	27
1955	2,633	10,969	42	449	41
1960	2,708	15,445	57	939	61
1961	2,641	17,075	64	1,090	64
1962	2,589	15,782	61	1,214	77
1963	2,544	14,374	56	1,353	94
1964	2,524	13,501	53	1,329	98
1965	2,527	13,514	53	1,322	98
1966	2,520	13,061	52	1,386	106
1967	2,519	12,364	49	1,265	102
1968	2,481	9,636	39	941	98
1969	2,444	9,154	37	1,142	125
1970	2,442	10,748	44	1,888	176
1971	2,466	10,326	42	1,917	186
1972	2,490	9,566	38	2,000	209
1973	2,567	9,345	36	2,299	246
1974	2,591	9,915	38	3,053	308
1975	2,659	11,432	43	4,380	383

[a] Excludes Alaska and Hawaii; excludes all railroad failures; excludes real estate and financial companies; includes voluntary discontinuances with loss to creditors and small concerns forced out of business with insufficient assets to cover all claims.
[b] Includes concerns discontinuing following assignment, voluntary or involuntary petition in bankruptcy, attachment, execution, foreclosure, etc.; voluntary withdrawals from business with known loss to creditors; also enterprises involved in court action, such as receivership and reorganization or arrangement which may or may not lead to discontinuance; and businesses making voluntary compromise with creditors out of court.
[c] Liabilities exclude long-term publicly held obligations; offsetting assets are not taken into account.

Sources: US Bureau of the Census, *Statistical Abstract of the United States: 1975*, Washington, DC, 1975, p. 507; Dun and Broadstreet, Inc., *Monthly Failures*, New York, 6 May 1976.

Table 3.2 Industrial and Commercial Failures – Number and Current Liabilities, by Industry and Size of Liability: 1960–75[a,b]

Industry and size of liability	Failures							Current liabilities ($ million)						
	1960	1965	1970	1972	1973	1974	1975	1960	1965	1970	1972	1973	1974	1975
Total	15,445	13,514	10,748	9,566	9,345	9,915	11,432	939	1,322	1,888	2,000	2,299	3,053	4,380
Mining and manufacturing	2,612	2,007	2,035	1,576	1,576	1,557	1,645	290	350	818	767	797	834	1,021
Wholesale trade	1,473	1,355	984	965	940	964	1,089	107	144	179	250	274	275	407
Retail trade	7,386	6,250	4,650	4,398	4,341	4,234	4,799	241	287	361	558	673	1,070	1,836
Construction	2,607	2,513	1,687	1,375	1,419	1,840	2,262	201	291	232	194	309	527	641
Commercial service	1,367	1,299	1,392	1,252	1,182	1,320	1,637	99	249	299	232	245	348	475

[a] Excludes Alaska and Hawaii: see footnotes [b] and [c] Table 3.1.

[b] Details may not add to totals because of rounding.

Sources: US Bureau of the Census, *Statistical Abstract of the U.S.: 1975*, Washington, DC, 1975, p. 508: ibid., 1974, p. 493.

Dun and Broadstreet, Inc., *Monthly Failures*, New York, 6 May 1976.

Table 3.3 Bankruptcy Cases Filed, by Type of Bankruptcy and Occupation of Debtor: 1940–74[a]

Item	1940	1950	1955	1960	1965	1966	1967	1968	1969	1970	1971	1972	1973	1974
Total	52,320	33,392	59,404	110,034	180,323	192,354	208,329	197,811	184,930	194,399	201,352	182,869	173,197	189,513
Type:														
Straight bankruptcies	45,654	26,632	48,899	95,710	151,137	163,005	175,125	165,593	155,000	162,451	168,364	153,934	145,914	157,967
Voluntary	43,902	25,263	47,650	94,414	149,820	161,840	173,884	164,592	154,054	161,366	167,149	152,840	144,929	156,958
Involuntary	1,752	1,369	1,249	1,296	1,317	1,165	1,241	1,001	946	1,085	1,215	1,094	985	1,009
Corporate reorganization	320	134	73	90	88	101	138	128	87	115	179	105	101	163
Arrangements	1,139	614	566	634	1,071	984	1,103	1,022	933	1,320	1,902	1,453	1,550	2,343
Wage-earners' plans	3,247	6,007	9,864	13,599	28,027	28,261	31,963	31,065	28,910	30,510	30,904	27,373	25,632	29,023
Other	1,960	5	2	1	[b]	3	[b]	3	[b]	3	3	4	[b]	17
Occupation of Debtor[c]														
Merchants	4,651	2,565	3,317	3,157	4,332	4,209	4,437	4,173	3,624	4,003	4,690	4,359	4,492	5,317
Manufacturers	921	803	750	624	688	624	635	635	579	731	992	688	649	710
Farmers	2,678	290	386	453	589	551	443	567	606	658	788	631	431	308
Employees	36,846	22,933	46,163	89,639	148,965	160,299	174,025	162,866	150,188	156,343	156,077	139,437	131,122	141,877
Members of professions	801	126	217	495	778	627	703	1,084	1,301	1,301	1,465	1,556	1,450	1,582
Other	6,423	6,675	8,571	15,666	23,628	24,871	26,652	27,469	27,669	30,264	36,106	35,081	34,056	38,699
In business	4,193	4,568	4,515	7,555	9,188	9,260	9,137	9,088	8,417	8,470	10,013	9,825	9,505	11,870
Not in business	2,230	2,107	4,056	8,111	14,440	15,611	17,515	18,381	19,252	21,794	26,093	25,256	24,551	26,829

[a] In thousands. For years ending 30 June. Covers all US District Courts. A bankruptcy case is a proceeding filed in a US District Court under the National Bankruptcy Act. 'Filed' means the commencement of a proceeding through the presentation of a petition to the clerk of the court. 'Pending' is a proceeding in which the administration has not been completed.
[b] Represents zero.
[c] Beginning 1965, excludes corporate and involuntary straight cases.

Sources: US Bureau of the Census, *Statistical Abstract of the U.S.: 1974*, Washington, DC, 1975, p. 508; ibid., 1974, p. 493; ibid., 1970, p. 485.

rising rapidly, as in 1970 and in 1974–5, they tend to overstate the case.[7]

Business bankruptcy filings rose 18.6 per cent to 20,746 in the year ending 30 June 1974 (a period of severe restraint), 'setting an all-time high record since comparable statistical records were maintained beginning in 1940.'[8] In this period, in the area of corporate reorganization,

there were 163 filings under Chapter X of the Federal Bankruptcy Act . . . against 62 cases in the previous year. . . .

The number of companies whose simpler structure permitted them to take advantage of the procedures of Chapter XI of the act, rose to 2171 from 1458. . . .[9]

Of course, one must bear in mind that the data reflect a multiplicity of causal forces. What the data would show without inflation or without the pressure of severe monetary stringency one cannot say.

3.1.2 Some Industry Experience

Monetary interest in the national income accounts took a sharp turn upward relative to debt beginning with the mid-1960s, with periods of credit squeeze being crucial in the process. Interest paid became an increasingly important factor in corporate costs and cash flow, with net interest rising from about $1\frac{1}{2}$ per cent of gross domestic product of non-financial corporations and about 22 per cent of their profits tax liability in 1965 to comparable figures in 1974 of about $3\frac{1}{2}$ and 68 per cent, respectively (see Table 2.1). In Chapter 2 the rising importance of interest in selected industry sectors was noted. Here we give some illustrations and additional detail.

There is general agreement that the area most strongly and unambiguously affected by severe monetary restraint is residential construction. No matter what appropriate data are examined, the facts stand out: residential construction falls in value; home mortgage funds decline in availability while mortgage interest rates rise; disintermediation develops at thrift institutions which supply mortgage credit. Liabilities in construction firm failures rise, and other financial institutions in the chain from home buyer to saver–lender may be severely affected, e.g. mortgage bankers and real estate investment trusts.[10]

One could go on at length here giving details of the plight and behavior of institutions in residential construction and related financing areas in 1973–4. Indeed, a calculation of the press coverage of events would show vast space devoted to a never-ending lament. One theme worth noting is that of REIT ensnarement in a web of complicated difficulties, some of which were noted in Chapter 2. They were driven from the commercial paper markets in the wake of, and adding to, their troubles. They were caught between borrowing at astronomical rates of interest (e.g. 130 per cent of extraordinarily high prime rates) and defaults of their builder/developer debtors. Thus, 'nearly 25% of the 200-odd REITs in existence today have cut, delayed, or omitted their second-quarter dividends, and the prices of virtually all the REITs are down on the floor.'[11]

Another industry hard-hit by severe restraint was retailing. Firm after firm reported difficulties or disappointing results in 1974. Important bankruptcies included those of Interstate Stores, reported then to be 'the largest in retail history,'[12] Mammoth Mart and Bohack Corporation. Even some of the best-known national leaders in retailing encountered disappointments in the face of rising dollar sales. Sears Roebuck and Woolworth were in this category,[13] as was J. C. Penney.[14] W. T. Grant, which filed for bankruptcy in October 1975 in the largest failure in retail history, was particularly interesting, reporting

for the six months ended July 31 [1974] ... a $10.9 million loss on sales of $806.8 million....
In the first half ... it had an interest expense of about $35 million. From fiscal 1973 to fiscal 1974, ended January 31, the chain said its interest costs rose to $51 million from about $21 million.[15]

High interest costs were cited generally by leading firms as an important factor in the case of disappointing results.

Enveloping not only key financial sectors such as depository and securities services and non-financial sectors such as retailing and residential construction, severe monetary restraint in the United States permeated sector after sector in the economy, attacking those most exposed by virtue of small size, traditional dependence on external funds, industry weakness externally or exogenously imposed, and/or firm weakness stemming from internal causes or newness. For example, the public utility industry – in addition to its inflationary burdens – was caught in a short-term liquidity squeeze. Dramatizing the industry plight vividly was the case of the Detroit Edison Company, which sold coal stocks and transportation equipment on a leaseback arrangement to raise funds.[16] Numerous electric utilities were reported reducing maintenance expenditures as a short-term expedient.[17] Utilities were reported finding it

nearly impossible to raise money anywhere at any price.

Commercial banks, already saddled with more business loan demand than they can handle, may be unwilling to extend credit to a utility. Nor can the utility float commercial paper on an open money market glutted with industrial issues.[18]

Finance companies, too, were in trouble, as might have been anticipated in view of their heavy dependence on external funds.[19] Life insurance companies, as in the 1966 and 1968–70 credit squeezes, were hard-hit by the growth of policy loans which they were required to give by regulatory requirement. As a proportion of life insurance company assets 'policy loans ... at the end of June [1974] rose to 8.3% ... the highest since the 10% recorded in 1940.'[20] The non-life insurance companies were faced with a different kind of threat, that from a collapsing stock market, for it is in common stocks that they hold their surpluses, which in turn are held for meeting claims.[21] Liquidations of such assets to meet claims could lead to disaster in adverse situations.

Another hard-hit group in the US credit squeeze were colleges and universities. Both public and private institutions borrow from banks to bridge the gap between payment of bills and receipts from sources such as tuition, government grants and investment income. Stiff rises in interest rates took sorely needed funds that presumably could have been used for operating expenses.[22]

One could go on at length here, citing sector after sector, firm after firm. Common to all firms or economic entities were very high rates of interest in recent US credit squeezes, especially that of 1973–4, and very frequently an inability to obtain the sums desired or needed even at very high rates. Worth noting in this micro-excursion are samples of terms and rates charged in the 1973–4 squeeze since they give perspective to some of the aggregative data cited earlier, as well as to industry or firm experience. For example, Penn Fruit Company, a regional supermarket chain that in 1975 filed a petition in bankruptcy, announced a $9 million credit with

Fidelity Bank and Girard Bank (of Philadelphia), which

provides for a $6 million reducing revolving credit maturing September 15, 1976, at an interest rate of 134 percent of the prime with no compensating balance, and a $3 million line of credit at 1 percent over prime with compensating balance requirements.[23]

At this time prime was 12 per cent! Somewhat similar was the experience of Phoenix Steel Corporation, which arranged a $15.5 million credit with First Pennsylvania Bank and Associates Capital Company (of South Bend, Indiana). Interest again was to vary with prime and 'based on current rates interest would be about 17 per cent. . . .'[24]

The reach of severe monetary restraint is very long. It does not stop at the profit-seeking enterprise sector of the economy, or at state and local government (discussed later). It reaches out to the very large, private, non-profit sector. Here are the philanthropic foundations, the private universities, colleges and other educational institutions, the art and scientific institutions, the symphony orchestras, the private hospitals, as well as potential donors to such organizations. The great security market deflation described earlier – and largely man-made by the monetary authorities – reduced the values of assets held by these institutions tremendously, reduced their spending ability and reduced sharply the ability of non-profit organizations to obtain contributions from private individuals.

The most publicized case was that of the Ford Foundation, which, with a fall in asset value 'from $3 billion to $2 billion in market value in the last year,' was reported 'considering a reduction of as much as 50 per cent in its annual grants.' Previously the Foundation had 'consistently given away twice the amount it earned through dividends and interest on its investments . . .'[25] The decline in asset value faced by the Ford Foundation was not unique. Between year-end 1972 and year-end 1974 total assets of US foundations were reported to have fallen from $39.5 billion to $29.5 billion, with common stock holdings falling $10.0 billion during this period.[26] Other foundations also found themselves required to reduce support in a vast array of fields such as performing arts, agriculture, health, humanities, education and community welfare.

Universities, colleges and other institutions had similar problems through endowment funds. A trend had developed towards use of capital gains for current funds, based on a recognition that capital gains reflect in part retained corporate earnings. The security market collapse of 1973–4 substituted losses for gains and so impaired the usable income of institutions. For example, the University of Pennsylvania 'began using up to nine percent of its capital gains for revenue under the authority of a "total return" bill passed by the state legislature in 1972.' In fiscal 1974–5 an already difficult financial situation was made worse by elimination of this source of spending.[27]

If the capital value effect of severe monetary restraint is extrapolated to every affected institution in the United States, there emerges a situation of great magnitude aggregatively and of harsh difficulty for a large number of individual institutions and their clients. Compounding all this travail is the adverse impact on potential philanthropic donors who in the United States often use corporate stock as the vehicle for giving, usually for tax reasons, and so prefer not to give in badly depressed security markets. Additionally, under such market conditions potential donors themselves may feel less wealthy or be strapped financially, and thus may feel unable or unwilling to give. If one adds to all of this the income effects of prolonged severe monetary restraint, the endowment income on investments may be reduced in addition to the incomes of potential donors (large and small) and their ability to give.[28]

3.1.3   The Waste of Talent

Severe monetary restraint sets in motion intensified searches for funds to replace or supplement normal sources. It also stimulates a more intensive search for uses of funds by those with cash to spare. Thus, every business borrower affected adversely by prolonged restraint must allocate additional man-hours to search for funds at competitive terms. Lending institutions may receive more applications as rejections multiply, again with a need for more man-hours. Non-professional lenders with temporarily idle cash (e.g. industrial firms) are likely to scrutinize competitive money-lending opportunities more closely. New organizations may be formed to institutionalize the emerging opportunities, e.g. the growth of money market mutual funds in the United States in 1974 with opportunities for daily commitment and withdrawal of funds. Bankruptcies and near-bankruptcies brought on by severe restraint create work for lawyers, financial experts and their staffs.

No reasonable quantification is possible of the incremental human and related material resources devoted to (1) hunting and allocating debt (and equity) funds in a credit squeeze such as that of 1968–70 or 1973–4, and (2) ministering to its casualties. Such resources are employed in substantial amounts even in the absence of severe monetary restraint. Nevertheless, a careful observer of the economic and financial scene cannot escape the conclusion that much incremental talent was employed in the aggregate and that it was talent of generally high quality. Given the view here that the net results of the two recent periods of severe, prolonged monetary restraint were generally adverse and largely self-defeating, one cannot help wondering about the potential for positive economic services, were all this valuable incremental talent released from defensive financial 'scrounging.'

3.2   The Household Sector

This section extends the argument of previous sections. We examine the consequences of severe general monetary restraint for the people employed by business and non-profit organizations, for people who are retired, for the existing unemployed, for those seeking to enter the labor force and for those in other categories.

The general economic setting is again that of inflation. The excess demand type of inflation is not at issue here. Adverse consequences of the type under consideration here would be of far less significance in a genuine demand-pull inflation. We are concerned with inflations classified in Chapter 4 in the categories of cost-push, demand-shift, functional and political. Combined with significant unemployment, such inflations have been referred to as 'stagflation'.

3.2.1   *Financial Defaults*

One measurable impact of prolonged, severe monetary restraint on persons is rising default rates on debts owed by individuals. The American Bankers Association makes surveys of delinquency rates on instalment credit at banks and reported that, in January and February 1974, the rate (number of delinquencies divided by number of loans) reached the highest level (2.69 per cent) since the start of the series in 1963. Inflation, unemployment and energy shortages were given as the chief reasons.[29] Another series '(see Figure 3.2) showed delinquency rates at a high since 1950. (Such peaks did not appear, however, in delinquency rates at sales finance and consumer finance companies.)[30]

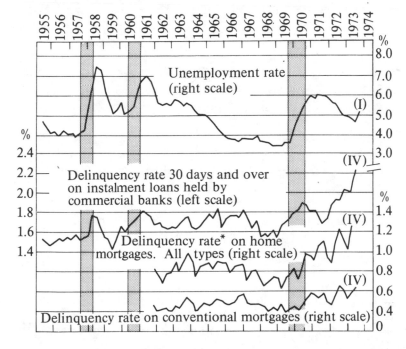

*60 Days and over

Figure 3.2   Unemployment and Delinquency Rates

A similar situation prevailed in real estate credit as mortgage delinquency rates reached the highest level in twenty years by the end of 1973 and continued to rise in 1974 and 1975 (see Figure 3.2).[31] Mortgage foreclosure rates on all mortgages also simultaneously reached record levels (see Figure 3.3). This reflected primarily foreclosures of government-guaranteed and insured mortgages rather than conventional mortgages.[32]

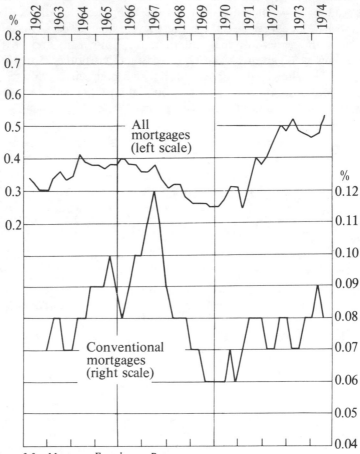

Figure 3.3   Mortgage Foreclosure Rates

Bankruptcies, as noted before, are another measurable phenomenon showing the impacts of prolonged severe monetary restraint.
Bankruptcies of all kinds – business, personal, etc. – increased by
9.4 per cent (reaching 189,513) in fiscal 1974 (ended 30 June 1974)
and another 34 per cent in fiscal 1975.[33] These overwhelmingly
reflected non-business failures. They include, however, a number of
bankruptcies declared by ex-students in connection with loans
contracted for education, and this may distort the significance of
the movements in the series. Even so, movements in student defaults

would inevitably reflect, albeit imperfectly, the state of the economy. With these reservations, we note that the data, at least in the 1970–1 and 1973–5 recessions, are cyclical (see Table 3.3).

3.2.2 Falling Capital Values

In the preceding chapter, estimates were given of the quantitative magnitudes of capital values wiped out in three periods of restraint. To be considered now are the consequences of such declines for the economic wellbeing of the members of society, whose improvement is generally considered a goal of society, but whose worsening is the most likely net outcome of severe monetary restraint under the conditions assumed here.

Let us examine first the situation of retired persons, who have grown enormously in absolute and in relative terms in recent decades.[34] These are, of course, a diverse lot. There are those who retire on a social security pension and nothing else. At the other end of the spectrum are those of great wealth with large investment incomes. To such extremes our analysis is not directed. It is directed at those with modest accumulated personal savings in marketable forms, normally securities and possibly real estate. It is directed also to those whose retirement income partly reflects institutional arrangements, typically involving employee pension funds that have benefits flowing from marketable securities and other marketable assets. Our question is then concerned with the consequences of falling capital values for persons who retire during periods of prolonged, severe monetary restraint or who are already in retirement when such restraint occurs and who are not at extreme positions in the income–wealth spectrum.

Those whose personal retirement assets included marketable bonds bought in less restrictive monetary circumstances may be adversely affected in a variety of ways, for example if bonds are used as collateral for loans. They are hurt if utilization of principal is required or is desirable to meet expected and unexpected living expenses, e.g. food, rent, large medical outlays. They may be hurt if bonds are sold to switch the composition of assets held. For example, there may be a switch from bonds to a home (assume that the retiree had been living in an apartment or rented home, or had living quarters that accompanied a job). Retirees may also be hurt if bonds are viewed as precautionary reserves whose value permits spending out of other resources on some predetermined, related scale.

The same possible consequences to retirees stemming from holdings of marketable bonds follow also in greater or lesser degree from holdings of other marketable assets. As noted earlier, high-grade preferred stocks are similar in character, as are common shares of public utility enterprises. Common shares of one type of real estate investment trust became a popular vehicle whereby individuals in the United States could, in effect, invest in a diversi-fied mortgage portfolio. Such shares may take on much of the capital value behavior of marketable, fixed-income debt instru-ments, but with even greater vulnerability to fluctuation. Other common stocks, as noted earlier, generally can become victims of prolonged, severe monetary restraint.

Individuals, of course, may invest in the above capital instru-ments indirectly through a mutual fund (open-end investment trust) or closed-end investment trust, and may buy specialized types of funds to suit their asset preferences – from a municipal bond fund to a high-risk common stock fund and all points between in pure form or in combination. Thus, although it may be argued that individuals are not substantial direct investors in corporate or municipal bonds or in preferred stocks in relation to their total asset holdings, still they may have substantial holdings indirectly via holdings in investment trusts.

Retirees, too, may be indirect investors in these assets via pension funds. Here they may have benefits related by formula to earnings levels of annuitants, or they may have retirement income related in either fixed or variable fashion to earnings of the pension fund, with a fairly fixed rate of contributions related to earnings. Where retire-ment income is related by formula to annuitant earnings, funds are likely to be invested in fixed-income obligations, which in turn are carried at face value by the fund administrators and so are not at issue here so far as falling capital values are concerned. At the other extreme, where retirement income is in the form of a variable annuity, the market value of equity instruments is involved, since the retirement income depends both on income of the pension fund and its capital gains and losses. Here the retiree is essentially in the same position as with direct ownership of, and dependence on, common stocks. Perhaps the simplest way to deal with this matter is by calling attention to the disastrous situation of such pension fund plans in 1974. Plan after plan was reported in trouble, with some firms giving supplemental benefits to retirees to compensate for falling pension fund distributions.[35] Unfortunately, too, if pensioners tried to supplement their annuity income by liquidating other securities, the pain was simply multiplied.

Residential real estate, too, may be part of a retiree's assets. It is much more difficult to isolate here the pure capital value impact of severe monetary stringency for reasons to be noted shortly. Suffice it to state that in terms of direction and magnitude, the effect on housing values of prolonged, severe monetary restraint alone should be parallel to that on marketable bonds, albeit with lags. These lags reflect the facts that the housing market is far less speculative than is the bond market (in the short-run), that it is far more 'imperfect' in character, that there is no unified national, or indeed unified local, market. Unless offset by other forces (which are discussed shortly), retirees may therefore suffer capital losses in severe monetary restraint should they have to dispose of their homes or income-producing residential real estate.

Close to the retirement situation is that of estates. Those who die in a period of very restrictive monetary policy may, in many cases, leave to their dependents less than intended. The argument here is simply that presented in preceding paragraphs. Worth adding, perhaps, is the translation of variable annuity-type benefits into a death benefit should an annuitant die prior to retirement age. In such situations a badly depressed equities market resulting from severe monetary restriction would again leave dependents in a financial state weaker than would otherwise be the case and possibly substantially weaker than intended.

In rebuttal, one might argue that what goes down can go up, so that retirees or legatees can postpone liquidation of assets or 'average out' values by liquidating gradually. This is all well and good for those not needing to liquidate assets to meet current needs, and if there is an available time-span adequate to 'average out.' Unfortunately, there is often no capacity to wait and a too short path to the grim reaper.

Much of the preceding argument has wider general application. Savings are employed for far more than retirement or building an estate and when those savings are accumulated in the marketable forms described in preceding paragraphs, large movements to the 'down side' stemming from prolonged, severe monetary restraint can bring distress and possibly disaster to various members of society. Some of the other major purposes and uses of building stores of value are obvious, e.g. large medical expenses, unemployment or decline in income resulting from economic factors, unemployment resulting from illness and convalescence, education of children, down payments on houses, major alterations or renewal expenses on houses, major household purchases including automobiles, major charitable contributions, travel, and collateral in borrowing for the foregoing.[36]

With respect to use of personal property for collateral in borrowing, insult is added to injury. An individual requiring use of savings that are embodied in a marketable instrument first finds its capital value badly eroded, then its collateral value in borrowing badly eroded, then must pay very high rates of interest on its dwindling borrowing power if he or she is unwilling to sell the instrument(s) at a large loss. Even worse is the case of the individual whose need to fall back on marketable assets results from unemployment created by monetary restraint. Overall, cumulative asset sales by distressed individuals and institutions may cause such asset prices to fall even further, thus compounding the difficulties for persons affected.[37]

3.2.3 Housing Sales and Purchases

On preceding and later pages, there is discussion of the impacts of severe monetary restraint on housing finance and values. Here the concern is with immediate impacts on individuals as they try to buy or sell houses. It was noted in the previous section that the pure capital value thrust of monetary restraint is the same for houses as for bonds, although there is considerable lag in adjustments in the housing markets. The pure capital value thrust (i.e. that involving capitalization of a stream of anticipated returns) may be offset, however, by forces at work that change the anticipated returns or that increase financial market imperfections. These forces include both monetary restraint as well as others. Thus, it may be impossible ultimately to disentangle from other influences the net effects of monetary policy.

Restrictive monetary policy itself pushes in more than one direction. On the one hand, severe restraint would be likely to lead directly to a reduction in the supply of housing credit, even without the major market imperfections and interferences that now prevail. This is amplified in practice by disintermediation resulting from market interferences and by market imperfections that prevent the upward adjustment of mortgage interest rates at a speed equal to that of bond interest rates, i.e. the availability effect.[38] In addition, there are the rising monthly costs of carrying mortgages and the unemployment stemming from severe monetary restraint. The combination of these several forces would act as a depressant on the demand side of housing, tending to produce lower prices. At the same time, difficulties for developers in obtaining financing during construction would act as a depressant on the supply side, and in combination with diseconomies resulting from lower output would tend to push up prices on new construction. Again there are the influences of movements in the general price level and the costs of new housing. In 1973–4, for example, the forces of inflation clearly outweighed any forces leading to lower prices on housing, and to such an extent, indeed, that there was a veritable explosion in construction costs which spilled over into the prices of old homes.

In any event, in the three periods of severe monetary restraint from 1966 through 1974, difficulties were encountered by those wanting to sell and buy existing houses. The degree of difficulty seems to have risen sharply in the second period compared with the first, while being probably most difficult in the third period.

The concern here is with the impact on individuals of all types who were required or wished to sell houses – or buy them – in periods of prolonged, severe monetary restraint. One suspects that the consequences for individuals varied widely within each of the three periods. Probably many an intended sale transaction died because the purchaser could not obtain mortgage financing from customary suppliers of real estate credit. Many another sale in the United States failed to be consummated by virtue of sellers being unwilling to absorb so-called discount points, i.e., in effect, to accept a lower price because of the mortgage-lender's refusal to accept a mortgage at face value. Overall, in the sharply curtailed fluidity of the housing market during those three periods of restraint, many an actual and potential house-buyer, and many an actual and potential house-seller, were injured. Undoubtedly, many of those who had to sell or buy without delay were forced to make sacrifices.

Many an individual who succeeded in buying did so by virtue of some tie with a lender: via an employer's relationships, via a preferred position owing to being a depositor, etc. Those with no ties came in last.[39]

3.2.4 Unemployment

By all odds, the most serious short-run consequence of prolonged, severe monetary restraint is unemployment. (The reader is reminded that an essentially demand-pull inflation is *not* the background condition assumed.) Of particular significance is the fact that unemployment is not regarded by policy-makers as simply an unfortunate by-product of the battle against inflation, public relations statements to the contrary notwithstanding. Instead, it is viewed as the weapon with the cutting edge. Underlying this view, of course, is the assumption that restraint of demand for goods and services through monetary and fiscal policies will result in (1) workers being more 'reasonable' in seeking wage increases, and (2) more resistance to wage demands and more restraint in raising prices on the part of the business community. It is a view that began to gain support in the 1950s and was in full bloom by the 1970s. Accompanying it was increasing disillusionment of many policy-makers and economists with the goal of full employment, which they more and more thought of as something to be approached very warily and slowly.

It is important, therefore, to look closely into some of the implications of unemployment. These are both economic and non-economic in character. The economic impacts are widely varied, including the behavioral responses of the public to events. Although the primary focus here presumably must be on economic elements, broad social aspects must also be considered. In some respects, indeed, social issues cannot be disentangled from economic issues.

Some Economic Implications of Unemployment

Various types of data are available concerning unemployment in the United States. Most comprehensive and widely used are the unemployment statistics of the Bureau of Labor Statistics (based on Bureau of Census surveys). Less comprehensive are data relating to unemployment among those covered by unemployment in-

Table 3.4   Major Unemployment Rates, 1965, 1969–75 (percentage of civilian labor force, persons aged sixteen years and over)

Category	Year							
	1965	1969	1970 (averages)	1971	1972	1973 (Oct.)	1974 (June)	1975 (May)
Total (all civilian workers)	4.5	3.5	4.9	5.9	5.6	4.6	5.2	9.2
Males, 20 yrs and over	3.2	2.1	3.5	4.4	4.0	3.0	3.5	7.3
Females, 20 yrs and over	4.5	3.7	4.8	5.7	5.4	4.4	5.1	8.6
Both sexes, 16–19 yrs	14.8	12.2	15.2	16.9	16.2	14.0	15.6	21.8
White	4.1	3.1	4.5	5.4	5.0	4.1	4.8	8.5
Negro and other races	8.1	6.4	8.2	9.9	10.0	8.4	8.8	14.7
Household heads	2.8	1.8	2.9	3.7	3.3	2.7	3.1	6.3
Married men	2.4	1.5	2.6	3.2	2.8	2.1	2.6	5.8
Full-time workers	4.2	3.1	4.5	5.5	5.1	4.1	4.7	8.8
Part-time workers	6.7	6.2	7.6	8.7	8.6	7.5	8.9	11.1
Occupation								
White-collar workers	2.3	2.1	2.8	3.5	3.4	2.6	3.1	5.4
Professional and technical	1.5	1.3	2.0	2.9	2.4	2.2	1.9	3.6
Managers and administrators (non-farm)	1.1	0.9	1.3	1.6	1.8	1.4	1.8	3.5
Sales workers	3.4	2.9	3.9	4.3	4.3	3.0	4.6	5.9
Clerical workers	3.3	3.0	4.1	4.8	4.7	3.6	4.4	7.8
Blue-collar workers	5.3	3.9	6.2	7.4	6.5	5.1	6.2	13.0
Craft and kindred workers	3.6	2.2	3.8	4.7	4.3	3.5	4.2	9.3
Operatives	5.5	4.4	7.1	8.3	6.9	5.4	6.8	14.4
Non-farm laborers	8.6	6.7	9.5	10.8	10.3	8.0	9.6	17.7
Service workers	5.3	4.2	5.3	6.3	6.3	5.1	5.8	8.7
Farm Workers	2.6	1.9	2.6	2.6	2.6	2.5	2.8	3.7
Industry (experienced wage and salary workers)								
Non-agricultural private wage and salary workers	4.6	3.5	5.2	6.2	5.7	4.5	5.4	10.1
Construction	10.1	6.0	9.7	10.4	10.3	9.0	10.2	21.8
Manufacturing	4.0	3.3	5.6	6.8	5.6	3.9	5.2	12.3
Transportation, public utilities	2.9	2.1	3.2	3.8	3.5	2.9	3.2	6.7
Wholesale and retail trade	5.0	4.1	5.3	6.4	6.4	5.1	6.1	8.9
Finance and service industries	2.3	2.1	2.8	3.3	3.4	4.1	4.3	7.2
Government workers	4.6	3.5	4.7	5.6	5.3	2.7	2.8	4.9
Agricultural wage and salary workers	1.9	1.9	2.2	2.9	2.9	6.7	7.5	9.4

Sources: US Dept of Labor, *Handbook of Labor Statistics, 1973*, Washington, DC, 1973, pp. 135, 147, 159; *Employment and Earnings*, September 1974, p. 43; March 1975, p. 45; December 1975, p. 44.

surance. Data attempting to place a different perspective on unemployment involve measurement of the intensity of demand by employers for workers. Techniques here include indexes of help-wanted advertising and job vacancy data obtained from business establishments. We shall focus on the broadest, basic official measures of unemployment rates (even though they understate the degree of unemployment by failing to cover discouraged persons no longer looking for work and partial unemployment, i.e. reductions in hours worked).

Very important is the wide variation that exists with respect to unemployment rates within the US economy. Presented in Table 3.4 are data showing for recent years movements in the aggregate unemployment rate and in crucial components. Here one finds that, with 4.6 per cent aggregate unemployment (the low point of 1973), white-collar workers faced only a 2.6 per cent unemployment rate, while construction workers had a 9.0 per cent rate and blue-collar, non-farm laborers had an 8.0 per cent rate; whites overall had a 4.1 per cent rate and Negroes and other races an 8.4 per cent rate. At the lowest annual average unemployment rate of the 1960s (3.5 per cent in 1969), the non-white rate was 6.4 per cent: the rate for professional and technical workers was 1.3 per cent, for non-farm laborers, 6.7 per cent and for the construction industry, 6.0 per cent. In May 1975 construction unemployment reached 21.8 per cent against an overall average of 9.2 per cent.[40]

As even these limited data suggest, the incidence of differentially high or low unemployment is not random in character.[41] For non-whites there appears to be at best a perpetual recession: the lowest average annual unemployment between 1954 and 1973 was 6.4 per cent and only one other time during that period was it below 7 per cent. The real variation for blacks was not between fairly full employment and recession, but between recession and major depression. Among whites, in stark contrast, in only two years in that period did the rate exceed 5.0 per cent.[42] For managers and administrators (except farm) the maximum unemployment rate between 1958 and 1972 was 1.8 per cent; for non-farm laborers it was 15.1 per cent.[43]

Regionally, variations by race are also very wide. Let us consider unemployment rates in a group of large US standard metropolitan statistical areas (SMSAs) for the years 1969–72, i.e. from a year of overall low unemployment levels to one of fairly high levels. In the

Cleveland SMSA, for example, non-whites in 1971 had an average unemployment rate of about 16 per cent, in contrast to a white unemployment rate about two-thirds less. In three others of the twenty largest SMSAs, non-white unemployment rates ranged from nearly 14 per cent to over 15 per cent in 1971–2, while maximum white rates in those years were between 7.3 and 8.7 per cent in the same SMSAs.[44]

What emerges from this is that to use unemployment as a vehicle for effectuating economic policy is to use a selective policy. Thus, to the industry-selectivity of monetary policy must be added a substantial class bias – against those least able to bear economic adversity. They are mainly the unskilled and semi-skilled, those on hourly pay arrangements.[45] To use prolonged tight money to fight non-demand-pull inflation is to use sectoral mass unemployment and sectoral major depression.

Additional variation in US unemployment rates is shown in Table 3.4 and illustrates well-known characteristics. Most important, perhaps, are disproportionately high unemployment rates among females and young people.

Another dimension can be added to the scarcity approach to the control of inflation by translating unemployment rates into output losses. For this purpose, let us use the widely used rule of thumb that a change of 1 percentage point in the US employment rate corresponds to a change of about 3 per cent in real GNP[46], and apply it to 1971. With unemployment at an average of nearly 6 per cent in 1971, the lost GNP for the year was perhaps $60 billion (at 1971 prices) compared with the GNP that would have been generated if a 4 per cent unemployment rate had prevailed. About $75 billion was lost if the comparison is with an output corresponding to the $3\frac{1}{2}$ per cent average unemployment rate of 1969. These magnitudes can be appreciated better by noting that $75 billion was the approximate GNP of Canada for 1970. For another comparison to put in perspective the meaning of $60–75 billion at that time, one might note that the total expenditures for goods and services by all state and local governments in the United States was estimated at about $122 billion for 1970. Thus, the lost GNP of 1971 and 1970 (with an average unemployment rate of 4.9 per cent for 1970) was probably roughly equal to total 1970 expenditures on goods and services by all states and local governments in the United States combined (estimating GNP losses in terms of departures from the average 1968–9 unemployment rate, which was under 3.6 per cent). For a more recent year, 1975, lost GNP was probably in the vicinity of $200 billion in 1975 dollars on the basis of an average unemployment rate roughly 4½ percentage points in excess of a goal of 4 per cent.

Rough as estimates of lost GNP may be, a change of several percentage points – or even 1 percentage point – clearly involves large absolute losses in GNP, with previously noted consequences. When such losses are distributed over the economy, belt-tightening is likely to be required of nearly all; and, as indicated earlier, the degree of impact may vary from serious to disastrous for those facing the full fury of unemployment.

For the unemployed there is obviously the immediate loss of income. For about half there is a temporary cushion in the form of unemployment insurance (covering 40 per cent or more of pay[47]), and in a few favored groups such as autos, steel and aerospace[48] supplementary private benefits may be paid by employers. For those not covered, and for those who have exhausted their benefits, there is public welfare. Admittedly, too, for those at the lowest end of the pay scales, welfare – tax-free – may involve not much change in income level. Overall, however, the unemployed, as a group, face severe losses in income.

Increasingly, fringe benefits are part of a pay package and unemployment destroys them, exposing affected persons and their families in some cases to dire consequences. As indicated in Table 3.5, health, insurance and pension plans are provided for the over-

Table 3.5   Percentage of Workers Employed in Establishments Having Formal Health Insurance and Pension Plans, 1971[a]

	Office workers	Plant workers
Life insurance	97	93
Hospitalization	97	95
Surgical	97	95
Medical	93	88
Major medical	91	69
Retirement pension	85	78

[a] Data are for manufacturing, public utilities and retail trade in 229 standard metropolitan statistical areas in late 1970 and early 1971. Establishment size is 100 or more employees in twelve largest SMSAs and 50 in others.
Source: *Statistical Abstract of the United States: 1974*, op. cit., p. 362.

whelming portion of employees in US industry and commerce (excluding very small establishments). Based on 1971–2 data, for example, 69 per cent of plant workers had major medical coverage, 95 per cent had hospital and surgical protection, and 93 per cent, life insurance. Office workers had even higher levels of participation. Thus, unemployment dealt a strong secondary blow in 1974 and 1975, one that received attention in the press.[49] Indeed, bills were introduced in Congress to assist the unemployed in retaining medical coverages. A dangerous side-effect of the situation concerned the finances of hospitals faced with clients unable to pay their bills. Beyond the medical field, cessation of group life policies removed for many of the unemployed critical low-cost family protection.

Common to most persons including the unemployed, is the problem of contractual, regular financial obligations. Most common and most important are mortgage payments, rents and life insurance premiums.[50] Very common, too, are instalment credit payments. Other contractual commitments include individual health insurance policies with public (non-profit) and private insurers, alimony and child support payments. With a rising ratio of divorces to marriages (37 per cent in 1972), alimony and child support commitments are serious in a macro, as well as in a micro sense.[51]

Finally, with steadily rising fees at colleges and universities, loans have been of increasing importance, burdening students and their families with substantial obligations. In turn, to the extent that unemployment leads to defaults on educational loans, financial pressure is placed upon the colleges and universities that have allotted their own resources for this purpose.

Certain consequences of contractual commitments were noted earlier. These included rising defaults on debts stemming from rising unemployment and related economic weakness. Noted also were rising mortgage foreclosures, rising delinquencies on consumer credit and rising bankruptcies. In addition, there are obviously sales of homes and cars and repossessions of goods by lenders where defaults on durable goods purchases have occurred. There is also additional borrowing, e.g. on life insurance policies and on houses. There is also dropping of policies, reduction in coverage, etc.[52]

While difficulties cited in preceding paragraphs focus on the unemployed, those difficulties in fact have wider incidence. Obviously, loss of purchasing power by the unemployed has adverse impacts on those whose fortunes are linked in some way to those of the unemployed. Most serious are cases of geographic locations where there is a high incidence of unemployment, with attendant distress to merchants, service people and others who themselves may then run into difficulties of the types described in preceding paragraphs. It should also be noted that the distinction between employment and unemployment is overdrawn. The fact is that short hours may give consequences much the same as unemployment.[53] In addition, when overtime becomes a way of life, its withdrawal can also give consequences similar to those of unemployment.

Beyond such problems as contractual financial commitments and loss of contractual fringe benefits are a host of often more immediate consequences of unemployment. These involve the belt-tightening in necessities, i.e. food, clothing, medical attention (other than that involved in fringe benefits) and housing. (Such belt-tightening would be required even in the absence of financial commitments and of a system of fringe benefits, although these items intensify the belt-tightening). Less important, of course, but painful to those involved is the reduction in spending on non-essential amenities and minor to major luxuries.

There may be losses of skills and work habits, although this is less likely in a very short period of unemployment. For young people newly entering the labor force, however, there is not only a lack of opportunity to build skills and work habits and an erosion of skills just learned, but a possible destruction of morale and the will to work. For older workers layoffs may mean discrimination in regaining employment. For workers who are unemployed for an extended period there may be difficulties in regaining employment even in recovery because of employer reluctance to hire the long-term unemployed. For close relatives of any unemployed, there may be financial burdens in helping out.

Children may be forced to abandon plans for college and other forms of post-secondary school training because one or both parents are made fully or partially unemployed, or even because they lose 'normal' overtime work. Others may be forced to discontinue existing education and training programs, not only beyond secondary school but even in secondary school. Of course, not only is there the immediate impact, which also adds to unemployment and competition for existing jobs, but for many of those affected there may be permanent economic damage to their careers. Even after re-employment, it may take a long time for a family to regain its full economic health, and children finishing secondary school then may also be deprived of further education and training. One will never know how many teenagers had their economic futures permanently impaired as a result of the deliberately created unemployment of 1974–5 and of 1970–1.[54] Society, too, becomes a heavy loser as a result of permanent damage to the quality of the labor force, and in this there is an element of irony. Those economists who have been least concerned about substantial US unemployment rates have tended to blame them on lack of suitable training. Their point of view can thus be self-fulfilling in a sequence going from deliberately created unemployment, to failure to obtain useful training, to future unemployment because of lack of training.

A further set of adverse economic consequences befalls the household sector as unemployment creates financial crises for state and local governments in the form of expenditure gaps. Current expenditures rise because of additional welfare problems, while revenues lag to the extent that they are related to income (e.g. wage taxes). Choices then have to be made, usually in terms of raising tax rates or cutting expenditures, both of which intensify the unemployment problem and help to create even more difficulties for all.

If one combines the costs of inflation and unemployment, one has the worst of all possible worlds, one illustrated by US experiences in 1974–5 and 1970–1. It is the world where expenditure gaps of cities and states created by inflation are compounded by sharply rising welfare rolls and shortfalls of tax receipts associated with unemployment.[55] It is a world of expenditure gaps in public educational institutions and school systems arising from inflation, plus a decreased capacity of state and local governments to pay for previously existing costs even if prices had not risen. At the college and university level, reduced appropriations (in real terms) may be a consequence, with fewer places available for students and less aid (in real terms) given directly by schools via grants and loans to students. In the recession of 1970–1, for example, the state of New York announced that 2,000 fewer students would be accepted in the state university system in the autumn of 1971.[56] In Philadelphia, those who followed the daily press closely during that recession were well aware, as was this writer, of the painful, losing struggle of the city school system to carry out plans for new facilities and renovation of old ones.

In the recession of 1974–5, one did not read much in the press of reductions in numbers of students to be admitted at public colleges and universities to save funds. Indeed, enrollments increased, partly apparently in response to the pressures of unemployment, which may have made college more appealing to those who could manage it financially.[57] However, there was a painful toll in the form of austerity imposed on college and university operations. References in the press were frequent concerning austerity budgets: increases in class sizes and hours of teaching, abandonment of programs, freezes on size of faculty, freezes on hiring of non-faculty. reductions in allowances for faculty travel, severe limitations on faculty pay increases resulting in reductions in real income, reductions in the real value of library support, cutting of library hours, reduction of building temperatures in winter and increases in summer.[58]

At the secondary and elementary school level, too, there were austerity budgets in the recession of 1974–5. Again, the casualties were programs (including summer school), salaries, class size and so on.[59]

Constantly during the 1974–5 recession, the press reported other spending cutbacks by state and local governments.[60] New York State, for example, reduced 'facilities and hours at 37 parks.'[61] In Detroit 'thirty-one recreation centers were shut for one month, city golf courses were opened a month late, hockey rinks were closed a month early.'[62] Garbage collections were cut in half by Cleveland and Albuquerque.[63] In Philadelphia, 'health, recreation and library services have been cut deeply.'[64] Dallas, Austin and other cities reduced their library services.[65]

During the 1970–1 recession, also, the press was filled with accounts of reductions of important services to the public. For example, New York State dismissed 8,250 employees, with heavy cuts in facilities for the mentally ill, for narcotics patients and for rat-control.[66] Cleveland was reported to have laid off 1,500 employees out of 13,000 and Pittsburgh, about 850 out of 6,950.[67] Meanwhile, cutbacks in education in city after city were reported continuously. Commonly cut, too, were playground and other recreational facilities.

The pressure on state and local governments to reduce spending in the environment of contrived scarcity is likely to backfire financially at the governmental level with little money saved. In the

1974–5 and 1970–1 recessions, for example, when museums partly closed their facilities, decreased hours and closed additional days because of insufficient money for guards,[68] the guards (and others laid off) in many cases must soon have gone on relief (along with guards laid off by private enterprise), which then increased public expenditures in the welfare sector while tax receipts fell. In this Alice-in-Wonderland world in which people are shifted from the guard rolls to the relief rolls, a scarcity of civilized public services is created, hurting the public and doing possibly irreparable damage to the unemployed and their families. Similarly, cities stay filthy because they can't pay people to remove trash frequently enough, but somehow money is found to pay relief to people who previously did these chores.[69]

To sum up, the financial backfire of contrived unemployment largely nullifies government efforts to economize and results in a dilution of fiscal efforts to spur recovery. Unemployment in the private sector is used to reduce demand. The spillover to the public sector causes pressures for increases in transfer-type expenditures at state and local government levels in the face of falling real receipts, with resulting cuts in non-transfer expenditures and, in turn, further unemployment-induced rises in transfer payments and pressure for higher taxes. The federal government, attempting to act as macro-regulator of the economy while also being 'financier of last resort,' finds its stimulative efforts largely dissipated by the offsetting state and local actions of opposite types. The upshot is reduced private output and income, reduced services rendered by and reduced income earned through state and local government purchases of goods and services, and increased transfers by all governments, especially federal. Society as a whole is a loser, not merely the unemployed, who instead of relying on themselves are forced to go on the dole by government policy.[70]

The world of contrived scarcity to fight inflation is also likely to backfire by generating further inflationary pressure. The so-called Phillips curve (describing a presumed trade-off between price or wage rises and unemployment rates) is a principal culprit here. According to those formulating policy proposals in terms of generalizations inferred from the Phillips curve, a rising unemployment rate should result in falling wage increases and so in lesser price increases. Evidence gathered by investigators in the early 1970s suggested that the Phillips curve was shifting to the right, implying greater upward wage–price pressures at given unemployment rates. Various explanations were offered for this phenomenon. One widely accepted explanation was in terms of the composition of the labor force; i.e., that women and young people constituted rapidly growing components, that they constituted disproportionate numbers of the unemployed, and that their unemployment did not exert the same downward force on wages as did that of prime-age males.[71] A second explanation was the accelerationist theory, according to which continuing, rising inflation led labor to bargain in terms of expectations of a rising inflation rate, with the inflation–unemployment trade-off then explainable in terms of the relation between the unemployment rate and the *change* in the rate of inflation. Thus, if unemployment fell to a rate that would generate inflationary pressures, that rate could remain relatively stable, while inflation accelerated.[72] A popular intuitive explanation was simply in terms of unions becoming more powerful, extending their influence into newer areas, especially public service employment, and becoming ever more aggressive. If one accepts the notion of a Phillips curve, another explanation should probably be added. Erratic job availability, including number of hours of work, probably leads unionized workers to seek higher hourly wages to compensate for falling hours of work. Added to this is the fact that during periods of rising unemployment some unions have sought to spread the available work by a reduction in the hours in the working week, again seeking higher hourly wages as an offset. These forces, in addition to efforts to compensate for inflation, were probably important in the very large increases in hourly rates plus shortened working weeks gained by various construction workers during the 1970–1 recession. (Thus a guaranteed minimum working year might curb the urge to seek higher hourly pay in order to generate adequate annual take-home pay.)[73]

Mark-up pricing during recessions, it is held by some, leads to inflationary consequences comparable to shifts in the alleged inflation–unemployment trade-off involving wages. It is argued that prices in industries characterized by substantial concentration are raised during recessions in order to meet profit targets. A variant of this puts the argument in terms of full-cost pricing, with declining output leading to rises in overhead costs per unit, which are then added to existing prices.[74]

Finally, the world of administered unemployment and contrived scarcity backfires in terms of the welfare, health, education and cultural programs of the federal government (and of other levels of government). For years there have been massive federal programs in the United States to improve the lot of the aged, the infirm and the less fortunate; to widen higher educational opportunities, especially in the face of escalating costs; to bring better health care to all, especially those least able to buy it themselves; to widen the availability of cultural facilities and opportunities. Unemployment merely adds to the numbers in need of help in the first three of these four categories, and, as noted, is likely to reduce the real resources available in all of them. To illustrate, in 1970, when administered unemployment was rising rapidly, the US Department of Commerce reported that the number of persons living in poverty, then defined as an income of $3,968 or less for a non-farm family of four, increased by more than 1.2 million or over 5 per cent, the first statistically significant increase since 1959, when data were first available. Improvement resumed in 1972 and continued in 1973, despite rapid inflation. With rising unemployment in 1974, however, the number of persons living below the poverty level (then defined as $5,038 for a non-farm family of four) rose by 1.3 million, or 5.6 per cent above 1973.[75] In short, a government professing to wish to eradicate poverty, and which established programs and agencies for this purpose, then used monetary policy to fight inflation by increasing poverty! At the same time, private charities dealing with the same problems were hit by falling contributions and rising needs.[76]

Social and Psychological Impacts of Unemployment
A large literature exists on this subject and it is beyond our province to try to develop a detailed analysis.[77] Although the subject is vital, it is, unfortunately, virtually ignored by economists. Hence, a short introduction is provided here.

Since the economic, social and psychological impacts of unemployment are closely intertwined, much of what was said on previous pages falls also under the present rubric. It should be emphasized that social and psychological impacts, like economic effects, may not disappear quickly, and so short-run problems may also have substantial long-run consequences.

The topic may be divided into effects on persons and effects on society. As the 1974–5 recession escalated rapidly, both of these aspects received attention in the press. A sampling of press titles conveys a sense of the problems creating concern: 'Economy Held Key to Child Suicides,'[78] 'The Hidden Costs of Unemployment,'[79] 'How Recession Is Driving People Off the Deep End,'[80] 'Down and Out in America,'[81] 'More Crime Forecast as Idleness Rises,'[82] 'Recession Kills Black Teen-Ager Hopes,'[83] 'The Recession Increases Racial Tensions in Detroit,'[84] 'Layoff and the Civil Rights of Minorities,' and 'Last Hired, and Usually the First Let Go,'[85] 'Hunger in U.S. a Problem of Want Amid Plenty,'[86] 'Tender Loving Care – In Europe the Jobless Get Special Treatment to Minimize Unrest.'[87]

With respect to individuals a major problem is the impact of unemployment on family life.[88] The psychological and social effects include the weakening and destruction of marriages and the impairment of parent–children relationships. Relations with other relatives are adversely affected for some, stemming from such factors as borrowing money or doubling up in housing. Social relations with others are likely to be seriously affected for many, and problems of maintaining confidence and self-respect may arise. Work habits and skills may be adversely affected – an economic impact, as noted earlier, but also with social and psychological implications. Interruptions to, and ending of, secondary and higher education may have short-run social and psychological effects, as well as leading to permanent downgrading socioeconomically.

Mental illness is created for some. In 1974–5 it was reported that 'community mental centers across country are . . . seeing a surge of patients,' and one specialist, Professor M. H. Brenner, was quoted as saying that 'for the past century and a quarter, every economic downturn, regardless of size, has brought about increased admissions to mental hospitals in every state.'[89] A link was also found running from economic conditions to family disintegration to teenager suicides.[90]

Obvious consequences of unemployment with respect to individuals include criminal acts along with other forms of anti-social behavior induced by forced idleness and the resulting despair, bitterness and alienation. Drug and alcohol use and addiction are further likely consequences for some. Health for many may be impaired because of poor or inadequate diets and the inability to obtain medical attention.[91] Evictions from housing rise, doubling up and overcrowding increase, and ceaseless moving from house to house create social and psychological upheaval for adults and children alike. Children of grade school age in some cases are likely to be stunted educationally as a result of all of the foregoing and of other implications of unemployment and poverty (e.g. inadequate clothing to go to school in inclement weather). One of the press items cited above captures the essence of the brutality of it all:

A 9-year old black youngster from a poverty-stricken home was asked to say the Pledge of Allegiance at the start of school on Monday morning. He refused and ran out of the class, hotly pursued by his teacher, determined to make him respect his country.

He ran into the arms of a school aide and said, 'That old teacher is trying to make me say the Pledge and I haven't had anything to eat all week-end.'[92]

Some broader social consequences of unemployment have already, in effect, been noted in the discussion of economic consequences. These social consequences are more than an aggregation of direct effects on persons. Society, too, is a loser: the collective effects on, and behavior of, directly affected individuals adversely affects the rest of us. The press stories of 1974–5 referred to were replete with accounts of difficulties for society. Crime rates were rising, with physical and material harm to victims and implications of needs for more police, jails and court facilities.[93] Drug addiction became an increasing problem, again taxing existing facilities and increasing various threats to society generally. Welfare agencies were swamped under an avalanche of relief cases, child welfare problems and family difficulties.

One of the most dangerous consequences of the 1974–5 recession was an apparent rise in racial tensions. Given the customary differentials in the impact of unemployment on blacks and whites, this was to be expected. It was compounded by the fact that hard-won gains of blacks under federal government prodding were endangered by conventional layoff procedures (i.e. last hired, first laid off). And, of course, the difficulties of continued progress were increased. There were also threats to the progress of other groups long subject to discrimination. These included Puerto Ricans, Mexicans, and women in the labor force.

Another consequence of substantial unemployment and accompanying massive relief payments – regardless of how disguised – may be a dangerous decline in the 'will to work' (noted earlier as an economic impact). Welfare payments may take on the character of narcotics, becoming habit-forming. A parasitic, able-bodied welfare group may reach dangerous proportions with self-perpetuating characteristics.

As noted above, one effect of unemployment, in the United States at least, has been to reduce the availability of civilized public services that mark and nourish a sophisticated society: museums, education at all levels, concerts, zoos, parks and public gardens, among others. The general level of cultural achievement and appreciation is thus adversely affected. Society is the loser when creative talents go to waste, be they literary, artistic, musical, scientific, political, architectural or other. Other casualties include recreational facilities, health facilities and standards, sanitation services, transportation and social services to the underprivileged, all of which are criteria of *the quality* of a civilization.[94]

FOOTNOTES

1. *Wall Street Journal*, 19 June 1974, p. 11.
2. *Federal Reserve Bulletin*, June 1974, p. 426; June 1975, p. 353.
3. *Wall Street Journal*, 28 May 1974, p. 39.
4. ibid.
5. For a picture of the deteriorating liquidity position of American business in the period 1964–74, see 'Recent Changes in the Liquidity of Major Sectors of the US Economy,' *Federal Reserve Bulletin*, June 1976, pp. 463–9.
6. See Table 3.1.
7. Long-run changes in business failure rates are particularly difficult to interpret causally. Business liquidity (and its causes in prior years), price behavior, differential movements in areas of economic expansion and contraction, structure of industry, foreign economic behavior, as well as other factors, enter the picture.
8. Administrative Office of the US District Courts, Division of Bankruptcy, *Director's Annual Report for Fiscal Year 1974*, Washington, DC, 1975, p. VIII–3.
9. *New York Times*, 21 September 1974, p. 36.
10. See also Chapters 2 and 4.
11. *Business Week*, 3 August 1974, p. 43. See also *New York Times*, 29 June 1974, p. 35; *Wall Street Journal*, 2 August 1974, p. 17 and 27 June 1974, p. 8.
12. *New York Times*, 30 June 1974, Section 3, p. 15.
13. ibid., 9 September 1974, p. 55.
14. *Wall Street Journal*, 20 August 1974, p. 5.
15. ibid., 28 August 1974, p. 8.
16. ibid., 17 July 1974, p. 10.
17. ibid., 5 September 1974, p. 30.

18. *Evening Bulletin* (Philadelphia), 6 August 1974, p. 31. See also *American Banker*, 8 July 1974, p. 1.
19. ibid.; see also *Business Week*, 8 May 1974, p. 70.
20. *Wall Street Journal*, 28 August 1974, p. 17, and 7 August 1974, p. 26.
21. *New York Times*, 12 September 1974, p. 57, and 23 December 1974, pp. 43–5.
22. See *Philadelphia Inquirer*, 23 September 1973, pp. 1-D, 2-D, for an account of the problems of Temple University.
23. *Evening Bulletin*, 10 September 1974, p. 35.
24. ibid., 21 August 1974, p. 46. For a survey of experiences in the credit crunch, see 'A Corporate Liquidity Crunch,' *Business Week*, 18 May 1974, pp. 68, 70.
25. *New York Times*, 22 September 1974, Section 1, pp. 1, 37.
26. Securities Exchange Commission, *Statistical Bulletin*, May 1975, p. 440.
27. *Daily Pennsylvanian*, 18 September 1974, p. 1. Losses in capital values aggravated a particularly severe situation at Brown University, whose financial problems led to the resignation of its president (*New York Times*, 18 July 1975, p. 48).
28. See *Wall Street Journal*, 29 November 1974, pp. 1, 17.
29. *New York Times*, 23 April 1974, p. 55 and 16 February 1974, pp. 1, 39.
30. See R. M. Giordano and R. B. Worley, 'The Erosion of Consumer Wealth,' in Goldman Sachs, *Economic Comments*, April 1974. (Data prior to 1955 are not shown in Figure 3.2.)
31. ibid. and *Federal Reserve Bulletin*, June 1974, p. 415. (Data prior to 1962 are not shown in Figure 3.2.) The Federal Reserve, quoting a different series than Giordano and Worley, cites much higher delinquency rates:

    By the first quarter of this year ... the delinquency rates on permanent mortgages held by institutions that report to the Mortgage Bankers Association of America averaged the highest for any quarter in the two-decade history of the series – 4.0 per cent, compared with 3.6 per cent a year earlier and with 3.2 per cent in the first quarter of 1971. While this uptrend has reflected mainly defaults on mortgages underwritten by FHA under special programs involving lower-income housing, it has also been associated with problems in the non-subsidized sector as well.

    See also *New York Times*, 19 May 1975, pp. 43–5.
32. Giordano and Worley, op cit.
33. Administrative Office of the US Courts, op. cit. and statistical release.
34. The percentage of the US population in the sixty-five-year and older group was 5.4 in 1930, 8.1 in 1950 and 10.5 in 1975 (US Bureau of the Census, *Current Population Reports*, Special Studies, Series P-23, No. 59, 'Demographic Aspects of Aging and the Older Population in the United States,' May 1976, p. 9).
35. *Wall Street Journal*, 10 September 1974, pp. 1, 42. Since 1969, book value of common stock has exceeded 50 per cent of the assets of private pension funds other than these administered by insurance companies (US Bureau of the Census, *Statistical Abstract of the United States: 1973*, Washington, DC, p. 298; 1974, p. 286). At market value this was the case even earlier (see SEC *Statistical Bulletin*, May 1975, p. 440).
36. Two recent econometric studies give evidence that spending in the US economy is strongly affected by the behavior of capital values. Barry Bosworth, 'The Stock Market and the Economy' in *Brookings Papers on Economic Activity*, Vol. 2, 1975, p. 289, calculates that the total depressive effect of the stock market 'on gross national product is very modest throughout most of 1973, but it rapidly builds to $28 billion (1958 prices) by the first quarter of 1975,' or about 25 per cent of the 'recession gap' (p. 290). However, he suspects that the decline in the stock market is owing more to changes in earnings expectations

than to interest rate changes. See also Franco Modigliani, 'Monetary Policy and Consumption,' in Federal Reserve Bank of Boston, *Consumer Spending and Monetary Policy* (Conference Series No. 5), 1971, pp. 9–84.

37. There is irony here in the sense that typically those who support prolonged, severe monetary restraint to fight even non-demand-pull type inflations also exhort the virtues of self-reliance and deprecate welfare activity by government. They seem not to see the connection between (1) government actions that create unemployment and falling capital values, and (2) the deterioration in the likelihood of survival of self-reliance as a viable choice for individuals.

38. It is in housing credit that the availability doctrine (i.e. credit rationing) has strongest empirical support. See OECD, *Monetary Policy in the United States*, Paris, OECD Publications, 1974, pp. 67, 76–7. For a review of the doctrine and its development, see R. V. Roosa, 'Interest Rates and the Central Bank,' in *Money, Trade and Economic Growth*, New York, Macmillan, 1951, pp. 270–95, and B. M. Friedman, *Credit Rationing: A Review*, Washington, DC, Board of Governors of the Federal Reserve System (Staff Economic Studies), 1972.

39. Much attention was paid by the press in 1974 to the plight of participants in the real estate credit markets. See, for example, *Wall Street Journal*, 19 September 1973, pp. 1, 19, which included a statement by

[a] senior mortgage officer of Trefoil Mortgage Co., a unit of Fidelity Corp. of Pennsylvania, which also owns Fidelity Bank in Philadelphia [who] says the favored applicants are those who have a strong cash balance on deposit at the bank, have received loans from the bank previously, or are connected with a company that does business with the bank.

40. In early 1976 the head of the AFL–CIO Building and Construction Trades Department stated that construction industry unemployment in Philadelphia was much higher: 35 per cent overall; bricklayers, 60 per cent; boilermakers, 45 per cent; operating engineers and laborers, 40 per cent – *Evening Bulletin* (Philadelphia) 17 January 1976, p. 1.

41. Cf. E. M. Gramlich, 'The Distributional Effects of Higher Unemployment,' *Brookings Papers on Economic Activity*, Vol. 1, 1975, pp. 293–336.

42. US Department of Labor, *Handbook of Labor Statistics, 1973*, p. 135; *Survey of Current Business*, July 1974, p. S–13.

43. *Handbook of Labor Statistics*, op. cit., p. 147.

44. ibid., pp. 117–18. For analysis of the unemployment experiences of Americans of Spanish origin or descent, whites and Negroes, see R. V. McKay, 'Employment and Unemployment Among Americans of Spanish Origin,' *Monthly Labor Review*, April 1974, pp. 12–16; C. G. Gellner, 'Regional Differences in Employment and Unemployment,' *Monthly Labor Review*, March 1974, pp. 15–24.

45. That race is involved in the United States is, in one sense, an accident. If non-whites did not fill this role, presumably whites would – as in Canada.

46. See A. M. Okun, 'Potential GNP: Its Measurement and Significance,' in American Statisitical Association, *Proceedings of the Business and Economic Statistics Section*, 1962, pp. 98–104. The actual figure given by Okun is 3.2 per cent. This has been revised downward to 2.7 per cent by G. L. Perry, in 'Labor Force Structure, Potential Output, and Productivity,' in *Brookings Papers on Economic Activity*, Vol. 3, 1971, pp. 533–65. A somewhat different approach is suggested by R. J. Gordon in 'The Welfare Cost of Higher Unemployment,' *Brookings Papers on Economic Activity*, (Vol. 1, 1973), pp. 133–95. He allows for the value of non-market activity by the unemployed, but this results in little change in the relationships.

47. See *Economic Report of the President*, 1975, op. cit., pp. 121–2, 280–1. There is actually wide variation in benefits by state and by income level: 'It has been

estimated that for unemployed insured male family heads in families with income below 150 percent of the poverty line, benefits may replace about 70 percent of lost income after taxes: for those with higher income, the replacement ratio may be about 40 percent.' (ibid., p. 123.)
48. See *New York Times*, 15 December 1974, Section 4, p. 1.
49. The number of adults entering the nation's hospitals has dropped for the first time in 15 years, apparently because laid-off workers who lost their health insurance benefits began postponing certain medical care, the president of the American Hospital Association said.

    The statistics alone didn't disclose why hospital admissions dropped in the nine-month period, but 'probably as much as anything was the postponement of elective procedures by the unemployed who've lost their health insurance', Mr McMahon said.

    In early 1975, Mr. McMahon and the AHA began pushing for federal legislation to provide health insurance for the unemployed who've exhausted both their health insurance and their unemployment benefits. It predicted that this year about 2.5 million Americans will be in this situation.
    In addition to the decline in admissions, the recession's impact was evident in the fact that paid visits to hospital outpatient clinics dropped 3.8% during the period, while unpaid visits to emergency rooms rose 5.5%, Mr. McMahon said. (*Wall Street Journal*, 15 January 1976, p. 17).

    See also, e.g. *New York Times*, 13 February 1975, Section 4, p. 19; *Evening Bulletin* (Philadelphia), 6 March 1975, p. 21.
50. In 1973 there were over 200 million life insurance policies in force in the United States (excluding group life insurance and credit life insurance) – *Statistical Abstract of the U.S.: 1974*, op. cit., p. 469.
51. ibid., p. 51. Conceivably, the rising divorce rate may have been accompanied by a falling rate of alimony and child support payments. Nevertheless, the magnitudes are great.
52. Cf. *Evening Bulletin* (Philadelphia), 'Layoff Poses Insurance Woe,' 27 December 1974, p. 15.
53. The average number of persons involuntarily on part time rose from 2,056,000 in 1969 to 2,675,000 in the recession year of 1971, receded to 2,519,000 in the incomplete recovery of 1973, then rose to 3,748,000 in the recession year of 1975 (see *Employment and Training Report of the President*, Washington, DC, 1976, p. 256).
54. In these recessions, newspaper articles noted the impact of unemployment on teenagers. The opening paragraph from 'Recession Kills Black Teen-ager Hopes' (*New York Times*, 19 May 1975, pp. 1, 48) is worth quoting:

    Tens of thousands of black and Puerto Rican teenagers are 'piling up at the bottom' of the recession. With no jobs and no prospects of jobs, they are abandoning their dreams of education, and their belief in the other institutions of a civilized society, and are slipping back toward the drugs and hustling of 'the street.'

55. ... the aggregate budgets of state and local governments moved from a $10 billion surplus in the second quarter of 1972 to a $12 billion deficit in the second quarter of 1975. ...
    Statistical estimates suggest that for every dollar decline in the Gross National Product during a business cycle, state and local revenues will eventually fall by about eleven cents, and expenditures will be pushed up by one cent. ...
    ... the Joint Economic Committee estimates that about $3.6 billion in tax increases will be enacted in 1975 alone, while a $3.3 billion cut in services is

expected. In addition, an estimated $1 billion of capital construction projects will be delayed or cancelled. . . .

Moreover, these tax increases and expenditure cutbacks are concentrated in states where the effect of the recession has been especially severe. (US Congress, Congressional Budget Office, *Temporary Measures to Stimulate Employment: An Evaluation of Some Alternatives*, Washington, DC, 2 September 1975, pp. 41, 43.)

56. *New York Times*, 20 April 1971, p. 1.
57. ibid., 3 September 1975, p. 41.
58. e.g. see *Evening Bulletin* (Philadelphia), 26 August 1975, p. 8.
59. e.g. see *Wall Street Journal*, 30 May 1975, pp. 1, 18; 18 August 1975, p. 1; *New York Times*, 13 July 1975, p. 46.
60. See, e.g. 'Fund-Short States Cut Services,' *New York Times*, 27 December 1975, pp. 1, 18.
61. *New York Times*, 24 May 1975, pp. 1, 26.
62. *Evening Bulletin* (Philadelphia), 11 June 1975, p. 2.
63. ibid.
64. *New York Times*, 29 November 1974, p. 66.
65. *Wall Street Journal*, 24 December 1974, pp. 1, 11; 14 October 1975, pp. 1, 45.
66. *New York Times*, 20 April 1971, pp. 1, 26.
67. ibid., 25 May 1971, pp. 1, 20.
68. See, e.g. *New York Times*, 11 July 1975, pp. 1, 10; 20 June 1975, p. 35; 30 November 1974, p. 29; 28 March 1971, p. 28. The Detroit 'Art Museum was closed for one month, and only 25 percent of its galleries are now open' (*Evening Bulletin* (Philadelphia), 11 June 1975, p. 2).
69. The sheer economic folly of firing needed government employees and putting them largely on relief would be readily apparent if a consolidated budget *for all levels of government combined* were possible, with a single ultimate collector and dispenser of funds. Now one unit can engage in the dubious luxury of firing only because another unit pays a large part of the resulting relief or other assistance. Thus, references to a possible elimination of 90,000 New York City jobs led to a forecast of 50,000 to 75,000 additional welfare cases being generated, with the cost being shared about 29 per cent each by the city and state, and the remainder by the federal government (*New York Times*, 9 May 1971, pp. 1, 31).
70. The 'backfiring' argument is well illustrated in a 1975 study of the Congressional Budget Office. Growth rates for the money supply of 7, 8½ and 10 per cent were assumed beginning in mid–1975 and consequences estimated by the fourth quarter of 1976. In relation to the 7 per cent growth rate, a 10 per cent rate resulted, at annual rates, in $46 billion greater GNP, $25 billion greater business fixed investment, $18 billion smaller federal deficit, and a *lower* price level (see Table 4.6).

European labor leaders were reported to be capitalizing on the budgetary aspects of rising unemployment by pressing for very high unemployment benefits 'to make costs burdensome enough "to insure that governments follow a high employment policy," says Peer Carlsen, deputy general secretary in the European Trade Union Confederation . . .' (*Wall Street Journal*, 28 May 1975, p. 29).

Another aspect of the 'backfiring' issue may be seen in fears for the 'solvency' of the US social security system. See, e.g. *Wall Street Journal*, 27 February 1975, pp. 1–3.
71. G. L. Perry, 'Changing Labor Markets and Inflation,' *Brookings Papers on Economic Activity*, Vol. 3, 1970, pp. 411–41.
72. Carried to its logical conclusion, the accelerationist position leads to rejection of

the notion of a Phillips curve. With fully anticipated inflation it is argued that a 'natural' rate of unemployment will prevail. Thus any observable trade-off is a short-run phenomenon, indicative of the fact that inflation is not fully anticipated. See E. S. Phelps, 'Introduction' and 'Money Wage Dynamics and Labor Market Equilibrium,' in E. S. Phelps (ed.), *Microeconomic Foundations of Employment and Inflation Theory*, New York, Norton, 1970, pp. 1–23 and 124–66, respectively; Milton Friedman, 'The Role of Monetary Policy,' *American Economic Review*, March 1968, pp. 8–11.

73. Some economists, on the other hand, simply reject the concept of a Phillips curve, or predictable relation between inflation and unemployment. See, for example, E. H. Phelps Brown, 'The Underdevelopment of Economics,' *Economic Journal*, March 1972, p. 6; G. D. N. Worswick, 'Is Progress in Economic Science Possible?,' *Economic Journal*, March 1972, pp. 81–3.

74. See M. M. Wachtel and P. D. Adelsheim, *The Inflationary Impact of Unemployment: Price Markups during Postwar Recessions, 1947–70*, in US Congress, Joint Economic Committee, *Achieving the Goals of the Employment Act of 1946*, Vol. 3, Paper No. 1, Washington, DC, 1976; John Blair, 'Market Power and Inflation,' *Journal of Economic Issues*, June 1974, pp. 453–78; Andrew Shonfield, *Modern Capitalism*, London, Oxford University Press, 1965, p. 359.

75. US Bureau of the Census, *Current Population Reports*, Series P–60, No. 99, 'Money Income and Poverty Status of Families and Persons in the United States: 1974' (Advance Report), July 1975, pp. 2, 3.

76. See, for example, *Wall Street Journal*, 19 December 1974, pp. 1, 21; *New York Times*, 15 December 1974, p. 29.

77. Some representative literature includes the following: Dorothy S. Thomas, *Social Aspects of the Business Cycle*, New York, Knopf, 1927; E. W. Bakke, *Citizens Without Work*, New Haven, Conn., Yale University Press, 1940; D. W. Tiffany, J. R. Cowan and P. M. Tiffany, *The Unemployed: A Social Psychological Portrait*, Englewood Cliffs, N.J., Prentice-Hall, 1970; M. Aiken, L. A. Ferman and H. L. Shepperd, *Economic Failure, Alienation and Extremism*, Ann Arbor, Michigan, University of Michigan Press, 1968; R. C. Wilcock and W. H. Franke, *Unwanted Workers: Permanent Layoffs and Long-Term Unemployment*, New York, Free Press, 1963; P. Flaim, 'Discouraged Workers and Changes in Unemployment,' *Monthly Labor Review*, March 1973, pp. 8–16; S. Schweitzer and R. Smith, 'The Persistence of the Discouraged Worker Effect,' *Industrial and Labor Relations Review*, January 1974, pp. 249–60.

78. *New York Times*, 20 June 1975, p. 34.

79. ibid., 9 June 1975, p. 31.

80. *Philadelphia Inquirer*, 11 May 1975, pp. 1–A, 16–A.

81. *New York Times Magazine*, 9 February 1975 (interviews with a series of mainly unemployed persons in Buffalo).

82. *New York Times*, 21 May 1975, p. 8.

83. ibid., 19 May 1975, pp. 1, 48.

84. ibid., 15 May 1975, p. 27.

85. ibid., 29 January 1975, p. 17.

86. ibid., 29 October 1974, pp. 39, 60.

87. *Wall Street Journal*, 28 May 1975, p. 1.

88. See, for example, *New York Times*, 28 July 1975, p. 17.

89. 'Recession Is Driving People off the Deep End,' op. cit.; cf. also M. H. Brenner, *Mental Illness and the Economy*, Cambridge, Mass., Harvard University Press, 1973, pp. ix, x, 77–9, 83, 108–9, 243.

90. 'Economy Held Key to Child Suicides,' op. cit.

91. See *Wall Street Journal*, 15 January 1976, p. 17 (cited earlier) for 1975 evidence.

92. 'The Hidden Costs of Unemployment,' op. cit.
93. A recent pioneering empirical study relates changes in unemployment to a group of 'social stress indicators': suicide, state mental hospital admissions, state prison admissions, homicide, cirrhosis of the liver mortality (reflecting alcoholism), and cardiovascular-renal disease mortality. Substantial and statistically significant' impacts were found for each indicator. The author in turn made quantitative estimates of the economic losses directly resulting from these impacts. See M. H. Brenner, *Estimating the Social Costs of National Economic Policy: Implications for Mental and Physical Health and Criminal Aggressions* (in US Congress, Joint Economic Committee, *Achieving the Goals of the Employment Act of 1946*, Vol. 1, Paper No. 5, Washington, DC, 1976).
94. The issue was put succinctly by San Francisco's budget director. After noting that 80 per cent of the city's expenditures were mandated for essential services, he observed, 'What are discretionary are libraries, recreational parks, culture and museums. . . . If those items are in trouble, then the quality of life really goes to hell' (*New York Times*, 29 November 1974, pp. 1, 66). An unusually severe case was that of Detroit, which illustrated most of the ills cited here (see *Wall Street Journal*, 25 July 1975, pp. 1, 17).

4 Efficiency, Effectiveness and Relevance of Severe General Monetary Restraint

4.1 Some Slippages in Monetary Policy

To begin, let us consider the meaning of, and conditions for, efficiency of restrictive monetary management via general instruments. Efficiency relates to the degree of effort expended in achieving a given monetary result. This amount of effort may be thought of in terms of (1) human energy expended and (2) forcefulness of financial action required to bring about a given financial result. The conditions appropriate for obtaining maximum efficiency include no ambiguity in the components of the money supply, a minimal number of liquid asset forms (money market instruments and non-negotiable near-monies), a stable or controllable ratio of money to bank reserves, and an easily controllable quantity of bank reserves. The heart of the matter is causing the supply of money and credit to move as desired with minimal opportunity for the system to generate money substitutes, minimum opportunity for activation of idle balances and minimum leakages in the system. (Although the focus here is on restraint, application of the principles is reversible.)

Now the fact is that monetary restraint provokes financial market reactions which seek to evade the restraint and which are destabilizing from the point of view of central bank control, thus diminishing efficiency. The central bank must then take stronger actions than would otherwise be necessary and must use more human energy policing additional variables and assessing their significance for policy. Since 1965 a host of developments have appeared in the United States along these lines, with clear deterioration in the efficiency of monetary policy. Some of these developments have involved the growth of money substitutes and bank reserve pyramiding; some have involved the growth in the volume of old and new credit instruments; some have involved exploiting accounting possibilities in commercial banking to reduce the recorded volume of deposits while leaving unchanged the volume of reserves; some have involved manipulating domestic and international flows of funds. Some of the developments presumably would have occurred in any event, unless prohibited; others owe their growth and/or invention to monetary pressures. In general, since they are well known in the financial world, they are examined here only briefly.

4.1.1   Money Market Innovations

An important device whose rate of growth was greatly accelerated by tight money is the negotiable certificate of deposit (CD), which is exploited mainly by large commercial banks. CDs serve to increase the volume of deposits – time plus demand – supportable by a given volume of reserves. They may be viewed essentially as demand deposits masquerading as time deposits and are of great importance quantitatively (see Table 4.1 for magnitudes of CDs and certain other of the items discussed here).

Table 4.1   Selected Money Market and Related Magnitudes at Year-End 1966, 1970 and 1974 ($ billion)

| Item | Year-end | | |
	1966	1970	1974
Negotiable CDs outstanding (large banks)	15.4	25.4	90.5
Commercial paper – total outstanding	13.6	33.1	49.1
Non-financial company issuer	0.8	7.1	12.7
Bank-related	0.0	2.3	8.3
Acceptances outstanding	3.6	7.1	18.5
Loans sold outright	n.a.	2.9	4.8
Federal funds sold[a]	4.1[b]	16.0	38.9

[a] Includes securities purchased under resale agreements.
[b] Year-end 1967.

Sources: *Federal Reserve Bulletin*, June 1970, p. A24; October 1974, p. A15; April 1976, pp. A12, A13, A25; Federal Deposit Insurance Corporation, *Annual Report, 1974*, p. 217.

Closely akin in spirit to negotiable certificates of deposit are certain large denomination time deposits at savings and loan associations. Such institutions have offered business accounts subject to withdrawal on several hours notice with funds placed in checking accounts at commercial banks designated by business depositors. In effect, there is activation of idle balances.

Also akin in spirit to negotiable certificates of deposit are the commercial paper issues of commercial bank holding company affiliates. These serve to reduce deposits at commercial banks as the proceeds are used to 'buy' loans from affiliated banks. In turn, excess reserves tend to rise. Of course, such commercial paper is virtually interchangeable with time deposits to the holder.[1]

A variant of the commercial paper issue is the floating rate note. Inaugurated in July 1974 by Citicorp, the parent holding company of First National City Bank of New York (now Citibank) and promptly issued by other bank organizations, it combined long-term maturity with semi-annual redemption privileges after a two-year waiting period.[2] The consequences of such issues for the volume of bank deposits are, in principle, the same as for issues of commercial paper.

Another product of tight money is the sale of loans by banks both with repurchase agreement and outright. Those sold outright are essentially the counterpart of issues of commercial paper by bank holding companies, just discussed. Those sold with repurchase agreements are in effect 'warehoused' with the non-bank public. The consequences for deposit aggregates are as with issues of bank-related commercial paper: unless offset elsewhere in the system, deposits decline as payment is made by the non-bank public while reserves remain unchanged and excess reserves tend to rise.

In recent years not only has there been explosive growth in bankers' acceptances, but a new, controversial bank obligation, the documentary discount note, has been invented. Commercial paper of ordinary non-bank businesses is given a guarantee by a commercial bank, creating a new class of very liquid short-term credit instruments, i.e., additional near-monies.

An area of growth in what may be called potential money has been the overdraft account for individuals. Individuals, in turn, can activate consumer credit in the form of new demand deposits simply by writing checks. This raises the question of whether unused lines of credit under overdraft facilities should be considered part of the money supply, since holders of such accounts must in large measure regard the unused credit as precautionary balances – or transactions balances – which release owned funds that would otherwise be held.

Related to the overdraft device is a cash management technique which permits operating on a very large scale at near-zero deposit balances. For example, stimulated by high interest rates, New York City instituted a statistical approach whereby cash is put into money market credit instruments and is converted back into demand deposits only hours before the estimated need to meet bank clearing requirements.[3] Thus, an economic unit (New York City) with a 1974 budget of roughly $10 billion operated with an average cash balance of not much over one-tenth of one per cent of that budget. The cash released, not only by New York City but by other organizations throughout the economy acting similarly, supplemented the loanable funds available at banks and elsewhere in the economy.

At the bank reserve level the all-out mobilization of resources began in the 1960s. From a system that basically owned its reserves, escalating interest rates (as well as other forces) brought about a transformation of the situation to one in which, for the system as a whole, most reserves were borrowed by banks from each other through the federal funds market (with the transactions legally disguised as purchases and sales of reserves).

The Eurodollar market also had explosive growth. US commercial banks borrowed from their branches and from others abroad to add to their domestic lending capacity. Moreover, in certain circumstances Eurodollars can lead to expansion of reserves in the US banking system. The usual impact of Eurodollar borrowing by domestic US banks, however, is an increase in bank lending and velocity of money as dollar deposits held abroad are loaned to borrowers desirous of spending in the United States.

Open market commercial paper sold by non-banking firms through dealers was also stimulated greatly by tight money. It was always an alternative to bank borrowing, and with high interest rates and lessened availability of bank credit it was an obvious source for high-grade clients. Some clients, however, finding the commercial paper market less receptive than desired, then sought bank guarantees, creating what was described above as documentary discount notes.

The net effect of aggressive bank actions to expand their lending power and of borrower actions to expand their sources of short-term borrowing has been to maximize the multiplying power of reserve balances and to permit the conventional, recorded money supply to turn over more rapidly. Part of the processes leading to increased velocity of money has involved accounting mechanisms that tend to reduce recorded deposits, as noted above. What one sees, looked at from the credit side, is a supply curve for short-term credit with considerable interest rate elasticity. The velocity of money (narrowly defined) had been rising almost continuously since World War II, and by the early 1960s was generally thought to be approaching an upper limit. In the credit crunches of 1966 and 1968–70, however, financial market responses managed to push both turnover of demand deposits and income velocity of the money supply (narrowly defined) to still greater heights. By 1974, however, the velocity figures for 1968–70 seemed relatively modest as banks pushed harder and harder to find funds lying idle – even momentarily. The most severe monetary restraint (combined with the worst peacetime inflation) of the twentieth century was driving velocity measures substantially higher again (see Figures 4.1 and 4.2).

4.1.2   Erosion of the Money Supply Concept

The hard fact of life for central banks in highly sophisticated financial societies is that there has been an erosion of the money supply concept. The sources of much of this erosion were discussed in the preceding section and can be summed up fairly well in the expression 'liabilities management,' so popular with commercial banks beginning in the 1960s. Banks' ability to reach out for non-deposit sources of funds with a resulting decline in recorded deposits impairs the usefulness of statistical data used as targets and indicators of monetary policy. The actions of commercial banks and other depository institutions in creating time and savings deposits with instant liquidity indicate that the narrow concept of money is becoming obsolete and that we should move on to broader concepts. Indeed, with negotiable certificates of deposit, rapid multiple expansion and contraction of time deposits takes place, just as with traditional demand deposits.[4] Meanwhile, there is in the United States a gradual movement by thrift institutions to confer checking account privileges on their depositors, with every likelihood of wide expansion of such privileges.

Parallel to the 'hidden' monies are the 'paddings' in the money supply. Here are the compensating deposit balance requirements imposed by commercial banks on their borrowers, causing borrowers to borrow more than they wish to spend, and leading to escalation

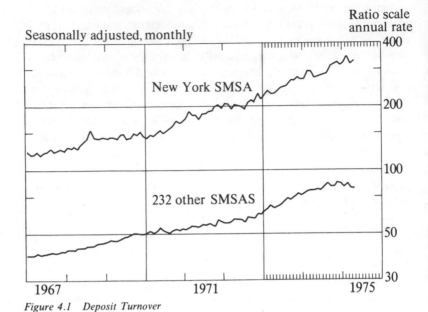

Figure 4.1   Deposit Turnover

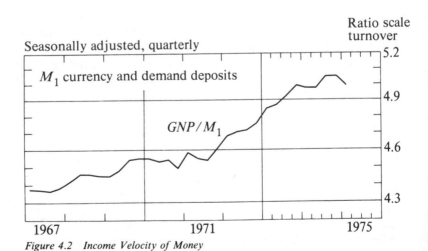

Figure 4.2   Income Velocity of Money

of the recorded money supply, assuming the presence of sufficient reserves.[5] In periods of tight money, these requirements tend to increase, thus to overstate the supply of usable money or, put differently, to cause the recorded money supply to exceed the usable money supply and to understate the degree of restraint.

A netting out of all these forces in quantitative terms is impossible. The upshot is an inability to measure the actual money supply and changes therein with any confidence, especially in periods of severe restraint. Comparisons of recorded data over time become less meaningful since the phenomenon being measured is partly hidden, partly padded, partly changing in character.[6] In turn, the usefulness of the money supply deteriorates as a device for managing the economy with any degree of precision.

Of course, there are other grounds for questioning the recorded values of the money supply, for example the statistical difficulties in gathering data in the United States. Then, too, with changing technology in funds transfers, it is difficult to visualize the character of the money supply that will be measured in the future, and in turn the behavior of its velocity. We shall not, however, pursue this avenue of inquiry further.

4.1.3 Immunization of the System

The financial system in some respects resembles the human body: when it is attacked by a disease and severe monetary restraint is used as the medicine, repeated dosages lead to the development of strains of germs that resist the drugs being used. So it is that the financial system has seen aggressive innovation and aggressive exploitation of existing institutional arrangements with each succeeding burst of tight money.[7] Once restraint ends and relaxation returns, the new financial mechanisms tend to remain and the areas of induced growth do not return to their former positions. They tend to be amalgamated into the system permanently, and permit a greater amount of credit to be supplied than before the squeeze at any given rate of interest and any given level of bank reserves, other things being equal. Thus, each succeeding period of tight money tends to require greater harshness to achieve a degree of restraint similar to that achieved in a previous period of tight money.

This necessity for increasing severity is also related to the fact that the high interest rates of severe restraint (especially longer-term) tend to become embedded in the system of institutional linkages, thus establishing a higher threshold from which each succeeding period of restraint begins. For example, the web of commitments made in financial institutions includes high interest guarantees to time depositors of four years and more, and medium- to long-term debt capital issues by banks bearing high rates of interest, in turn making it difficult to lower lending rates on longer-term credit. Added to this is the psychological factor that exposure to extraordinarily high rates (such as high-grade corporate bond rates of 10 per cent, 7 per cent on high-grade tax-exempt securities, prime interest rates of 12 per cent with effective rates often well above, home mortgage rates of 10 per cent) tends to make merely high levels seem reasonable and so reinforces the pressures resisting reductions to previous lows. This, of course, is simply an application of the oft-held position that interest rates are largely a psychological affair, the products of expectations whose base is in part what the public has become accustomed to.[8] Interest rate behavior after the squeezes of 1966, 1968–70 and 1973–4 supports this thesis: long rates declined relatively little compared with short rates.

The conclusion follows that the successive, extraordinarily high levels of interest rates reached beginning in 1966 have had the long-run effect of making it very difficult for longer-term rates to fall back to levels that might be viewed as reasonable historically. These high rates tend to permeate the economy and important questions are then raised for the longer-run performance of the economy. These questions involve such issues as levels of investment and income, and the allocation of resources.

4.1.4   Institutional Contradictions

The fact is that severe monetary restraint – of the type experienced since 1966 in the United States – has serious elements of incompatibility with the subtle assumptions upon which the US financial–economic system operates. That system is a highly complex one, with layerings of financial claims, with interest rate and related linkages among layers and institutions, bound often by contracts, both long- and short-term. All of the layerings of claims, all of the interest rate and related linkages, involve delicate relationships more or less geared to a range of values rooted in historical experience. Much of this was implicit in preceding pages. For example, savings and loan institutions issue mainly short-term claims upon themselves (savings accounts) at rates of interest bearing roughly average historical relationships to the average rates on the long-term assets (mainly mortgages) held by those institutions. Central bank actions which push interest rates beyond any reasonable range of expectation based on historical experience create disintermediation and liquidity problems of a type described earlier. The situation is made especially anomalous by the fact that the institutional arrangements of the savings and loan industry were encouraged and facilitated by the government, which then, through its central bank, proceeded to make the industry's survival difficult. Cited in an earlier chapter was the plight of casualty insurance companies, caught in a liquidity squeeze involving falling stock prices in which monetary policy was a major factor. One could cite also the plight of capital-intensive industries that rely heavily on external, long-term financing, mainly debt. Such debt is usually issued on the expectation that at maturity refinancing on reasonable terms will be possible. In a sense, one could argue that no industry would finance itself in this way if it envisioned the possibility of a prolonged series of government-sponsored credit crunches arising in the future. Given such unanticipated credit conditions, the financial–economic system then struggles to innovate and adapt successfully to the new environment in order to survive. The central bank, as noted, is then likely to find itself in a new environment to which its instruments are not adapted and, in turn, to have to develop new tools or apply the old ones at excruciating levels of intensity.

4.1.5   Conclusions

By almost any test, monetary management via general instruments was declining in efficiency in 1973 and 1974 *vis-à-vis* 1968–70, and in 1968–70 *vis-à-vis* 1966. The Federal Reserve found itself resorting to multi-tiered graduated reserve ratios, to policing monetary aggregates more closely than ever, to imposing the highest interest rates in more than a century, despite which credit still grew rapidly. The endless speeches and pronouncements of the authorities in these periods gave a picture of confusion, frustration and never-ending *ad hoc* actions to plug one hole after another as financial market innovation continued aggressively. It was on-again, off-again for interest rate ceilings on certain deposits, then multiple rate ceilings by time dimensions, then reserve requirements against non-deposit sources of funds ('hidden' deposits), then graduated reserve ratios against negotiable certificates of deposit related to increments of such certificates in individual institutions, and behind all such actions much effort and analysis to appraise the meaning and significance of innovative money market developments and how to deal with them.

4.2   Inflation in Advanced Commercial Societies

4.2.1   Types of Inflation

Before dealing with the details of recent inflation, let us review briefly the principal variants of inflation that may beset society.[9] The type of inflation most prominent in economic history is the classic, demand-pull variety related to very rapid growth in the money supply. Highly publicized cases include the European inflations of the sixteenth century attributed to the importation of gold and silver from newly discovered and exploited Latin America, the early eighteenth-century French inflation associated with John Law's paper money issues, the eighteenth-century inflations of colonial Massachusetts and Rhode Island involving paper money issues, the hyperinflations in the US Revolutionary War and in post World War I Germany.

After World War II cost-push inflation leaped to the fore as a type of equal and even greater prominence in the highly complex Western industrial societies. Big labor and big business were viewed as oligopolistic agencies arbitrarily setting prices on their services and products in a setting in which they gave leadership to non-union areas and business units of lesser size. They could respond to excess demand (demand-pull) by raising prices if they wished, or they could leave them unchanged, and they could raise prices in periods of slack. Thus, prices and wages overall could rise in periods of expansion and fail to fall, or even rise, in periods of contraction.

Big government, meanwhile, strengthened the hands of all labor (union and non-union) in resisting falling wages via minimum wage laws, unemployment compensation and welfare. Big government, too, interposed obstacles to falling prices by agricultural price supports, actions of regulatory agencies, stockpiling practices and subsidies in some sectors.

It was suggested that modern inflation could also be of a hybrid character which came to be known as demand-shift or structural inflation.[10] Demand-pull pressures in competitive sectors were viewed as spilling over into non-competitive areas having considerable slack, tending to draw resources away from the slack area. The latter area, having market power, would resist by raising its bid prices for the resources. For example, mechanics in railway repair shops with disguised unemployment might react to wage temptations in boom areas by demanding matching wages in union contract negotiations; railways, confident of obtaining compensating rate increases from regulatory agencies, might yield. Reverberations would make their way to the areas of excess demand and the process would continue as a wage–price spiral. Of course, the initial thrust could come from excess demand in a booming, non-competitive sector. Theoretically, it would also be possible for the process to begin with a cost-push thrust in a slack area with very inelastic demand, with a spillover of increased demand into competitive areas.

In a quite different framework, there has been discussion of 'functional' inflation, or what might be called scarcity inflation. This was viewed as a general rise in prices in a situation in which resources were becoming relatively scarcer, with resulting restraint of standards of living.[11] Examples would include exhaustion of the most economically obtained supplies of iron ore, coal, oil and copper. A price inflation in products or services requiring the use of the raw materials produced under conditions of increasing difficulty would serve to effect the necessary restraint in standards of living. Wage increases designed to catch up with such inflation would presumably be fruitless and would lead only to a wage–price spiral. (The restraint in standards of living could also obviously be effected by wage decreases.)

What may be thought of as a variant of functional or scarcity inflation relates to temporary scarcities. Here are natural or man-made failures of supply on a scale sufficient to affect the price level.

Examples might be massive crop failures or massive supply errors.

Finally, let us go backwards in time and note briefly a category of cost-push inflation that is older than is often realized. This is the type in which a government or several governments set prices on internationally traded products of strategic importance and either restrain production or withhold output from the market to sustain those prices. The resulting inflation might indeed be called 'political' inflation and be regarded as an independent type. Early examples of inter-governmental cartel agreements are found in the 1920s in rubber and tin.[12] Surplus coffee has been burned or dumped in the ocean for years by Brazil in order to maintain prices. The United States has withheld from world markets supplies of raw materials in its stockpiles. (Obviously, the extent of impact of such actions on price levels depends on a number of factors, including relative importance of the items involved, elasticities of demand for those

Table 4.2   Price Increases in Developed Countries, 1960–74 (percentage changes in GNP deflators)

	Annual average[a]			Change from preceding year				
	1960–70	1960–5	1965–70	1970	1971	1972	1973	1974
Industrial countries[b]	**3.4**	**2.6**	**4.2**	**5.9**	**5.4**	**4.8**	**7.0**	**11.7**
Canada	3.0	1.9	4.2	4.7	3.2	4.9	8.4	13.8
United States	2.7	1.4	4.1	5.5	4.5	3.4	5.6	10.3
Japan	4.8	4.9	4.7	6.7	4.6	5.0	11.1	20.9
France	4.3	4.1	4.4	5.5	5.6	6.0	7.2	9.6
Germany, Federal Republic	3.5	3.6	3.4	7.1	7.9	5.9	5.9	6.6
Italy	4.4	5.5	3.5	6.6	6.6	5.9	10.3	16.3
United Kingdom	4.3	3.6	5.0	7.3	8.9	7.7	7.4	12.6
Other industrial countries[b,c]	4.5	4.4	4.5	5.9	7.2	7.3		
More developed primary producing countries[b]	**4.8**	**4.7**	**4.9**	**6.2**	**9.0**	**9.4**	**14.0**	**16.5**
Australia	2.9	2.2	3.6	4.6	6.5	7.6	11.8	16.2
Spain	5.8	6.6	5.0	4.9	7.4	8.9	13.8	12.9
Other countries[b,d]	5.2	5.0	5.4	7.4	10.6	10.2	16.8	19.5

[a] Compound annual rates of change.
[b] Average of percentage changes for individual countries weighted by the US dollar value of their GNPs at current prices in the preceding year.
[c] Austria, Belgium, Denmark, Luxembourg, the Netherlands, Norway, Sweden and Switzerland.
[d] Finland, Greece, Iceland, Ireland, Malta, New Zealand, Portugal, South Africa, Turkey and Yugoslavia.
Source: International Monetary Fund, *Annual Report, 1975*, p. 4.

items, the availability of substitutes and the costs of substitutes.)

We conclude our excursion into types of inflation even though we have not exhausted all the possibilities. One could, for example, add exchange rate inflation as a distinct type, one that attracted increasing attention after the regime of floating exchange rates appeared among leading commercial countries beginning in 1971. Illustrative materials concerning the various types of inflation appear in subsequent sections describing the inflation of 1973–4 and examining the pitfalls of monetary restraint as a remedy. Important to note in all of this is that in the world of modern commercial–industrial economies the varieties of inflationary elements tend to intermix, making for complexity of analysis as well as complexity of therapy.

4.2.2   The Inflation of 1973–4

A goal of this study is to evaluate the efficacy of severe general monetary restraint in dealing with inflations of the type found in complex commercial societies beginning with the mid-1960s. (See Table 4.2 for a picture of price behavior in a group of countries in that period.) We shall focus on the most severe portion of that inflation – that beginning as 1973 approached – on the assumption that the issues can be put in boldest relief by so doing. The purpose of this section is to describe the major causes of the accelerated inflation, thus to lay the groundwork for the critique that follows (and which, indeed, precedes in earlier chapters).

Of course, the 1973–4 portion cannot be isolated from the inflationary conditions of the preceding years, but there are distinct features in it. As indicated in Table 4.3 and Figure 4.3, inflationary forces in the United States accelerated until 1970, subsided somewhat in 1970 through mid-1972, then accelerated with great vigor in late 1972 through 1974. Thus quantitatively the third phase was distinct. There were also very distinct causal forces at work. The first phase in the United States was traceable overwhelmingly to the very costly Vietnam War – its devouring of resources, including manpower and its method of financing. Demand-pull was the principal originating force. The deceleration in 1971–2 was probably due mainly to the incomes policies pursued. But inflation does not wind down quickly in the present world: forces are unleashed, both cost-push and demand-pull, which must seep gradually through the in-

Table 4.3 Prices in the United States, 1960–74

A. Consumer prices (1967 = 100)

Period	All items	Food	Housing							Apparel and upkeep	Transportation	Health and recreation				Other goods and services
			Total	Rent	Home-ownership	Fuel oil and coal	Gas and electricity	Furnishings and operation			Total	Medical care	Personal care	Reading and recreation	
1960	88.7	88.0	90.2	91.7	86.3	89.2	98.6	93.8	89.6	89.6	85.1	79.1	90.1	87.3	87.8
1965	94.5	94.4	94.9	96.9	92.7	94.6	99.4	95.3	93.7	95.9	93.4	89.5	95.2	95.9	94.2
1966	97.2	99.1	97.2	98.2	96.3	97.0	99.6	97.0	96.1	97.2	96.1	93.4	97.1	97.5	97.2
1967	100.0	100.0	100.0	100.0	100.0	100.0	100.0	100.0	100.0	100.0	100.0	100.0	100.0	100.0	100.0
1968	104.2	103.6	104.2	102.4	105.7	103.1	100.9	104.4	105.4	103.2	105.0	106.1	104.2	104.7	104.6
1969	109.8	108.9	110.8	105.7	116.0	105.6	102.8	109.0	111.5	107.2	110.3	113.4	109.3	108.7	109.1
1970	116.3	114.9	118.9	110.1	128.5	110.1	107.3	113.4	116.1	112.7	116.2	120.6	113.2	113.4	116.0
1971	121.3	118.4	124.3	115.2	133.7	117.5	114.7	118.1	119.8	118.6	122.2	128.4	116.8	119.3	120.9
1972	125.3	123.5	129.2	119.2	140.1	118.5	120.5	121.0	122.3	119.9	126.1	132.5	119.8	122.8	125.5
1973	133.1	141.4	135.0	124.3	146.7	136.0	126.4	124.9	126.8	123.8	130.2	137.7	125.2	125.9	129.0
1974	147.7	161.7	150.6	130.2	163.2	214.6	145.8	140.5	136.2	137.7	140.3	150.5	137.3	133.8	137.2
1974—Mar	143.1	159.1	144.9	128.4	157.2	201.5	140.0	132.6	132.2	132.0	135.4	144.8	131.8	129.5	132.8
Apr	143.9	158.6	146.0	128.8	158.2	206.5	141.9	134.0	133.6	133.7	136.3	145.6	133.1	130.4	133.6
May	145.5	159.7	147.6	129.3	159.4	211.0	143.9	137.0	135.0	136.3	137.7	147.2	134.9	132.0	134.4
June	146.9	160.3	149.2	129.8	161.2	214.2	144.5	139.2	135.7	138.8	139.4	149.4	136.5	133.5	135.8
July	148.0	160.5	150.9	130.3	163.2	218.5	146.2	141.4	135.3	140.6	141.0	151.4	137.8	134.6	137.7
Aug	149.9	162.8	152.8	130.9	165.4	220.9	148.5	143.9	138.1	141.3	142.6	153.7	139.3	135.2	139.4
Sept	151.7	165.0	154.9	131.4	167.9	222.7	150.2	146.6	139.9	142.2	144.0	155.2	141.2	137.0	140.4
Oct	153.0	166.1	156.7	132.2	170.1	225.5	151.5	149.0	141.1	142.9	145.2	156.3	143.0	137.8	141.4
Nov	154.3	167.8	158.3	132.8	171.7	229.2	154.0	151.0	142.4	143.4	146.3	157.5	144.2	138.8	142.7
Dec	155.4	169.7	159.9	133.5	174.0	228.8	156.7	152.3	141.9	143.5	147.5	159.0	145.3	139.8	143.9
1975—Jan	156.1	170.9	161.2	134.0	175.6	228.9	160.2	153.2	139.4	143.2	148.9	161.0	146.5	141.0	144.8
Feb	157.2	171.6	162.7	135.1	177.3	229.5	162.7	154.7	140.2	143.5	150.2	163.0	147.8	141.8	145.9
Mar	157.8	171.3	163.6	135.5	178.2	228.3	164.0	155.6	140.9	144.8	151.1	164.6	148.9	142.0	146.5

NOTE.—Bureau of Labor Statistics index for city wage-earners and clerical workers.

B. Wholesale Prices: Summary (1967 = 100, except as noted)

Period	All commodities	Farm products	Processed foods and feeds	Industrial commodities Total	Textiles, etc.	Hides, etc.	Fuel, etc.	Chemicals, etc.	Rubber, etc.	Lumber, etc.	Paper, etc.	Metals, etc.	Machinery and equipment	Furniture, etc.	Nonmetallic minerals	Transportation equipment[a]	Miscellaneous
1960	94.9	97.2	89.5	95.3	99.5	90.8	96.1	101.8	103.1	95.3	98.1	92.4	92.0	99.0	97.2	—	93.0
1965	96.6	98.7	95.5	96.4	99.8	94.3	95.5	99.0	95.9	95.9	96.2	96.4	93.9	96.9	97.5	—	95.9
1966	99.8	105.9	101.2	98.5	100.1	103.4	97.8	99.4	97.8	100.2	98.8	98.8	96.8	98.0	98.4	—	97.7
1967	100.0	100.0	100.0	100.0	100.0	100.0	100.0	100.0	100.0	100.0	100.0	100.0	100.0	100.0	100.0	—	100.0
1968	102.5	102.5	102.2	102.5	103.7	103.2	98.9	99.8	103.4	113.3	101.1	102.6	103.2	102.8	103.7	—	102.2
1969	106.5	109.1	107.3	106.0	106.0	108.9	100.9	99.9	105.3	125.3	104.0	108.5	106.5	104.9	107.7	100.8	105.2
1970	110.4	111.0	112.0	110.0	107.2	110.1	105.9	102.2	108.6	113.7	108.2	116.7	111.4	107.5	113.3	104.5	109.9
1971	113.9	112.9	114.3	114.0	108.6	114.0	114.2	104.2	109.2	127.0	110.1	119.0	115.5	109.9	122.4	110.3	112.8
1972	119.1	125.0	120.8	117.9	113.6	131.3	118.6	104.2	109.3	144.3	113.4	123.5	117.9	111.4	126.1	113.8	114.6
1973	134.7	176.3	148.1	125.9	123.8	143.1	134.3	110.0	112.4	177.2	122.1	132.8	121.7	115.2	130.2	115.1	119.7
1974	160.1	187.7	170.9	153.8	139.1	145.1	208.3	146.8	136.2	183.6	151.7	171.9	139.4	127.9	153.2	125.5	133.1
1974—Apr	152.7	186.2	159.1	146.6	137.5	145.4	197.9	132.3	129.4	200.2	114.4	161.2	130.8	122.9	146.7	119.4	128.2
May	155.0	180.8	158.9	150.5	139.1	146.3	204.3	137.0	133.7	198.0	146.6	168.7	134.1	124.5	150.7	121.4	133.2
June	155.7	168.6	157.4	153.6	141.7	146.0	210.5	142.8	135.6	192.2	147.5	174.0	137.2	126.1	152.3	122.8	134.3
July	161.7	180.8	167.6	157.8	142.1	146.6	221.7	148.4	139.5	188.6	153.3	180.3	140.3	128.2	156.4	125.1	135.2
Aug	167.4	189.2	179.7	161.6	142.3	146.2	226.0	158.5	143.4	183.7	162.9	185.6	144.3	129.8	157.6	126.7	135.4
Sept	167.2	182.7	176.8	162.9	142.1	148.1	225.0	161.7	145.6	180.4	164.2	187.1	146.8	132.8	159.8	127.7	136.3
Oct	170.2	187.5	183.5	164.8	140.5	145.2	228.5	168.5	147.5	169.4	166.0	186.9	150.0	135.5	162.2	134.2	137.1
Nov	171.9	187.8	189.7	165.8	139.8	144.5	227.4	172.9	148.5	165.8	166.9	186.7	152.7	136.9	163.4	135.1	140.7
Dec	171.5	183.7	188.2	166.1	138.4	143.2	229.0	174.0	149.4	165.4	167.2	184.6	154.0	137.7	164.3	137.0	142.4
1975—Jan	171.8	179.7	186.4	167.5	137.5	142.1	232.2	176.0	149.6	164.7	169.8	185.5	156.6	138.8	168.5	137.1	145.5
Feb	171.3	174.6	182.6	168.4	136.5	141.7	232.3	178.1	150.0	169.3	169.8	186.3	157.7	139.1	170.3	138.2	146.4
Mar	170.4	171.1	177.3	168.9	134.3	143.2	233.0	181.8	149.7	169.6	170.0	186.1	158.8	138.5	170.8	139.5	146.8
Apr	172.1	177.7	179.4	169.7	134.4	147.5	236.5	182.4	149.4	174.9	169.7	185.7	159.7	138.5	173.0	139.9	147.3

[a] Dec. 1968 = 100.
Source: *Federal Reserve Bulletin*, May 1975, p. A53.

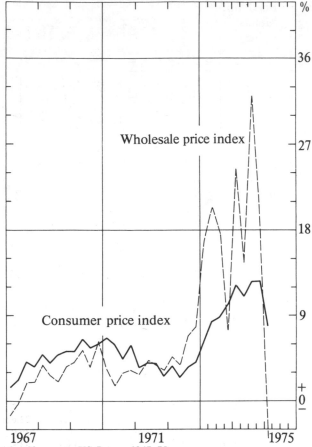

Figure 4.3   Changes in US Prices, 1967–75

numerable interconnections in the economy before all the embers are burned out. Before all those embers died out, however, new forces were unleashed in late 1972. The nature of the forces fueling the subsequent 1973–4 inflation were recounted almost continuously in the press and in the specialized literature in economics and finance. Therefore we will be brief, summarizing the situation based on readily available analyses.[13]

The severe inflation of 1973–4 had its origins in the agricultural shortages of 1972 in combination with a gathering worldwide

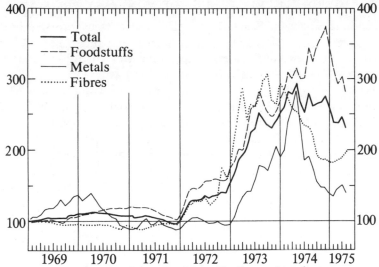

Figure 4.4   *World Market Commodity Prices:* The Economist *Indicator*

Table 4.4   Food Prices in the OECD Consumer Price Index (CPI)

	Weight of food in CPI	Change in food prices	1972–3 Weighted contribution to rise of total CPI	March 1973–March 1974 Change in food prices	March 1973–March 1974 Weighted contribution to rise of total CPI
	%	%	%	%	%
Canada	30.8	12.5	51.3	15.3	45.3
United States	22.2	14.5	51.6	18.3	39.8
Japan	43.1	12.4	45.3	25.8	46.3
Australia	38.6	15.3	62.1	19.8[a]	56.2[a]
France	40.2	9.7	53.4	12.5	41.2
Germany	33.3	7.6	36.2	5.1	23.6
Italy	43.3	12.0	48.1	14.4	39.0
United Kingdom	41.6	11.5	52.2	14.4	44.4
Belgium	30.0	8.0	34.3	7.8	24.9
Denmark	36.9	10.8	43.0	13.0	34.8
Ireland	48.1	16.5	69.3	11.1[a]	39.5[a]
Netherlands	35.1	7.3	32.5	7.1	27.1
Austria	39.2	7.5	38.2	7.2	31.4
Finland	39.8	11.2	39.5	9.4	21.1
Norway	35.4	7.2	33.3	7.4	29.1
Portugal	53.8	9.0	37.2	25.2	47.2
Spain	55.2	12.6	61.4	15.2	53.4
Sweden	33.3	6.8	34.3	7.2	22.2
Switzerland	36.0	6.1	25.3	6.4	24.0

[a] First quarter 1973 to first quarter 1974.
Source: OECD, *Economic Outlook*, July 1974, p. 30.

economic expansion. The failure of the Russian wheat crop received the greatest publicity, but other countries and other agricultural products, too, had difficulties. India, China and Australia had grain failures. Most of the anchovy 'crop' in the Pacific Ocean off Peru vanished, eliminating an important source of protein for the world. Pressures were transmitted to all grains, to soybeans, to meats and to processed foods embodying grains and protein components. The prices of basic foodstuffs then reflected these supply pressures (see Figure 4.4 and Table 4.4). Meanwhile rising economic activity throughout the world brought rising pressure on prices of raw materials, including wool, hides and skins. Prices of lumber and plywood also rose very rapidly.[14]

In 1973 reverberations continued and flowed through the entire economy. Pressures accelerated as US price controls were simultaneously weakened in January by resort to an essentially self-administering operation. The situation was succinctly summarized by the US Council of Economic Advisors as follows:

There is no simple explanation for this behavior which was the most extraordinary in almost a generation and which confounded the Council and most other economists alike. The simultaneous upsurge in demand in the United States and in foreign countries, the shortfall in agricultural production of 1972 and early 1973, the decline in the international exchange value of the dollar, the unexpected capacity problems in materials industries, the increases in petroleum prices late in the year as a result of the Arab oil embargo, the shifting character of domestic price controls – all these tell part of the story of last year's inflation.[15]

Shortages existed in gasoline, heating oils, natural gas, fertilizers, textiles, paper, petrochemicals and in a vast assortment of end products embodying these and other raw materials.[16] The resulting behavior of prices in a number of important areas is shown in Table 4.5.

What transpired from mid-1972 through 1973 involved an extraordinary series of apparent coincidences on a global scale superimposed on the worldwide economic expansion beginning in 1972 and reaching boom proportions as 1973 was approaching. Not only were there the grain crop failures of 1972 in Russia, China and India, and in Australia in early 1973; Argentina, too, had lowered grain output.[17] Anchovy supplies continued very low in 1973, after the 1972 failure. Droughts in Asia caused rice production to fall seriously. Weather developments also had unfavorable effects in the

Table 4.5   Changes in International Commodity Prices, 1971–4[a]

| | Percentage price change from[b] | | | | | |
| | December 1971–
December 1972 | | December 1972–
December 1973 | | December 1973–
April 1974 | |
Commodities	£ terms	$ terms	£ terms	$ terms	£ terms	$ terms
Coffee	+ 20	+ 12	+ 14	+ 13	+ 23	+ 27
Cocoa	+ 66	+ 54	+ 81	+ 79	+ 81	+ 87
Tea	+ 1	− 6	+ 7	+ 6	+ 32	+ 36
Sugar	+ 62	+ 50	+ 42	+ 40	+ 70	+ 76
Wheat	+ 50	+ 39	+120	+118	+ 2	+ 5
Maize	+ 39	+ 29	+ 95	+ 92	− 5	− 2
Beef	+ 27	+ 18	+ 31	+ 29	+ 3	+ 7
Lamb	+ 33	+ 24	+ 57	+ 55	− 13	− 10
Soybeans	+ 19	+ 10	+ 81	+ 79	− 14	− 12
Groundnut oil	+ 19	+ 10	+ 75	+ 73	+ 39	+ 44
Wool	+140	+123	+ 58	+ 57	− 19	− 16
Cotton	+ 9	+ 1	+120	+118	− 18	− 15
Rubber	+ 46	+ 35	+143	+140	− 20	− 18
Softwood	+ 13	+ 5	+111	+109	+ 6	+ 9
Wood pulp	− 6	− 12	+ 30	+ 28	+ 17	+ 21
Newsprint	+ 4	− 3	+ 25	+ 23	+ 22	+ 25
Aluminum	− 11	− 17	+ 19	+ 17	+ 16	+ 20
Copper	+ 7	− 1	+118	+115	+ 32	+ 36
Lead	+ 44	+ 34	+ 95	+ 93	+ 14	+ 18
Nickel	+ 15	+ 7	− 1	− 2	+ 12	+ 15
Tin	+ 12	+ 4	+ 76	+ 74	+ 37	+ 41
Silver	+ 53	+ 42	+ 60	+ 58	+ 54	+ 59
Iron ore	− 3	− 10	+ 16	+ 15	+ 10	+ 13
Steel scrap[c]	+ 42	+ 32	+ 59	+ 57	+ 37	+ 41
Crude oil (light)	+ 21	+ 12	+106	+104	+128	+135

[a] Quotations in the United Kingdom; end-of-period prices.
[b] The difference between price changes in sterling and dollar terms reflect relative movements in the sterling/dollar exchange rate.
[c] US quotation.
Source: Bank of International Settlements, *Annual Report, 1973–74*, p. 16.

United States, causing delay in harvesting the 1972 corn and soybean crops.[18] Bad weather affected US output of fruits and vegetables in late 1972 and much of 1973 and likewise cotton production.[19] Supplies of wool 'were limited as a result of bad weather and a declining world sheep population.'[20]

In addition to the extraordinary series of coincidences, there was a failure of the petroleum refining industry to expand capacity in the several years prior to 1973, despite the ever-growing use of petroleum products as (1) raw materials in a vast variety of industries – from packaging to textiles to electronics to drugs to construction, and (2) a fuel source vital to production and transportation globally. There were other failures to expand capacity in vital areas, for example natural gas and steel. In the latter case, an interesting link leads to the apparent over-valuation of the US dollar prior to August 1971, causing foreign steel supplies to hang heavily over the US market.

We need not go on restating that which is quite commonplace. Suffice it to state that all of the above, coupled with rising global demands, rising global aspirations and expectations of better standards of living, rising import prices for key countries involved in currency devaluations and depreciations and rising export demands for the products of those countries stemming from their devaluations and depreciations, led to the most severe worldwide inflation of the twentieth century (other than those associated with wars).

4.3   Severe General Monetary Restraint and Inflation After 1965

4.3.1   Quantitative Impacts: Econometric Evidence

It is most unlikely that we will ever know the consequences of specific changes in the money supply within a margin of error small enough for purposes of close prediction and control. Econometric studies relating income and prices to changes in the money supply, besides leaving substantial amounts of unexplained variation in incomes and prices, suffer by virtue of being portraits of a specific period of time in the past. The real world, on the other hand, is constantly changing, and will not stand still for the convenience of the monetary authorities. The slippages in the real world are not static: there is constant change in the relative importance of the package as a whole and its components, and part of the change is in the new elements – the unborn slippages – still to arrive. As observed earlier, the authorities, by their continuous, severe pressure on the financial system, cause irreversible change in the system and in the psychological adaptation of society to the levels of the variables in the system. Thus society adapts to changes with new notions of 'norms.' In turn, prediction via equations fitted to previous data, involving values that society had partly incorporated into its range of experience, thinking and planning, but partly had not because it was so new, cannot be expected to hold up within a narrow range of accuracy when applied to a future period which simultaneously is digesting previous change and coming forth with new, unpredictable change to which society must begin adapting.

Despite these caveats, let us nevertheless consider some recent statistical results to see what they would imply for the efficacy of monetary policy if by chance the caveats were based on groundless fears. The evidence currently available includes econometric simulations of the movements of the economy in response to varying rates of change in the money supply. Let us consider the evidence briefly, first for income and second for prices. In terms of a monetarist equation (Federal Reserve Bank of St Louis) the simulation for impacts on GNP show fairly nominal effects for changes in rates of money supply growth in periods up to about six months. By the end of a year, however, pronounced effects would be evident. For example, it is suggested that an increase in the annual rate of growth of the money supply from 6 to 10 per cent for three consecutive quarters, even if followed by a fall to a 2 per cent growth rate in the fourth quarter, would lead to GNP being about 2 per cent greater than would have been the case with a steady 6 per cent money supply growth rate.[21]

Results quite consistent with those obtained from the monetarist equation were also obtained by the Congressional Budget Office in an analysis utilizing three prominent large-scale econometric forecasting systems. These are shown in Table 4.6.

Operationally, the conclusions in the preceding paragraphs have another dimension, namely the period of time required for central bank action on selected bank reserve aggregates or interest rates to be translated into fairly full impact on the money supply. Here, lags are again substantial, perhaps 'of the order of six to eight months to work themselves out fully.'[22] The two lags combined thus suggest that it may be about one-and-a-half years before major effects of Federal Reserve actions are felt.

Additional caveats are in order concerning the econometric evidence cited. First, with the monetarist equation, the correlations

Table 4.6 Estimated Effects of 10 and 7 Per Cent Growth Rates of Money Supply in Relation to Effects of 8½ Per Cent Rate[a]

Economic variable	10%−8½%			7%−8½%		
	1975-IV	1976-II	1976-IV	1975-IV	1976-II	1976-IV
Current dollar GNP ($ billion)	+ 2.0	+ 8.5	+ 20.8	− 1.6	− 9.8	− 25.5
Real GNP (1958 $ billion)	+ 1.5	+ 5.3	+ 12.0	− 1.1	− 5.2	− 12.8
Price level (percentage changes in GNP deflator)	− 0.1	− 0.2	− 0.3	0	+ 0.1	+ 0.1
Unemployment rate (percentage points)	0	− 0.1	− 0.3	0	+ 0.1	+ 0.3
Business fixed investment ($ billion)	+ 0.9	+ 4.7	+ 11.9	− 0.5	− 4.7	− 12.8
Federal deficit (NIA basis) ($ billion)	− 0.9	− 3.3	− 7.9	+ 0.6	+ 3.9	+ 9.7

[a] All quantities are seasonally adjusted; dollar magnitudes are expressed at annual rates. Money supply assumptions cover 1975-III through 1976-IV (18 months).

Source: US Congress, Congressional Budget Office, *Inflation and Unemployment: A Report on the Economy*, Washington, DC, 30 June 1975, pp. 65–8.

between changes in measures of the money supply and changes in GNP generally show changes in the money supply accounting for somewhat less than half to a little over half of the changes in GNP. In other words, forecasting errors would have been substantial even when forecasting retrospectively in terms of a known data base and known outcomes.[23] Secondly, there are also substantial errors in predicting relationships between Federal Reserve actions (on selected reserve aggregates or interest rates) and measures of the money supply.[24] It follows that, if these forecasting uncertainties are allowed for, not only may it be about one-and-a-half years before major effects on GNP of Federal Reserve actions are felt, but those effects will be subject to large prediction errors.

A second type of econometric simulation is intended to give evidence concerning the quantitative impact of changes in the money supply on prices rather than income. Here, use is made of a monetarist formulation (that of the Federal Reserve Bank of St Louis) and a non-monetarist formulation (the SSRC–MIT–Penn model). Results of both formulations are shown in Table 4.7 and each indicates little short-run differences in price implications associated with substantial differences in rates of growth of the money supply. Significant differential impacts appear if substantial differences in money growth rates are sustained for a period approaching two years.[25] However, worth noting are the relatively small differential impacts of 3 v. 5 per cent and 5 v. 7 per cent in two of the formulations over even a two-year period. One should note, too, the relatively large differences between the several formulations in the price predictions related to specific rates of growth in the money supply, a warning of lack of reliability. At the same time, they 'project an unemployment rate at least one full percentage point higher with a constant 3 per cent growth rate v. a constant 7 per cent.'[26] If these findings can be relied upon, despite the previously noted limitations of econometric projections, 'changes in the rate of growth of the money supply appear to be of limited usefulness as a short-run weapon in the battle against inflation.'[27] In the longer run, however, price stability has far more relation to behavior of the money supply.

Again, analysis of impacts on price levels by the Congressional Budget Office using other large-scale econometric forecasting models gives results consistent with those just cited (see Table 4.6).

While the evidence just cited (again assuming its validity) shows relatively little short-run differential impact of modest differences

Table 4.7 Simulated Inflation in Two Models of the US Economy

	1973-I–1974-I	1974-I–1975-I	Projected annual rates of change of the price level							
			1973-II	1973-III	1973-IV	1974-I	1974-II	1974-III	1974-IV	1975-I
SMP model Assumed annual rates of growth of M1[a]										
3%	5.0	4.5	5.0	4.5	4.8	5.9	4.6	4.6	4.4	4.5
5%	5.1	5.0	5.0	4.5	4.9	6.0	4.9	5.0	4.9	5.1
7%	5.2	5.6	5.0	4.6	5.0	6.3	5.2	5.5	5.7	6.0
StL model Assumed annual rates of growth of M1										
3%	3.3	2.3	3.6	3.4	3.2	2.9	2.6	2.4	2.1	1.9
5%	3.4	2.7	3.6	3.5	3.3	3.1	2.9	2.7	2.6	2.6
7%	3.5	3.1	3.6	3.5	3.4	3.3	3.2	3.1	3.1	3.2
Alternative StL model Assumed annual rates of growth of M1										
3%	4.8	3.2	5.3	5.0	4.5	4.2	3.9	3.4	2.9	2.5
5%	5.1	4.4	5.4	5.2	5.0	4.8	4.7	4.5	4.2	4.0
7%	5.5	5.5	5.5	5.5	5.4	5.5	5.6	5.6	5.5	5.4

[a] M1 identifies the narrowly defined supply as currency plus demand deposits.

Source: Federal Reserve Bank of Kansas City, *Monthly Review*, July, August 1973, p. 6.

in rates of growth of the money supply on either economic activity
or price levels, the consequences for interest rates are another story.
A 7 v. a 3 per cent or even a 7 v. a 5 per cent rate of growth of
the money supply are likely to imply great differences in interest
rate levels.[28]

4.3.2   Quantitative Impacts: Other Evidence and Considerations

Recent evidence available from non-econometric sources is not fully
comparable with that cited from econometric sources. For one thing,
the former relates essentially to restraint, with monetary ease being
viewed as a point of departure or a base from which to measure
the consequences of restraint. Another element that lacks compara-
bility is price performance, where, with non-econometric evidence,
one cannot really begin to estimate the consequences of a hypothetical, alternative course of action in recent US experience.

Given these qualifications and limitations, the evidence available
from non-econometric sources is consistent with that cited from
econometric sources. In the short run, survey studies in the United
States and United Kingdom have generally suggested a relative
impotence of tight money, except with respect to residential
construction. Prior to the US 'credit crunch' of 1966, such surveys
were impressionistic in character, consisting of views of business
interviewees on how they would react to hypothetical monetary
policy actions. They were set implicitly in a short-term framework
and, in the United States at least, in the context of interest rate
levels of generally low and modest proportions such as characterized
the period from the early 1920s to the mid-1960s and in the context
of generally relatively high business liquidity. Although corrobora-
tive of short-term findings here, further discussion of them will be
avoided.

The 1966 'credit crunch' was in some respects almost a laboratory
experiment in the application of monetary restraint. It was brief,
severe, and lent itself to serious statistical analysis. Monetary
restraint began towards the end of 1965 and was intensified sharply
in the spring of 1966, then relaxed beginning in the autumn 'as
certain additional Federal fiscal actions of a restrictive nature were
taken and as evidence of moderating tendencies in economic activity
and commodity prices accumulated.'[29] Following this episode,

careful statistical surveys were made by the Department of Commerce and the Federal Reserve Board concerning the impact of the restraint on actual capital expenditures (non-farm, non-residential) of business and non-federal governmental units in relation to planned expenditures. The results indicated that tight money was responsible for only nominal cutbacks in business capital expenditures in 1966 in relation to original plans, less than 1 per cent, while the lagged impact on capital spending plans for 1967 was higher, slightly over 1 per cent.[30] Results were similar in the case of actual capital expenditures by state and local governments and state colleges:

Allowing for a variety of added expenditure reductions and postponements stretching into 1967 by both large and small state and local governments, it is estimated that stringent credit market conditions in 1966 reduced state and local government spending by somewhat over $400 million. This probably is equal to less than 1 per cent of state and local government capital outlays for 1966 and 1967 combined.[31]

In contrast, there was severe short-term impact on the US housing market, with housing investment falling $6.1 billion (annual rate), or 23 per cent, between the first and fourth quarters of 1966.[32]

Extrapolating from short-run impacts on economic activity to short-term impacts on prices, one would have to agree on logical, *a priori* grounds with the econometric results cited. If little can be expected of monetary restraint – except in housing – in curbing aggregate economic activity, little should probably be expected of it in curbing inflation in the short run.

The somewhat longer run, say one or two years, is another matter. The non-econometric evidence is less factual and more impressionistic than in the shorter run. Nevertheless, hard as it may be to relate cause and effect conclusively, that evidence is consistent with the econometric evidence. Money *does* matter in the real world as well as in the financial world. The prolonged credit squeeze, lasting roughly from November 1968 to May 1970, was of historically unprecedented severity, driving interest rates to levels outside the range of historical experience except for the Civil War period. In this fierce squeeze was another laboratory case of the application of restrictive monetary policy, and this may be used to illustrate its consequences. The prime, very short-run casualty, residential construction, was joined after a while by state and local governments. Withdrawals of security offerings and postponements were gradually translated into reduction of capital expenditures below planned levels. The tentacles of severe restraint spread nearly everywhere, hitting hard and restricting achievement of planned financing generally.

Clear evidence exists with respect to state and local governmental units in the 1968–70 squeeze, thanks to a Federal Reserve study of fiscal 1970. Capital spending projects of 'an estimated $1.60 billion remained suspended at the end of fiscal year 1970 . . . 5.6 per cent of total capital expenditures by state and local governments in the preceding fiscal year.'[33]

For other sectors of the economy, some idea of the impact of the credit squeeze may be gleaned from Table 4.8, which shows funds raised from 1966 to 1974, with shares of individual sectors. Home mortgage funds borrowed actually rose slightly in 1969, but then fell sharply in 1970. Quarterly data indicate that home mortgage funds borrowed fell beginning in the third quarter of 1969 (1969-III), reached a trough in 1970-I and did not reach the previous peak until 1971-II. Total residential mortgage credit granted acted similarly except that it reached its previous peak in 1971-I.[34] Expenditures for non-farm residential structures showed a very similar pattern with a decline in 1969-III, a trough in 1970-II and attainment of the previous peak by 1971-I.[35] Another series, private housing starts, more sensitive than expenditures (i.e. with less lag) began to fall in 1969-II, reached a trough in 1970-I, and by 1970-IV had regained its previous peak.[36]

The basically pervasive impact of the credit squeeze is shown in Table 4.8 with the grand total of all non-federal government credit raised by non-financial business down substantially in 1970. Examination of quarterly data tends to show general declines beginning in 1969-III, lasting through 1970-I.[37]

Ultimately, of course, there is no way to measure the extent to which a credit squeeze reduces funds raised, and in turn spending. One would have to know the amount of funds sought and spending plans for each sector of the economy as well as the amount of funds obtained and realized spending in each sector.[38] That business received less than it desired in 1969 and early 1970, however, is fairly obvious. The historically unprecedented interest rates and the frenzied movements of funds in the money markets reflect in good measure the effects of borrowers' wanting more credit than was

Table 4.8 Funds Raised in the United States by Non-Financial Sectors, 1966–74[a]

	1966	1967	1968	1969	1970	1971	1972	1973	1974
					($ billion)				
State and local governments	6.3	7.9	9.8	10.7	11.3	17.8	14.2	12.3	16.6
Households	22.7	19.3	30.0	31.7	23.4	39.8	63.1	72.8	44.0
Farm	3.1	3.6	2.8	3.2	3.2	4.1	4.9	8.6	7.8
Non-farm non-corporate	5.4	5.0	5.6	7.4	5.3	8.7	10.4	9.3	7.2
Corporate	25.3	29.6	31.6	38.9	39.5	46.8	55.3	67.2	77.1
Foreign	1.5	4.0	2.8	3.7	2.7	4.6	4.3	7.5	15.4
Total	64.3	69.4	82.6	95.5	85.4	121.9	152.1	177.7	168.1
Home mortgages	11.7	11.5	15.1	15.7	12.8	26.1	39.6	43.3	31.7
Multi-family residential mortgages	3.1	3.6	3.4	4.7	5.8	8.8	10.3	8.4	7.8
Commercial mortgages	5.7	4.7	6.4	5.3	5.3	10.0	14.8	17.0	11.5
Farm mortgages	1.8	2.3	2.2	1.9	1.8	2.0	2.6	4.4	4.9
Total mortgages	22.3	22.1	27.1	27.6	25.7	46.9	67.3	73.1	55.9
					Percentage of total				
State and local governments	9.8	11.3	11.9	11.2	13.2	14.6	9.3	6.9	9.9
Households	35.3	27.8	36.3	33.2	27.4	32.6	41.5	41.0	26.2
Farm	4.8	5.2	3.4	3.4	3.7	3.4	3.2	4.8	4.6
Non-farm non-corporate	8.4	7.2	6.8	7.7	6.2	7.1	6.8	5.2	4.3
Corporate	39.3	42.7	38.3	40.7	46.3	38.4	36.4	37.8	45.9
Foreign	2.3	5.8	3.4	3.9	3.2	3.8	2.8	4.2	9.2
Total	100.0	100.0	100.0	100.0	100.0	100.0	100.0	100.0	100.0
Home mortgages	18.2	16.6	18.3	16.4	15.0	21.4	26.0	24.4	18.9
Multi-family residential mortgages	4.8	5.2	4.1	4.9	6.8	7.2	6.8	4.7	4.6
Commercial mortgages	8.9	6.8	7.7	5.5	6.2	8.2	9.7	9.6	6.8
Farm mortgages	2.8	3.3	2.7	2.0	2.1	1.6	1.7	2.5	2.9
Total mortgages	34.7	31.8	32.8	28.9	30.1	38.5	44.2	41.1	33.3

[a] Excluding the US Government.

Source: *Federal Reserve Bulletin*, February 1976, p. A56.

available on current terms and bidding steadily higher for accommodation, influencing bank and other lenders to engage in a scramble to find funds for their business customers. Although it may be impossible to quantify the unsatisfied margin, key market participants attested to its reality and to the fact that it was large.[39]

The credit squeezes of 1966 and 1968–70 seem in historical perspective to have been but rehearsals for the credit squeeze of 1973–1974. As noted earlier, the financial system, partially 'innoculated' by previous medications, again showed its capacity to elude control and so the dosages had to be greater, with much higher interest rates. Income velocity, already very high in 1970, was about 4.7 in 1972, 4.9 in 1973 and over 5.0 in 1974. Demand deposits (excluding New York City) turned over in a large number of standard metropolitan statistical areas 52.2 times per annum in February 1970 (a peak at the time) and by November 1974 reached a staggering 87.5.[40]

Despite the extraordinary ingenuity of the US financial system and its participants, the credit squeeze of 1973–4 produced severe consequences. Some of these were described in Chapters 2 and 3 and bear at least brief, partial repetition in the present context. Sectorally the results were much the same as in 1969–70 (see Table 4.8), with residential mortgages and households generally bearing the main brunt. However, the credit squeeze gradually spread its effects in all directions. The financial press gave a vivid picture of industries and firms forced to contract spending plans. Most dramatically caught, probably, were the public utilities, as inflation drove up their costs of supplies and tight money raised their costs of capital to levels difficult to absorb. Dramatic, too, were the accounts of liquidity problems in banks and other financial institutions (savings and loan associations, savings banks, real estate investment trusts, securities firms, finance companies, factoring firms). Overall, outside the financial field, there was also a general deterioration of liquidity positions of corporations, with some measures of corporate liquidity reaching obviously dangerous levels.[41] The nature of the general impact of severe restraint was placed in bold relief in mid-1974, when

one of the country's largest retail apparel chains, Robert Hall, recently notified its Seventh Avenue suppliers that it was adopting a policy of paying 30 days later than usual.

The reason, it told its shocked suppliers, is that it would not borrow money at 10 to 12 percent interest to pay its bills. By avoiding this interest, the chain's management said, the company could earn more money than it earned from its regular retail business.[42]

The writer follows with the astute observation, 'Can a businessman do better by not carrying on his regular business?' It should be added, moreover, that in mid-1974, with prime rates of 12 per cent and more and with compensating balance requirements added, interest costs on money used for many firms were more on the order of 15 per cent or higher, rather than the 10–12 per cent quoted.

4.3.3   The Logic of Severe Monetary Restraint in Modern Peacetime Inflations

In an earlier day, say much of the nineteenth century, it could be argued that monetary policy would have been thoroughly adequate to deal with inflation, since inflation was reasonably close to a demand-pull affair and cost-oriented forces were of nominal strength. Moreover, there was far less sophistication in banking and credit systems, with far fewer money substitutes, far less ambiguity in the nature of money, only a nominal power (relative to today) to mobilize bank reserves speedily over national and international boundaries, only nominal power (relative to today) to mobilize deposit and non-deposit sources of funds, domestically and internationally. Thus there were far fewer opportunities for slippages in the application of monetary policy.

In modern peacetime inflations in advanced economies, logic would dictate a dissection of each inflation, with weights assigned to the forces in each. Multiple policies would then be applied with relative policy weights determined by the strength of the various inflationary forces. Simple restraint of aggregate demand via monetary and fiscal policy would *not* be the solution. Illustrations of this last point follow immediately, while positive suggestions appear in Chapter 5.

If, in fact, crucial natural resources such as iron ore, natural gas and petroleum are *relatively* scarcer in supply than in the past, functional inflation is present. The ultimate solution to such an inflation is a fall in the growth path of money incomes relative to prices (possibly with an actual decline in real income in the short run) and, if possible, the development of substitutes for raw materials of increasing scarcity. The latter, of course, is by far the preferred solution, and to it severe monetary restraint can make no contribution; in fact, it inhibits this preferred solution by restricting access to financing, and in this sense it is inflationary. The preferred solution is all-out easy financing for substitutes! If, nevertheless, severe monetary restraint is employed, it presumably should work by restraining aggregate demand so that funds are siphoned to areas of relative scarcity (characterized by rising prices and profits) from areas of plenty (with falling prices and profits). Ideally, the overall price level would remain the same but the growth of real income would have fallen. In the real world, however, cost-push forces would in all probability emerge in the adversely affected areas, restraining price decreases; and with public consciousness of the restraint of or decline in real income, cost-push forces would probably spread generally. Monetary restraint would then be left with administered unemployment as its weapon to deal with cost-push forces – and nothing immediate to deal with scarcities.

What has been said concerning functional inflation is largely applicable to food and other temporary scarcity situations arising from droughts, floods or other causes. The essential difference is that the temporary shortage does not imply any long-term restraint on the standard of living. The strict theoretical logic of severe monetary restriction again implies a shift of spending from areas of plenty to areas of relative shortage, with declines in prices and in turn supplies in the affected areas of plenty, and a temporary decline in real income. In practice, again, prices are unlikely to fall in the areas adversely affected by the shift of spending; and, in practice, labor is likely to exert cost-push pressure to maintain real income. Severe restraint, however, will produce not an iota of additional crops, but again may restrict farmers' access to credit to finance the next crop and so be a force adding to inflation. Moreover, at extreme rates of interest, crop storage and distribution costs may be pushed significantly upward, again adding to inflation.

Another example of a temporary scarcity situation is electric power in the early 1970s. A shortage of power does not ordinarily cause a rise in its price, given the presence of regulatory bodies, but it may contribute to a shortage of other materials for whose production electricity is essential, in turn leading to inflationary forces in other economic sectors. Unfortunately, as noted earlier, curtailments of capital spending plans were announced almost continuously in the spring and summer of 1974.[43] Easier money, not severe restraint, would have been the anti-inflationary solution.

In terms of a *pure* cost-push situation, little need be added to the earlier analysis. Public examination of this issue has been prolonged and intense. It is worth repeating, however, that in all likelihood severe restraint, by causing unemployment, escalates the use of cost-push mechanisms. During the escalating unemployment of 1970–1, for example, certain very large wage settlements developed out of union negotiations. To this writer at least, as suggested in the previous chapter, it appeared that administered unemployment in the construction industry led labor to seek hourly wage increases sufficient to offset, in part at least, the income lost through reduced hours of available work, thus to push the so-called Phillips curve to the right.

When severe monetary restraint is used to deal with cost-push inflation, unemployment is the cutting edge. Its target is the efforts of people to maintain their original slice of the economic pie intact, while the authorities constrain the size of the pie (aggregate supply), that is use scarcity. Here then is a startling phenomenon: while *increased* supply is generally acknowledged to be an antidote for inflation, our authorities have had the opposite solution, to produce less! Their intentions have been clear, to reduce aggregate demand, so to put pressure on labor to reduce demands, and so to raise the resistance of business to labor's demands. A previously noted flaw in the use of contrived scarcity to stop inflation with heavy cost-push elements is that, given income supplements, it reduces aggregate supply more than it reduces aggregate demand and so embodies inflationary elements.

Finally, we turn to governmentally (politically) generated inflation. The situation here, to some extent, resembles that of functional inflation. To illustrate, the oil-exporting countries that in 1973–4 contrived to restrain production in order to keep prices elevated were forcing a reduction in real incomes of oil-importing countries. The exporters were simply requiring the oil-importing countries to deliver much more of their domestic output in exchange for given quantities of oil. In addition, such an inflationary force could have further repercussions through depreciation of an importing country's currency against both the oil exporter's currency and possibly other currencies. Higher import prices generally would then appear and export prices would ordinarily rise under the pressure of foreign demand for goods. Application of severe monetary restraint, if effective in keeping the overall price level constant, could do so only by causing other prices to fall. Given cost-push pressures, however, the more likely outcome would be rising prices for goods not involved in imports and exports and increased unemployed resources. The preferred solution, on the other hand, as with scarcity inflation, would be the development of alternative sources of supply, but again severe monetary restraint would inhibit their financing.[44]

In another sense logic vanishes, giving way to assorted monetary charades in the application of severe general monetary restraint. Selectivity prevails without the application of formal selective controls – a selectivity based on a combination of non-price credit rationing and high interest rates hitting financial and real sectors most sensitive to them. The main victim, despite the widening tentacles of persistent restraint, has been and continues to be residential housing. (Suburban shopping centers, duplicating many already probably surplus facilities and eroding further the viability of central city districts, in 1974 continued being built at a merry pace.[45]) The authorities, alarmed by the sledgehammer selectivity of the restraint imposed by their monetary subdivision in such episodes, have had other subdivisions take action to cushion somewhat the impacts on housing finance. Thus, the governmentally sponsored Federal National Mortgage Association and the Federal Home Loan Banks poured billions into the mortgage markets in 1969, and the state of New York set up a state mortgage financing agency to cushion the impact on housing. In 1973–4 billions were again poured into the mortgage markets by quasi-government agencies in the United States in the form of both principal and subsidies for interest.[46] These billions, of course, were demand-pull elements in so far as taxes were not raised to offset them. Presumably these subsidies and injections of principal helped stave off total collapse of the residential building industry, but still the industry was left in a shambles and serious questions remained concerning the future ability of the general US public to pay for decent housing without government assistance.

The monetary charades go further. In other industries of importance to the national wellbeing that have been severely hurt by extreme monetary restraint, governmental agencies have taken offsetting action that diluted the intended effects of monetary restraint. A good example in the early and mid-1970s was the electric utility industry, where in some cases rate increases were granted to offset cost increases, including interest cost.

Selective in an important sense and worth emphasizing are the previously noted negative implications of severe monetary restraint for the ability of governments at all levels to finance their operations. A monetary policy sufficiently restrictive to cause recession or depression also causes tax revenues of state and local governments to fall and expenditures for welfare and related services to rise. In effect, the Federal Reserve authorities have a powerful voice in determining the quantity of school construction, the level of school operating budgets, the degree of financial support for public libraries and museums, the availability of recreational facilities for children in inner cities, the quantity of garbage and trash collection services.

At the federal government level, the impact of monetary policy on fiscal conditions and policy may be enormous. The great federal deficits of fiscal 1975 and 1976 and the resulting large rises in the national debt were the product of recession – in which the Federal Reserve authorities played a major role. Ensuing governmental actions to reduce various programs and services thus had their causes in good measure in the government's own stringent monetary policy.

Ironically, the financing of deficits was then made much more difficult for non-federal governments as a consequence of the high interest rates that are the earmark of monetary stringency. The higher interest charges also then affect refundings of maturing securities. To apply this analysis concretely, the problems of New York City were partly the result of Federal Reserve behavior.

Let us conclude this discussion of the logic of severe monetary restraint by noting briefly some of the longer-run implications of the foregoing. An unfortunate by-product of the off-again, on-again character of housing construction activity (caused mainly by monetary policy) has probably been a sharp braking of the ability of the housing industry to improve its efficiency.[47] Private business organizations – especially in a fragmented, small-scale industry such as residential construction – have sufficient risk and problems already to inhibit development of efficient producing units. To add the use of the industry as a sacrificial lamb of contra-cyclical policy is to present overwhelming odds. Over the longer run, the effect is to lower real income and to reduce society's welfare.

The contra-cyclical use of prolonged severe monetary restraint implies a 'stop-and-go' economy generally. This is a deterrent to the development and implementation of long-run investment plans in even large-scale, efficient organizations. Analogous to the case of the housing industry, other private business must consider government-created recession a further risk.[48]

The general inhibition to real investment may lead to retarding the growth of technology, and in turn the quality of investment. The production of capital goods presumably involves attempts to find new technological improvements to embody in those goods. Lethargy in demand for capital goods is likely to have a soporific effect on related innovational activity.[49] Moreover, there appears to be a cumulative process in kindling and maintaining innovational technological drive.

Under persistently tight money, new businesses may be particularly affected. Not only may they be unwilling or unable to pay the high price of credit, but the increased risk of their inability to pay those costs in an environment of restraint of business activity may lead lenders to favor more seasoned prospects. All of this obviously would tend to maintain the *status quo* among industrial and commercial enterprises, thus favoring older firms.

In some circumstances, there may be shifts from real investment to financial investment, both blue chip and speculative. At a 10 per cent yield on high-grade bonds, for example, many an industrial or commercial firm may find it sensible to limit feasible, socially desirable expansion and to put available funds into financial investment. At 10 per cent, too, there may be strong inducement for many to borrow, not for relatively routine purposes, but for highly leveraged, speculative operations in financial claims or existing real estate.

Where use of credit stays within the real sector, it may in part move from the industrial and commercial areas to highly leveraged investment in fields such as commercial real estate development.

4.4   International Consequences of Severe US Monetary Restraint

Let us call attention briefly to the international impacts of severe monetary restraint, focusing on the high, long-term interest rates that tend to persist as a result of repeated cyclical doses. Among the unhappier consequences of a prolonged period of very high interest rates in leading commercial societies is the fallout on other coun-

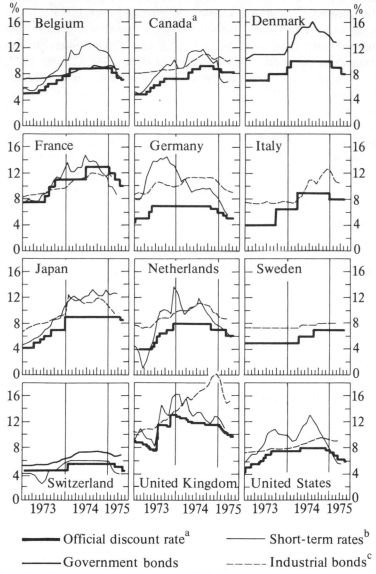

Figure 4.5   Short- and Long-Term Interest Rates

tries, especially poorer ones. The United States is in a particularly influential position with respect to world levels of interest rates and can export rising or falling rates. There are limits to this capacity, and in some circumstances, the power may be nominal. Germany, for example, with huge balance of payments surpluses year after year and itself a haven for speculative international balances, if it wished could have withstood fairly easily the tight money pressures emanating from the United States in 1966, 1968–70 and 1973–4. Switzerland has financial characteristics giving a large degree of freedom from US pressures. Nevertheless, as a general rule most advanced commercial countries with close links to the US economy cannot escape the influence of US interest rates, particularly on the high side (see Figure 4.5). Given the linkages between great commercial banks, the linkages between financial markets and the role of multinational corporations (including banks), high interest rates in the United States tend to spread as foreign creditors send funds here in search of them and US firms try to increase borrowing abroad at lower rates. Given the size and numbers of leading US corporate borrowers *vis-à-vis* the lending capacities of foreign private creditors, the impact of severe US monetary restraint on foreign interest rates tends to be strong. (This tends to be the case, moreover, even under floating exchange rate systems.)

Thus, the unhappy truth is that in the absence of special circumstances, or in the absence of some variant of foreign funds control, most other countries cannot maintain significantly lower interest rates in the face of persistent, high US interest rates. Foreigners must then share in the economic consequences of high domestic and foreign interest rates.[50] The degree to which individual countries are affected by the level of interest rates will, of course, vary in relation to differences in their structural and institutional characteristics. Presumably, the larger the size of the public sector, the smaller the degree of impact of high interest rates, since fiscal measures can supplement credit transactions; i.e. taxation can be used to provide capital funds. Since Western European countries generally have larger state sectors than the United States, it follows that the adverse consequences of a persistent high interest rate level are likely to be somewhat muted compared with the effects in the United States. Nevertheless, even public sectors may be affected unfavorably by high interest rates, not just in terms of cost of debt service, but also in terms of criteria for undertaking public projects, whose

Table 4.9 86 Developing Countries – External Public Debt Outstanding, by Region, 1967–73 ($ million)[a]

	Africa	East Asia[b]	Middle East[c]	South Asia	Southern Europe[d]	Western Hemisphere	Total
Total debt outstanding end of year							
1967	9,223.6	5,315.7	3,762.9	11,705.8	5,677.8	15,061.6	50,747.4
1968	10,154.0	6,361.6	4,587.3	13,070.3	6,269.5	16,782.6	57,225.4
1969	11,061.4	7,823.5	5,512.7	14,082.8	7,206.7	18,454.0	64,141.1
1970	12,905.0	9,254.3	7,474.1	15,416.6	7,832.3	20,856.2	73,738.6
1971	14,811.7	11,394.6	9,330.2	16,746.8	9,290.6	24,557.7	86,131.5
1972	16,660.3	13,985.4	11,243.9	18,260.5	10,311.4	29,532.5	99,993.9
1973	21,774.7	16,851.7	13,308.4	20,379.4	11,174.5	35,404.1	118,892.7
Debt outstanding by type of creditor							
31 December 1967							
Bilateral official	5,835.1	2,832.4	1,884.5	7,858.3	3,237.8	5,800.4	27,448.4
Multilateral	1,051.7	710.8	320.9	2,298.3	966.5	3,297.8	8,646.2
Private							
Suppliers	1,465.1	1,263.9	406.5	783.5	710.3	2,573.7	7,202.9
Banks	313.3	146.1	429.8	111.5	402.4	1,378.2	2,781.4
Other	558.4	362.4	721.1	654.2	360.8	2,011.5	4,668.4
Total	9,223.6	5,315.7	3,762.9	11,705.8	5,677.8	15,061.6	50,747.4
31 December 1968							
Bilateral official	6,312.6	3,455.5	2,346.8	9,499.2	3,341.8	6,284.8	31,240.9
Multilateral	1,233.0	825.6	344.6	2,485.2	1,097.3	3,849.6	9,835.2
Private							
Suppliers	1,628.2	1,602.6	594.8	930.9	736.8	2,928.9	8,422.2
Banks	419.4	137.9	482.6	139.0	670.5	1,617.1	3,466.6
Other	560.8	340.0	818.5	16.0	423.1	2,102.2	4,260.6
Total	10,154.0	6,361.6	4,587.3	13,070.3	6,269.5	16,782.6	57,225.4

31 December 1969							
Bilateral official	6,673.0	4,114.5	2,582.8	10,187.2	3,738.0	6,601.6	33,897.0
Multilateral	1,612.7	1,179.9	388.7	2,734.7	1,225.2	4,279.9	11,421.2
Private							
Suppliers	1,747.6	1,849.1	912.4	1,016.1	907.6	3,156.6	9,589.3
Banks	495.8	261.4	720.3	132.0	899.9	2,090.2	4,599.6
Other	532.3	418.6	908.6	12.8	436.0	2,325.8	4,634.1
Total	11,061.4	7,823.5	5,512.7	14,082.8	7,206.7	18,454.0	64,141.1
31 December 1970							
Bilateral official	7,435.3	4,969.6	3,635.9	11,361.9	3,997.7	6,737.4	38,137.8
Multilateral	1,968.5	1,653.8	636.6	3,027.7	1,438.7	5,027.5	13,752.9
Private							
Suppliers	2,138.6	1,709.2	1,241.0	868.4	882.6	3,938.1	10,778.0
Banks	513.3	481.6	863.1	146.6	1,087.3	2,460.1	5,552.0
Other	849.3	440.1	1,097.4	12.1	426.0	2,693.1	5,518.0
Total	12,905.0	9,254.3	7,474.1	15,416.6	7,832.3	20,856.2	73,738.6
31 December 1971							
Bilateral official	8,366.4	6,236.3	4,813.5	12,278.6	4,527.1	7,228.7	43,450.7
Multilateral	2,334.0	2,179.1	745.6	3,431.5	1,757.0	5,979.1	16,426.4
Private							
Suppliers	2,425.7	1,978.0	1,310.3	881.1	925.9	4,401.3	11,922.3
Banks	780.2	542.9	1,121.9	143.6	1,624.9	3,848.1	8,061.6
Other	905.3	458.3	1,338.8	11.9	455.7	3,100.5	6,270.5
Total	14,811.7	11,394.6	9,330.2	16,746.8	9,290.6	24,557.7	86,131.5
31 December 1972							
Bilateral official	9,024.8	7,776.8	6,299.3	13,153.5	4,852.9	8,357.0	49,464.2
Multilateral	2,968.5	2,724.6	840.5	3,999.2	1,967.4	7,227.7	19,727.8
Private							
Suppliers	2,554.4	1,925.7	1,341.5	979.6	977.8	4,542.6	12,321.6
Banks	1,227.5	927.2	1,235.6	118.1	2,015.4	5,963.7	11,487.4
Other	885.1	631.1	1,527.1	10.2	497.9	3,441.5	6,992.9
Total	16,660.3	13,985.4	11,243.9	18,260.5	10,311.4	29,532.5	99,993.9

Table 4.9 —cont.

	Africa	East Asia[b]	Middle East[c]	South Asia	Southern Europe[d]	Western Hemisphere	Total
31 December 1973							
Bilateral official	10,603.8	9,483.1	7,558.0	14,136.2	5,197.5	9,361.5	56,340.0
Multilateral	4,007.4	3,434.4	1,064.7	4,815.2	2,369.1	8,393.7	24,084.5
Private							
Suppliers	2,788.3	2,055.0	1,213.4	997.4	1,007.0	4,707.7	12,768.9
Banks	3,649.6	1,255.6	1,558.6	121.5	2,070.6	9,167.4	17,823.2
Other	725.6	623.5	1,913.7	309.1	530.4	3,773.9	7,876.1
Total	21,774.7	16,851.7	13,308.4	20,379.4	11,174.5	35,404.1	118,892.7

[a] Items may not add to totals due to rounding. *Includes the countries listed below*:
Africa – Algeria, Botswana, Burundi, Cameroon, Central African Republic, Chad, Congo (People's Republic of the), Dahomey, Egypt (Arab Republic of), Ethiopia, Gabon, Gambia (The), Ghana, Ivory Coast, Kenya, Lesotho, Liberia, Malagasy Republic, Malawi, Mali, Mauritania, Mauritius, Morocco, Niger, Nigeria, Rwanda, Senegal, Sierra Leone, Somalia, Sudan, Swaziland, Tanzania, Togo, Tunisia, Uganda, Upper Volta, Zaire, Zambia, plus East African Community.
East Asia – China (Republic of), Fiji, Indonesia, Korea (Republic of), Malaysia, Philippines, Singapore, Thailand, Vietnam.
Middle East – Iran, Iraq, Israel, Jordan, Syrian Arab Republic.
South Asia – Afghanistan, Bangladesh, Burma, India, Pakistan, Sri Lanka.
Southern Europe – Cyprus, Greece, Malta, Portugal, Spain, Turkey, Yugoslavia.
Western Hemisphere – Argentina, Bolivia, Brazil, Chile, Colombia, Costa Rica, Dominican Republic, Ecuador, El Salvador, Guatemala, Guyana, Honduras, Jamaica, Mexico, Nicaragua, Panama, Paraguay, Peru, Trinidad and Tobago, Uruguay, Venezuela.
[b] Does not include publicly guaranteed private debt of the Philippines estimated at $363.7 million as of the end of 1973.
[c] Does not include the undisbursed portion of the debt of Israel for the years 1967–70.
[d] Does not include the non-guaranteed debt of the 'social sector' of Yugoslavia contracted after 31 March 1966.

Source: World Bank, *Annual Report 1975*, p. 91.

desirability may be judged partly by relating implied rates of return to market interest rates.

Probably more important in terms of world welfare are the consequences of a sustained high level of interest rates in the United States and other advanced countries for the great masses of people living in less developed countries. In this case the basic problem is not in any important degree likely to be the consequences of high internal interest rates in less developed countries. Typically, such countries already live with high rates as an indigenous phenomenon applicable to indigenous firms of small to medium size.[51] To less developed countries the basic problem of high levels in advanced countries is thus likely to come from borrowing abroad. Massive infusions of foreign capital have reached the less developed countries since World War II and total external debt outstanding was vast in the 1970s (see Table 4.9). While much of the capital flow has represented outright grants and much has involved lending by international or governmental agencies on a subsidized basis, there are still large non-subsidized components, and even in subsidized lending by official agencies the net interest paid may be relatively large.

A key problem here is the vulnerability of poor countries to adverse blows because of the fragility of balance of payments positions. A fall in exports because of depressed conditions in industrialized countries can mean disaster. A sharp fall in export prices of a basic export commodity (or a sharp rise in prices of crucial imports) may have the same effect. Large external debts at high interest rates thus constitute a formula for serious difficulties. The degree of exposure for a large number of less developed countries is suggested in Table 4.10, relating debt service to export earnings.

Even if no threat arises from exports and imports, high levels of interest rates may have substantial impact on wellbeing in a poor country. Marginal increments of interest of a given sum in a poor country will use up a fraction of national output far greater than an identical sum in a rich country (of similar population). For example, when a small country has a *per capita* annual income of less than $100 per year,[52] an extra several million dollars of interest payable by the government on foreign debt may be oppressive. If external borrowing is done by the private sector, higher interest is presumably added to costs and passed on to customers. To the extent that the customers are domestic, there again is the squeezing of interest out of a very small national income. The upshot, other things being equal, is reduced ability to obtain foreign debt capital for developmental purposes.[53]

Table 4.10   Service Payments on External Public Debt as Percentage of Exports of Goods and Non-Factor Services,[a] 1967–73[b]

Country	1967	1968	1969	1970	1971	1972	1973
Africa							
Algeria	6.0	5.8	6.2	7.4	9.7	10.9	11.3
Botswana[c]	6.0	4.8	3.1	2.1	1.4	2.0	2.5
Burundi	2.6	3.2	3.3	1.9	2.2	7.0	3.0
Cameroon	2.3	3.0	3.4	4.6	4.9	7.7	5.4
Central African Republic	n.a.	2.2	4.1	3.2	2.1	1.5	4.0
Chad	4.4	4.7	5.4	3.2	8.1	1.7	n.a.
Congo, People's Republic of the	5.0	6.4	5.2	7.8	8.0	8.3	10.7
Dahomey	2.8	5.1	2.6	2.9	4.4	3.1	n.a.
Egypt, Arab Republic of	19.5	19.4	24.5	26.2	19.4	31.5	34.6
Ethiopia	9.7	9.4	11.0	11.6	10.6	8.7	6.4
Gabon	4.7	6.0	5.2	5.2	7.1	7.0	7.3
Gambia, The	d	d	d	d	d	d	d
Ghana	7.2	10.6	9.8	5.0	7.1	3.0	2.3
Ivory Coast	6.5	5.7	4.9	6.0	6.8	7.2	6.3
Kenya[c]	6.8	7.5	5.9	5.3	5.8	5.7	5.2
Lesotho[c]	5.8	3.4	4.4	8.5	7.1	5.1	3.2
Liberia[f]	5.9	6.3	7.4	8.0	7.1	6.7	6.3
Malagasy Republic	4.9	5.1	4.0	3.6	4.4	3.9	5.0
Malawi	6.9	7.6	6.4	8.7	8.8	8.9	9.0
Mali	10.9	8.9	8.6	1.8	0.7	1.2	1.6
Mauritania	1.3	1.3	2.2	3.1	3.0	5.5	2.1
Mauritius	3.6	6.8	3.2	3.7	5.1	2.1	1.7
Morocco	7.3	7.9	8.5	8.3	11.6	10.7	9.7
Niger	2.5	3.7	4.5	3.9	3.1	2.9	n.a.
Nigeria	5.0	6.0	5.6	4.0	2.8	2.4	2.1
Rwanda	6.3	2.6	3.4	1.2	1.8	2.4	1.3
Senegal	1.9	1.9	2.3	2.3	5.1	3.7	8.1
Sierra Leone	8.3	5.7	7.2	9.0	8.5	8.6	8.4
Somalia	2.1	1.9	1.5	2.1	2.5	3.0	3.6
Sudan	5.6	6.8	8.0	9.2	12.1	12.3	11.1
Swaziland[c]	n.a.	4.3	3.8	4.7	5.3	9.5[f]	10.5
Tanzania[c]	4.6	7.3	7.6	7.2	8.4	11.6	6.7
Togo	2.4	4.0	2.0	3.2	2.9	4.9	4.7
Tunisia	20.8	24.0	21.2	19.5	16.9	16.3	13.8
Uganda[c]	5.4	8.2	9.6	4.6	6.2	6.0	5.6
Upper Volta	1.8	4.5	5.1	5.9	5.9	5.1	8.3
Zaire	2.4	2.9	3.9	4.0	4.6	7.5	7.0
Zambia	2.4	2.7	1.9	5.1	10.0	10.7	28.0
East Asia							
China, Republic of	3.3	3.4	4.2	4.6	4.5	4.0	3.5
Fiji	0.7	0.6	0.7	0.9	0.7	0.9	0.8
Indonesia	5.3	5.6	5.7	6.6	7.6	6.7	7.1

Country	1967	1968	1969	1970	1971	1972	1973
Korea, Republic of	8.2	9.4	12.1	23.4	21.7	18.8	13.9
Malaysia	2.1	2.2	2.2	3.0	2.7	2.7	2.3
Philippines	7.2	5.3	4.6	7.5	7.0	9.9	6.3
Singapore	0.1	0.3	0.3	0.4	0.4	0.9	0.4
Thailand	3.6	3.8	3.8	3.6	3.4	2.9	2.6
Vietnam	1.9	2.1	0.9	0.8	0.9	2.2	2.7
Middle East							
Iran[g]	4.9	7.2	9.3	11.5	11.5	17.1	10.6
Iraq	0.9	1.4	2.2	2.1	1.9	2.7	3.0
Israel	15.7	16.9	17.2	18.6	13.4	17.7	20.8
Jordan	1.8	1.7	1.7	3.6	3.8	4.7	3.7
Syrian Arab Republic	11.6	6.9	7.7	9.2	8.9	8.1	7.3
South Asia[h]							
Afghanistan[g]	12.6	14.9	19.3	20.1	19.2	26.0	19.9[i]
Burma[g]	6.4	9.2	21.0	16.1	14.2	17.5	18.6
India[g]	24.9	25.1	26.5	28.0	25.9	24.5	20.1
Pakistan[i]	16.7	19.5	22.4	24.3	19.4	23.4	16.1
Sri Lanka	3.5	7.0	8.6	9.7	10.8	14.2	12.6
Southern Europe							
Cyprus	2.3	2.1	2.1	2.5	2.9	2.2	2.0
Greece	5.7	5.7	7.3	8.4	10.2	9.1	9.7
Malta	1.4	1.4	1.7	2.0	12.5[j]	0.7	0.6
Portugal	6.7	5.5	6.0	5.6	4.9	3.8	n.a.
Spain	1.8	2.4	3.1	4.0	5.2	3.5	3.6
Turkey	16.4	20.0	19.2	22.5	19.0	18.8	10.4
Yugoslavia[k]	12.7	13.9	10.0	9.6	6.5	6.4	6.9
Western Hemisphere							
Argentina	25.9	28.3	24.1	21.0	19.5	20.3	18.3
Bolivia	5.9	6.5	6.8	10.9	12.2	17.9	14.8
Brazil	16.0	15.6	16.6	15.3	15.8	14.3	13.9
Chile	12.6	19.8	15.9	18.3	21.0	11.6[i]	11.0[i]
Colombia	14.2	13.1	11.8	11.9	14.8	12.6	13.0
Costa Rica	12.0	11.9	10.5	9.7	10.1	10.0	10.2
Dominican Republic	7.3	7.7	8.6	5.1	6.7	4.1	4.5
Ecuador	6.7	8.8	10.0	9.1	12.2	10.6	7.5
El Salvador	2.6	2.6	2.8	3.7	5.8	3.1	5.3
Guatemala	7.4	7.8	8.0	7.7	8.2	10.6	3.8
Guyana	5.2	6.1	3.5	4.0	2.8	4.9	5.4
Honduras	2.1	1.7	2.3	2.8	3.2	3.4	3.9
Jamaica	2.2	3.2	3.0	3.2	3.9	5.2	5.0
Mexico	23.8	26.3	23.3	25.2	24.1	23.5	25.2
Nicaragua	6.4	7.6	10.0	10.6	13.4	10.3	17.8
Panama[c]	2.9	3.2	3.7	7.8	9.3	10.8	16.4
Paraguay	7.4	10.3	9.4	11.0	13.1	13.2	9.5
Peru	11.1	14.6	12.0	13.7	20.0	19.3	32.5[j]
Trinidad and Tobago	3.0	3.0	3.7	3.7	3.3	3.0	4.1
Uruguay	17.0	18.9	18.5	18.4	22.2	34.0	30.1
Venezuela	1.8	1.8	1.7	2.6	3.3	4.4	4.2

[a] Except where otherwise indicated, includes all goods and non-factor services. Data for some countries are partially estimated.

[b] Debt–service ratios are based on debt service actually paid as reported by the countries and not on contractual debt service due. If a country did not pay the entire debt service due during a year, this may be reflected in a lower debt–service ratio than would have been the case if contractual debt service had been used in computing the ratio. The debt–service ratio is, by itself, an inadequate and incomplete indicator of a country's debt situation. Many other factors must also be considered, such as the stability and diversification of the country's export structure, the prospects for future growth, the extent to which imports can be reduced without adversely affecting current production, the time profile of the country's debt outstanding, the size of foreign-exchange reserves and available compensatory financing facilities, and the debt–service record of the country. For these reasons, international comparisons of debt–service ratios have only limited meaning.

[c] Because of special monetary arrangements peculiar to countries such as this, the debt–service ratio must be regarded with more than usual caution in considering the country's external financial situation.

[d] The debt–service ratio is less than 0.1

[e] One-third of the service payments of the East Africa Community has been added to the service data of Kenya, Tanzania, and Uganda.

[f] Export data for exports of goods only.

[g] Data are for fiscal years.

[h] Excludes Bangladesh.

[i] Data are for Pakistan, which through 1971 included East Pakistan. The ratios for 1971, 1972 and 1973 reflect debt relief.

[j] Service payments for this year reflect prepayments. For Peru, the ratio without prepayments would be about 23 per cent.

[k] External public borrowing declined and was replaced by non-public borrowing beginning 1967.

[l] Service payments for this year declined due to debt reorganization.

Source: World Bank, *Annual Report 1975*, p. 94.

FOOTNOTES

1. Eventually the Federal Reserve Board placed reserve requirements against such issues.
2. See, e.g., *New York Times*, 26 July 1974, p. 47. See also Chapter 2 above.
3. See *New York Times*, 5 December 1971, Section 1, p. 49.
4. Dispute over the definition of money has existed for many years. R. S. Sayers noted 'the artificiality of any legal definition of money ... the fact that there is no hard and fast line between what is money and what is not money' (*Central Banking after Bagehot*, London, Oxford University Press, 1958, p. 5). Events of recent years have strengthened his position greatly. See also James Tobin, 'Commercial Banks As Creators of "Money",' in Deane Carson, *Banking and Monetary Studies*, Homewood, Illinois, Richard D. Irwin, 1963, pp. 408–19.
5. For a discussion of this and similar issues, see Tilford Gaines, 'Will the Real

Money Supply Please Stand Up,' in *Morgan Guaranty Survey*, April 1970.

6. The monetary authorities are clearly aware of this despite their policy statements and actions which indicate confidence in their data. One need only note their references to five possible money supply definitions, M-1 to M-5, for which data are published in the *Federal Reserve Bulletin*. Indeed, according to the *New York Times* (23 March 1975, Section 3, p. 2) eight definitions of money were referred to by the chairman of the Federal Reserve Board.

7. Cf. W. L. Silber, 'Towards a Theory of Financial Innovation,' in W. L. Silber (ed.), *Financial Innovation*, Lexington, Mass., D. C. Heath, 1975, pp. 53–85.

8. Cf. Joan Robinson, *The Rate of Interest and Other Essays*, London, Macmillan, 1954, pp. 5, 30. One is reminded here of the 'three gears' approach described in the *Radcliffe Report* (Committee on the Working of the Monetary System: *Report*, Cmnd 827, London, HMSO, 1959, pp. 153–4).

9. Classification schemes for inflation vary, depending in part on theoretical approaches. For a review of inflation theory, see A. J. Hagger, *The Theory of Inflation*, Melbourne, Melbourne University Press, 1964.

10. C. L. Schultze, *Recent Inflation in the United States*, US Congress, Joint Economic Committee, *Study of Employment, Growth, and Price Levels*, Study Paper No. 1, Washington, DC, 1959.

11. The term 'functional inflation' was suggested many years ago in a talk by E. L. Bernstein, Director of Research at the International Monetary Fund.

12. See, e.g. J. W. F. Rowe, *Markets and Men*, New York, Macmillan, 1936.

13. See, e.g. *Economic Report of the President*, February 1974, Washington, DC, 'Price Changes in 1973 – An Analysis,' *Monthly Labor Review*, February 1974, pp. 15–25; Bank for International Settlements, *Forty-Fourth Annual Report, 1973–74*, Ch. I; *IMF Survey*, 5 August 1974, pp. 241–7.

14. Board of Governors of the Federal Reserve System, *Fifty-Ninth Annual Report 1972*, Washington, DC, pp. 33–4.

15. *Economic Report of the President*, op. cit., p. 65.

16. *New York Times*, 6 January 1974, Section 3, pp. 49, 67, 71, 75.

17. Federal Reserve Bank of Kansas City, *Monthly Review*, January 1973, p. 6.

18. ibid., December 1973, p. 15.

19. *Monthly Labor Review*, February 1974, pp. 20, 22.

20. ibid., p. 24. The coincidences of 1972–3 extended even to economically insignificant areas with what amounts to irony. Thus, by the autumn 1973 planting season, US wholesale grass-seed prices had reportedly risen three to five times in the previous year, reflecting 'drought, foreign buying, environmental controls on production, and a switch by some farmers from grass-seed production to crops like wheat ...' (*New York Times*, 18 September 1973, p. 45).

There is irony, too, in the declining sheep population mentioned above. It has been attributed to declining wool prices associated with a strong shift of consumer demand to double-knit synthetic fabrics in the early 1970s. That shift was apparently short-lived, however, and return shifts of demand to wool found smaller flocks of sheep available to meet the demand.

21. R. G. Davis, 'Implementing Open Market Policy with Monetary Aggregate Objectives,' Federal Reserve Bank of New York, *Monthly Review*, July 1973, p. 175. (Results are taken by Davis from simulations by James Pierce and Thomas Thomson.)

22. ibid., p. 180.

23. ibid., p. 173.

24. ibid., pp. 176–80. See also 'Tracking Fed Policy,' in *Morgan Guaranty Survey*, September 1975, pp. 8–9.

25. D. M. Bechter, 'Money and Inflation,' Federal Reserve Bank of Kansas City, *Monthly Review*, July–August 1973, pp. 3–6.
26. ibid., p. 6.
27. ibid.
28. Cf. James Tobin, 'Monetary Policy in 1974 and Beyond,' *Brookings Papers on Economic Activity*, Vol. 1, 1974, p. 221.
29. Board of Governors of the Federal Reserve System, *Fifty-Third Annual Report 1966*, Washington, DC, p. 25. For details concerning interest rates, bank reserve positions, money supply, etc., see pp. 25–42.
30. Jean Crockett, Irwin Friend and Henry Shavell, 'The Impact of Monetary Stringency on Business Investment,' *Survey of Current Business*, August 1967, p. 25.
31. J. E. Petersen and P. F. McGouldrick, 'Monetary Restraint, Borrowing and Capital Spending by Small Local Governments and State Colleges in 1966,' *Federal Reserve Bulletin*, December 1968, p. 954.
32. Crockett, Friend and Shavell, op. cit., p. 26.
33. J. E. Petersen, 'Response of State and Local Governments to Varying Credit Conditions,' *Federal Reserve Bulletin*, March 1971, p. 210.
34. *Federal Reserve Bulletin*, March 1971, p. A71.1; December 1971, p. A72.
35. *Survey of Current Business*, July 1972, p. 16.
36. US Department of Commerce, *1971 Business Statistics*, Washington, DC, 1971, p. 52.
37. *Federal Reserve Bulletin*, March 1971, p. A71.1.
38. A further difficulty in assessing the impact of monetary policy is basic un-reliability of key data that are available. Flow-of-funds data, for example, are the source of Table 4.8 above, and lack stability over time, since revisions are made in them from time to time, presumably as additional details become available. These revisions are of sufficient magnitude at times to question earlier inferences one may have drawn. Compare, for example, the *Federal Reserve Bulletin*, April 1974, p. A62 with April 1973, p. A70 concerning 1968–1971 figures for total funds raised by all non-financial sectors, excluding US government. Such changes, of course, also have important implications for the reliability of econometric evidence.
39. Although existence of credit rationing beyond the world of housing credit has been challenged, accounts in the press and by participants in the credit markets support it strongly. This was true both in the 1969–70 and 1973–4 credit squeezes. For an examination of the argument, see B. M. Friedman, *Credit Rationing: A Review*, Washington, DC, Board of Governors of the Federal Reserve System (Staff Economic Studies), 1972 and OECD, *Monetary Policy in the United States*, Paris, OECD Publications, 1974, pp. 67, 76–7.
40. *Federal Reserve Bulletin*, July 1975, p. A11; June 1970, p. A15. See also Figures 4.1 and 4.2.
41. Cf. *Wall Street Journal*, 28 May 1974, pp. 1, 39.
42. *New York Times*, 30 June 1974, Section 3, p. 15.
43. Within the last 12 months the investor-owned electric utilities have seen profits dwindle because of rising costs.... The high cost of money ... added to ... other problems has caused these companies to postpone more than $2.5 billion in planned construction mostly for electric generating plants (*New York Times*, 28 August 1974, p. 37).
44. By early September 1974, evidence appeared of considerable agreement among economists on the dangers that severe restraint posed to supplies in at least some areas. See *New York Times*, 5 September 1974, pp. 1, 24. For an analysis stressing the need to avoid impeding supplies of goods and services when attack-

ing inflation, see Arthur Smithies, 'The Control of Inflation,' *Review of Economics and Statistics*, August 1957, pp. 272–83.
45. See 'Construction, Real Estate and Mortgage Markets,' *Federal Reserve Bulletin*, June 1974, pp. 410–11.
46. For some details, see ibid., pp. 408–09; *Economics Report of the President*, op. cit., p. 87; *Wall Street Journal*, 1 July 1974, p. 22 and 22 January 1974, p. 4.
47. Cf. *Financial Times* (London), 4 July 1974, p. 9.
48. Cf. W. A. Eltis, 'Investment, Technical Progress, and Economic Growth,' *Oxford Economic Papers*, March 1963, p. 48.
49. Cf. Jacob Schmookler, *Invention and Economic Growth*, Cambridge, Harvard University Press, 1966, Chs. VI, VII, pp. 204–09.
50. For accounts of efforts of France and the United Kingdom to achieve 'interest rate disarmament,' see *New York Times*, 14 September 1974, p. 35 and *Financial Times* (London), 31 July 1974, p. 12. In mid-1974 the United Kingdom sought to relax monetary conditions, but was caught in the tight money web of the rest of the world and so could not proceed to the extent desired. The Chancellor of the Exchequer commented, 'The running in most of the world's main financial centres is at present being made by the US' (ibid).
51. Low levels of interest rates in advanced commercial countries may be transmitted to the more commercialized sectors of less developed countries through branches of foreign banks or through pressures of money transfers from abroad by large local enterprises controlled locally or abroad. Those low levels are likely to be confined to a relatively narrow commercial sector, while elsewhere high rates remain normal.
52. This was estimated to be the case for 'probably close to 1,000 million people in the developing world' (*World Bank/IDA Annual Report 1973*, Washington, DC, 1973, p. 7).
53. Big debts at high interest rates in poor countries, especially in Latin America, led to disaster after 1929. Although the institutional circumstances were considerably different in the late 1960s and 1970s, many of the dangers, risks and pressures of 1929 were present.

5 Alternatives to Severe General Monetary Restraint

A handicap in dealing with difficult economic problems is the wide-spread belief that solid and reasonably quick-acting solutions exist within the existing economic framework and that the task of investigators is to search until they find them. Different investigators do search, and they usually make claims on behalf of a particular wonder drug. Unfortunately, in the economic world, where ills may be set in motion not just by economic forces but by domestic and international political forces, by natural environmental forces and by the expectations, fears, desires, attitudes, actions and reactions of human beings and the collective groups through which they function in important areas, the dynamics involved may prevent achievement of full cures. This appears to be the case with the inflation–unemployment illness. Given the existing economic framework, it should perhaps be looked upon as a disease comparable to diabetes, with no known cure, but with remedies available to hold its impact within reasonable bounds. Our inability to control inflation with any certainty of solid success, except at prohibitive costs, indicates that a rigid anti-inflation goal should give precedence to full employment, achievement of which is attainable.[1] Other objectives of economic policy should be coordinated with these, e.g. economic growth and achieving a more equitable distribution of income, both for their own virtues and because in some instances they may aid in fighting inflation and unemployment. In the pages that follow, an attempt is made to find a solution to the inflation–unemployment dilemma that is consistent both with the realization that perfection is impossible and with the complexity of forces giving rise to the inflation generated beginning in the mid-1960s. At the same time consistency with achieving other pressing goals is sought.

5.1   Institutional Reforms

Before proceeding to proposals aimed solely at our problem, let us briefly refer to certain institutional arrangements which act as constraints in dealing with inflation and whose reform would give minor instant help. These institutional constraints include a multiplicity of governmental and private anti-competitive devices protecting (not always successfully) specific private economic interests. They range from government quotas on the imports of goods and restrictions on purchases of foreign-owned services (e.g. shipping) to private restrictions on supply and private floors on prices of domestically produced and imported goods and services. Governmental instances in the United States include import quotas (formal or informal) on sugar, meat, steel and textiles; freight rate fixing; state fixing of milk prices; federal protection of monopolistic practices via regulatory commissions (the Interstate Commerce Commission and the Civil Aeronautics Board, among many others).[2] From the standpoint of fighting inflation, as well as in terms of meeting other generally accepted criteria of economic performance, many such governmental restraints should be removed or revamped. Likewise, more vigorous enforcement of anti-trust laws is desirable to deal with anti-competitive institutional arrangements in the private sector.

Institutional reform of a variety of private and public practices that restrain competition, however, is in a sense a one-shot affair with respect to the control of inflation. If it were accomplished to a desirable extent, the problem of inflation would still be with us if all other factors facing the US economy remained unchanged.

Moreover, no matter how vigorous anti-trust enforcement might be, monopolistic elements would necessarily still be significant in the United States and other modern, industrial economies: the requirements of large-scale, efficient production alone would cause this in important sectors of the economy. In Galbraithian terms, destruction of large-scale business units would eliminate a sector where much planning efficiency exists. Nor can one see, for example, either likelihood of, or net gain from, the ending of labor unions. Nevertheless, regardless of one's basic approach to dealing with the inflation–unemployment problem, certain institutional restrictive practices – public and private – are impediments to the general welfare and should be removed or revamped.

5.2   The Choices

One obvious choice is 'more of the same,' that is, demand management mainly in terms of monetary policy with the dials set for substantial unemployment in order to contain inflation (along with institutional reform). The uncompromising judgement in previous chapters was that society cannot afford this solution, that it represents bad economics and bad social policy, and ultimately is immoral.

A second solution was both implicit and partly explicit in earlier chapters. It is a demand management policy too, but with the dials set for full employment (and again includes institutional reform). This is treated in the next section as a phase of planning, and so we touch on it only briefly here. It is a route involving much easier monetary policy coordinated with fiscal policy. It would involve fiscal reform to coordinate actions of federal, state and local levels of government so that federal fiscal policy would not be neutralized by offsetting policies at state and local levels. This could be done by such devices as liberalized, anti-cyclical revenue-sharing, guarantees of federal grants to lower levels of government to offset declines in revenues resulting from unfavorable economic conditions, and federal grants to lower levels of government to expand expenditures when unemployment is excessive. (Needless to say, should excess demand be the problem, comparable coordination of governmental fiscal policies would be required.)

Other possibilities should be considered in connection with this second solution. For example, the view here is that it would be important to strip the Federal Reserve authorities of their independence so that they could no longer veto solutions opted for by the elected branches of government. In addition, the federal government should have the stand-by role of employer of last resort for use in cases where general fiscal and monetary policies fail to solve the unemployment problem satisfactorily. It would also be very desirable to add an incomes policy and initiate vigorous stockpiling programs.

Great as is the superiority of the second solution to that of 'more of the same,' the fact is that we can still do much better in terms of the inflation–unemployment problem and in terms of other essential economic goals; in other words, the second solution still has important deficiencies. To rely on demand management and ignore supply (other than institutional reform) is dangerous. An economy could fail to reach full employment because of an inadequate infrastructure, a lack of reliable supplies of natural raw materials or other basic items. Key materials might be subject to random shocks emanating from the weather or other phenomena. At the same time supplies of basic materials as well as the infrastructure, to some extent, would be subject to the planning of great domestic private enterprises and the private planning of great multinational firms whose goals and time horizons might be quite different from those that would appear in the best interests of society. Likewise, basic materials might be subject to the planning of state enterprises in socialized and other economies elsewhere, again with possibly adverse implications unless elementary planning exists.

Not only does leaving basic supply planning to the private sector have deficiencies of the types just suggested, but it lacks coordination with the means of paying for the supplies when foreign sources are involved. If, for example, a large volume of raw materials must be developed abroad, a private enterprise cannot be expected to plan in terms of developing the foreign exchange necessary to pay for them over the years to come. Yet, such supply planning should be linked to balance of payments planning. Moreover, foreign supply planning often involves what is really foreign policy, with strong political overtones. The dangers of delegating this to private business firms have been criticized for generations, even as great enterprises have been given virtual licenses to conduct foreign policy.

Enough has been said above to suggest that supply-oriented inflationary forces of key types described in Chapter 4 could still run amuck in a demand-management–institutional-reform approach to the inflation–unemployment problem. It must be admitted, too, that demand-pull inflation would remain a risk, both in terms of domestic and foreign forces. We conclude that a broader approach is necessary, one that embraces management of both demand and supply in coordinated fashion. It is a form of elementary economic planning and guidance, and to this we turn next.

5.3 Planning as the Key

Given the maintenance of a basically private enterprise system with a large measure of free market activity, the most promising key to the dilemma of maintaining full employment while keeping inflation within reasonable bounds is elementary economic planning or what is popularly referred to as indicative planning. This is not complete mandatory planning, as in a fully socialized country, or planning as comprehensive as that in World War II in private, market-oriented economies.

In a strict sense, indicative planning implies that the planners draw up a comprehensive package of desired, mutually consistent and reasonably attainable goals or targets. These are, in effect, forecasts of what may be reasonably expected of an economy as a whole and by sector over short periods and in the longer run. The private sector, it is then hoped, will have a good view of what markets should look like over the specified periods of time and, given government commitments to carry out its share of the plan, will act in harmony with the forecast. If the private sector by and large does this, and if the forecasts prove to be basically correct, the plans ought to have a substantially self-fulfilling character.

In France, where such planning has been practiced most extensively, broad governmental use of inducements and intervention in economic processes has been part of the package and the process as a whole has been referred to as indicative planning. We proceed similarly here.

Indicative planning is thus a 'half-way house' in which the government begins by determining desirable overall goals (employment, prices, consumption, housing construction, investment in key plant and equipment, balance of payments, etc.). In turn, it analyzes the supply requirements of its goals and then brings into play the tools of fiscal policy (including selective taxes, loans and subsidies), monetary policy (including selective credit aspects), foreign trade policy, exchange rate policy, wage–price policy and, in certain key supply situations, direct intervention in market processes to achieve the desired outcomes and prevent failure of the plan.

Macro-fiscal policy would be assigned the task of regulating aggregate demand to keep it within range of full-employment requirements. Selective taxes and changes therein would be used to influence sectoral demand and resource use; selective credit controls would be used similarly. General monetary control would be used somewhat passively, normally to provide sufficient money (however defined) to accommodate the rest of the plan, including the levels of interest rates.

Direct government intervention would be called for in certain marketing and pricing situations where now private profit-making organizations possessed of enormous concentrated powers (even quasi-governmental) make decisions affecting national or international wellbeing purely in terms of profit potentials. In such situations the private organizations concerned must be treated as quasi-public utilities in which responsibility for major decisions is shared with government.

Direct government intervention in market processes is required to cope also with production goals. This is important in several respects, to assure that supplies of key facilities and commodities are sufficient to support full employment, to restrain inflationary pressures, and to insure meeting basic or important needs of society. Such government intervention may be required even in relatively competitive sectors of the market if market mechanisms do not assure meeting production goals deemed essential for the wellbeing of the community.

The suggested approach here would resemble French indicative planning.[3] It would have much less resemblance to economic management in Japan, which has been referred to as indicative planning, but which has been regarded by most observers as too informal to fit such a classification. It would have facets, however, resembling that aspect of Japanese economic management that has been described as 'supply management.'[4] The elements in such economic guidance may be examined under five categories: (1) goals, (2) aggregate supply, (3) aggregate demand, (4) pricing and (5) organization.

5.3.1   Goals

For the United States and other modern industrial economies the view here is that first priority must be accorded to meaningful full employment. This includes an unemployment rate of 2 to 3 per cent, that is, useful full-time and part-time jobs for essentially all who seek them. Second is containment of inflation to manageable proportions or, if possible, attainment of price stability. Third is improvement in the allocation of resources over that now prevailing, which is subject to a combination of market forces (competitive and monopolistic) and government forces, with the latter uncoordinated with respect to their parts in terms of predetermined goals and in some respects the products of bureaucracies behaving much like private organizations. Fourth, and very helpful and probably necessary to achieving goal (2) is an improvement in distributional equity. (Criteria of distributional equity and methods of achieving it, however, are beyond the scope of this study and will not be pursued.)

5.3.2   Aggregate Supply

Probably the most important role of government in aggregate supply is to assure an adequacy of basic raw materials and an adequate infrastructure to support full-employment levels of production and distribution. Full-employment supply capabilities may be obtained through (1) wholly private action, (2) private action aided or induced by government action such as tax favors, loans and purchasing behavior, or (3) government acquiring and owning factors of production in whole or part. The government should also take measures to stimulate and possibly assure the existence of *efficient* productive capacity in key industries and not merely quantitative potential.

To illustrate, if there is insufficient capacity to meet full-employment needs in steel, aluminum, natural gas, oil refining or electrical capacity, the government should investigate to determine the cause. If there is a real difficulty inhibiting unaided private expansion, the government should step in. If the difficulty is inability to raise capital on feasible terms, the government can use allocational (selective) means to favor the industry concerned. It can also use loan guarantees and direct credits. Tax benefits, too, are obviously available, as are government contracts to purchase output. If all else fails, the government can build the capacity itself, as it did on an enormous scale in World War II. The government-owned facilities may then be put into use in various ways, perhaps most acceptably politically by leasing it to private enterprise, or, if not needed initially, kept in government hands as stand-by capacity.

Avenues such as these are pursued by the French, although in some cases a transplant of the specific French techniques to the United States may be unrealistic. Especially noteworthy, but probably least acceptable politically in the United States, the government is a big entrepreneur, with ownership or shares in numerous industries, including coal, oil, gas, electricity, railroads, shipping, chemicals, fertilizers, automobiles, trucks, aircraft, airlines, banking and insurance. It controls much of the available credit and directly supplies most of the investment funds of the country, including those available to lower levels of government. As a result of all this, the French government has powerful levers to persuade private firms to conform generally to government plans.[5]

In the case of Japan, supply management is very important, with preferred credit facilities, tax favors and import protection made available to industrial sectors being pushed by the government.[6]

There would appear to be no reasonable excuse for certain US supply failures of the early 1970s had government engaged in the activities suggested. For example, freight car shortages were reported to be an obstacle to shipments of grain – and obviously could have been avoided. Electrical capacity was clearly under strain for several years and, despite the difficulties stemming from environmental considerations, could have been dealt with decisively through one or more of the avenues suggested. The shortages of natural gas could also have been avoided or offset had the government engaged in appropriate planning and followed through with effective action. It should be noted, moreover, that appropriate, far-sighted planning, followed by appropriate implementation, would have contributed to coping with unemployment, welfare and inflation simultaneously. For example, according to press reports, natural gas shortages contributed to severe shortages of fertilizer in 1974, with presumably adverse consequences in terms of nutrition, inflation and unemployment.

In the case of items subject to vagaries of the weather and those requiring importation, old principles suggested in the past and partially implemented from time to time (even if accidentally) point to obvious solutions. An ever-normal granary plan in the 1930s called for well-designed stockpiling programs for food. Beginning in the 1930s and continuing for many years, large-scale *ad hoc* stockpiling of basic agricultural items occurred as a by-product of price-support programs. In a planning context, the United States (and other countries) should stockpile sufficient basic foods and raw materials to insure for a reasonable, extended period against a reduction or cut-off of supplies, whatever the reasons. Included should be such items as wheat, corn, rice, soybeans, cotton, wool and rubber. Non-agricultural raw materials should be treated similarly, e.g. oil, tin, copper, bauxite. Indeed, given the capacity of the food-processing industry to freeze and can perishable food products, a case can be made for stockpiling meats, fish, fruits and vegetables to soften the blows of weather vagaries.

The concept of deliberate stockpiling is not new. The United States has practised it for a long time with respect to defense needs.[7] At the non-governmental level it goes on continuously, presumably as part of 'strategic' planning. Oil companies, for example, in effect stockpile gasoline station locations. Reportedly, this type of stockpiling may involve sites to be utilized perhaps ten years in the future. Oil companies, steel companies, non-ferrous metal companies, giant agricultural firms and others engage in continuous exploration as part of their production planning for the distant future. Research at private corporations is analogous to the foregoing items in the sense of stockpiling technology and new and revised products for future use. At the national level, where governments take responsibility for levels of economic activity, for defense against inflation (and deflation) and for overall welfare, it seems almost superfluous to have to argue that governments must take an active, critical role in ensuring the continuing availability of the supplies essential to a nation's wellbeing.

5.3.3   Aggregate Demand

Full-employment demand is consistent with a variety of spending–saving frameworks, from very high consumption of frivolous and luxury items and items requiring heavy use of foreign exchange, along with neglect of important, real social needs and virtually no saving, to very high levels of saving and investment with consumption restrained to an austerity level focused on basic needs. Ideally, demand should be managed with an eye to public needs, national resources, government needs, as well as public desires. The planning body should draw up a general 'bill of particulars' showing a forecast of private demand by major categories, government demand, both federal and non-federal, and foreign demand. The government sector requires particular attention and should involve a detailed breakdown of society's needs, including educational, recreational, cultural, health and others. To repeat a point made at the outset of this study, it is in the area of civilized public services that the United States has been most deficient. The federal budget should be drawn to meet these needs in coordination with state and local governmental units.

In terms of macro-fiscal considerations, it is vital in aggregate demand planning that close attention be paid to the role of governments below the national level. In the United States national income and product accounts, total purchases of goods and services by state and local governments far exceed those by the federal government, although the opposite relationship exists for total expenditures inclusive of transfer payments.[8] Thus, non-federal spending must be dovetailed with federal spending, both to prevent overspending relative to capacity and to prevent underspending. As noted earlier, for example, it is sheer folly to have the federal government embark on a program of fiscal stimulus in heavy unemployment while state and local units raise taxes and lower expenditures on goods and services to cope with fiscal difficulties created by unemployment (i.e. falling tax receipts and rising relief loads). Needed is an overhaul of the financing mechanisms for state and local governments, perhaps partly along the lines pursued in Australia. There the major share of all taxes is collected at the federal level with allocations by formula to lower governmental units. In essence, this is full-scale revenue-sharing. Using existing machinery, the United States could easily move in a similar direction, expanding greatly the present sharply limited revenue-sharing scheme. Another approach is that of Canada, in which provincial governments are guaranteed 100 per cent of previous years' revenue by the federal government.[9]

Effective planning, however, goes beyond simple revenue-sharing or revenue guarantees: it must involve the fixing of approximate total spending quantities by the entire public sector and provision of funds for this purpose. Only a national government with dominant taxing power and the power to create money can accomplish this.

The federal government, using whatever state and local arrangements are most suitable, must be the employer of last resort. There are enough serious needs in society to be met so that this is feasible. All those willing and able to work should be guaranteed jobs, not relief.[10] It should be emphasized that with appropriate fiscal and monetary policies, and with the government's role in acquiring and financing basic supply requirements, both short- and long-term, the employer-of-last-resort role should not be one of vast proportions. The scale of that role should be limited, too, by psychological factors; the fact that government is committed to a firm jobs-for-all policy should limit declines in spending at all levels (consumption and investment) that might otherwise develop because of fears of substantial unemployment. This is akin to the role of deposit insurance in minimizing runs on banks by minimizing fears of bank failures.

Another aspect of government planning for demand stems from government intervention in supply. Government stockpiling of critical materials and building of stand-by or immediately operational capacity not only assures supplies of goods and/or services in the future, but creates current demand for goods and services.

Let us turn now to the private sector. Government influence over the bulk of private spending would not differ a great deal under indicative planning from what it is now, but the exceptions would be important. General fiscal policies would relate to apparent relationships between planned saving and investment in the non-federal sector of the economy. Interest rate and money supply levels would be set to accommodate desired, anticipated levels of private spending and planned levels of public spending. Within such a framework the public would have generally broad freedom of choice in its spending and saving decisions, although selective tax and credit mechanisms would tend to push some choices away from those adversely affecting society.

One may think of government influence on the composition of private demand as operating at two levels, consumer demand and business demand. Preparation of the overall plan would lead to the determination of certain areas where consumer demand is to be stimulated or, oppositely, restrained in order to deal with national goals. For example, to deal with demand aspects of a national energy policy, one might assemble a variety of fairly obvious fiscal and credit tools. Automobile purchases could be subjected to taxes graduated by weight and horsepower. Credit terms on automobiles could be regulated with variation in severity determined by similar criteria. Use of mass transportation could be stimulated through subsidies. (Action with respect to consumer demand could be complemented by direct action on the supply side, e.g. low-interest loans and tax credits to automobile manufacturers to expand their capacity for making cars with low fuel consumption.) The tax mechanism might be used to discourage purchase of relatively frivolous – or at least less essential – oil-consuming vehicles such as snowmobiles, motorboats, yachts and private airplanes. It could be used to discourage inefficient fuel-using devices, e.g. low-efficiency air-conditioning units.

Indicative national planning would logically incorporate goals for housing consistent with other national goals and use selective fiscal and credit devices for this purpose. For example, to conserve energy there might be excise taxes geared to the size of new houses constructed or tax credits related to construction characteristics that conserve fuel. Selective credit regulation could be used similarly. To achieve national goals in units of housing constructed, the existing financial machinery of the government could be used. Obviously any other areas of the economy requiring special attention could be treated similarly, e.g. manpower training and education.

Turning to government influence on the composition of business demand, we find a situation where the supply aspect is significant, with demand partly a reflection of supply activity. The fairly pure demand element is evident mainly at a macro-level where the government employs credit and fiscal devices or direct loans and subsidies to stimulate – or vice versa – *general* business investment in plant and equipment. The supply element is dominant when government uses selective incentive devices to influence capital spending in specific sectors. The supply element would similarly be dominant if the government selectively used incentive credit or fiscal measures to bring about private stockpiling of critical inventories.

Government influence and intervention with respect to the directions of demand and supply exist now on a vast scale. For example, there are subsidies to shipping, tax credits for general capital expenditures, accelerated depreciation, tax shelters in real estate, tax shelters for domestic oil production (very large until recently), tax benefits on home ownership, a myriad of other government devices to stimulate home ownership, and government loans and guaranteed credits in the export sphere. These subsidies (direct and indirect) and loans of federal government agencies are a major force in the US economy.[11] The point is that we already have on hand – and use – machinery to influence the character of private demand and private supply, and thus the allocation of resources. The difference under indicative planning would be that these and other planning devices would be used to promote achievement of coordinated, publicly planned goals, rather than used piecemeal, often simply in response to lobbying pressures.

5.3.4   Pricing

Government intervention in the pricing process in the United States has occurred in a number of forms throughout the mid-twentieth century. Aside from wartime wage–price controls and 'emergency' price controls, the intervention has been in two principal forms: first, public utility-type controls over essential services delivered (in theory) by monopolistic or semi-monopolistic units; and second, agriculture price supports, which involved government stockpiling as a by-product.

Economic planning logically requires intervention in pricing to a wider extent than has been the case in ordinary peacetime. Public utility-type controls would clearly continue, perhaps with a somewhat wider frame of reference. Since these are so widely used and accepted, no further discussion of them follows.

With stockpiling activities extending to all important basic raw materials and commodities whose supply is subject to the vagaries of weather or the possibility of interruption from abroad, government logically would use the price mechanism to influence their production and would also normally perform a price-stabilizing function in its buying and selling activities. Government intervention in pricing would also reach out to cases where, on a large-scale, essential commodities are sold to, or bought from, countries which engage in state trading or quasi-state trading. Finally, government intervention via incomes policies, which is on an intervention level higher than any of the preceding, should logically be part of indicative economic planning.

Let us illustrate some of the above situations of direct governmental intervention in markets and prices other than incomes policies. (All, it should be emphasized, would be logical even in a 'no-planning' situation). We do so in terms of recent case histories. Grain exporting is an example of a prime candidate for such treatment since it is an activity in which five great dealers were reported to control about 90 per cent of the trade.[12] In an earlier chapter, our analysis of the 1973–4 inflationary surge laid much emphasis on the grain situation in 1972 as an initiating factor in the accelerating inflation of 1973. It was totally devoid of economic logic for dwindling reserves of basic grains to be sold to a foreign government by several private US dealers at prices and in quantities basically determined by those private firms and the foreign government. This represented a non-competitive situation in which one monopsonistic buyer negotiated with several oligopolistic sellers for one-quarter of the US wheat crop and other grains. Even in an overall 'no-planning' situation, this should have been handled by intergovernmental negotiation concerning prices, quantities and delivery schedules, all considered in relation to US and world economic conditions. Far preferable, however, would have been a US economic plan in which exports and imports of basic commodities crucial to world health and world price structures and subject to quasi-monopolistic conditions of purchase and/or sale would have been negotiated at the governmental level in terms of short- and longer-run considerations. (Here, too, is the obvious case where it would have been desirable to have had a governmental stockpiling program to even out conditions of supply in commodities subject to the vagaries of weather.)

Among those strongly wedded to free market principles, some would doubtless be concerned that governmental intervention in price setting would lead to distortions in the allocation of resources. In fact, the case may be turned around. One should be more concerned with the distortions in the allocation of resources, let alone the inflationary effects caused by the gyrations in grain prices which took place in the absence of US government intervention. For example, after wheat rose from $1.66 per bushel in mid-1972 (weighted average, all grades) to a peak of $6.27 per bushel in February 1974, it moved downward to $4.59 in May 1974, then resumed rising.[13] Meanwhile, soaring grain prices led almost simultaneously to soaring prices for meat and fish. The initial burst of rising beef prices gave large windfall profits to cattle ranchers (amidst much protest by consumers and replies of 'long overdue justice' by ranchers). By late 1974, however, anguished cries of distress were emanating from the ranchers, caught between falling cattle prices, grain prices falling far less, and continuing high retail beef prices along with mounting inventories in the beef processing industry. Reports of rancher failures grew in numbers, with dire predictions concerning the economic fate of many.

It is difficult to see how direct government intervention in the pricing and marketing of grains in the period 1972–4 would not have improved the allocation of resources in agriculture (including livestock production), restrained the explosive spread of inflation, and acted as a general stabilizer of prices, production and distribution in an area vital to world health and welfare. As part of the process, if need be, the government could have subsidized grain prices, rather than allow violent rises to penetrate the entire price structure, leading in turn to accelerated demands for wage increases to offset the rapidly rising cost of living, all in an environment of speculative reactions of an inadequately informed network of participants in the futures markets.

A somewhat similar argument can be made in the case of the behavior of the sugar markets in 1974. Again there is a picture of control of marketing by a handful of great, oligopolistic firms, the sugar refiners. Again there was a price explosion which penetrated into all the food products using sugar. Refined sugar prices at wholesale, for example, rose from \$0.122 per pound in January 1973 to \$0.592 per pound in December 1974, then began falling, reaching \$0.194 per pound in December 1975.[14] The consequences of this price behavior were both inflationary and inimical to any sound planning of resource allocation. The private control of sugar prices caused needless distortions in the uses of sugar and stimulated a probably wasteful search for substitutes. Much or all of this could presumably have been prevented by government intervention in the sugar markets, with the most effective solution including stockpiling.

The foregoing can be applied to the oil situation beginning in late 1973. Supplying oil to most of the great consuming areas of the world was in the hands of a small number of giant international companies, and, again in a total departure from economic logic, those few companies were left to bargain with sovereign governments of the producing nations, while governments of the chief consuming countries, in effect, stood by seemingly helpless. Oil, it should be remembered, is as basic to world welfare as steel and probably more important to price levels. It involves, in a sense, the reverse of the Midas effect (which turned all that Midas touched into gold): now almost all one touches uses oil, either as a raw material or in the production process – food, clothing, tires, consumer appliances, furniture, dishes, construction and so on almost *ad infinitum*. Again, the case for government intervention in pricing and supply was over-whelming.

Let us now move on to the more complex level of government intervention in pricing. Given the adoption of indicative planning, direct influence on key components of the general price structure becomes an ingredient for success in meeting objectives of plans, including dealing with inflation. Although in recent years such action has been commonly referred to as incomes policies, the latter is a somewhat inadequate expression. Perhaps more adequate would be incomes and prices policies. Though these have received much publicity in the press in recent years, with consequent widespread familiarity with their characteristics, let us take a moment to indicate their scope. At one extreme are the severe US World War II-type controls in which virtually all prices are controlled by law even with use of subsidies if necessary. Wages, too, are controlled, and profits are handled by an excess profits tax. At the other extreme would be the use of persuasion to attempt to obtain voluntary restraint, as in the United States in the 1960s, also as in Austria in the 1960s and 1970s, and in the United Kingdom in the mid-1970s – the last two in terms of a 'social contract' approach. The essence of an incomes policy, then, is the attempt to direct or influence the decision-making process with respect to incomes and prices. The process may range from total voluntarism to rigid control, from nearly complete coverage of the economy to coverage of one or a few key sectors.

An incomes policy may be used in inflations of all types, any of which may occur despite the use of indicative planning. In theory, however, an incomes policy should be unnecessary and undesirable in moderate, peacetime, excess-demand inflation, since it would lead to 'suppressed' inflation with all its attendant woes; general monetary and fiscal policies should be sufficient. In principle, incomes policies are thus most compatible with cost-push and other supply-oriented situations which appear to be dominant under contemporary conditions. In practice, an incomes policy is best used not only where supply restriction is dominant, but in a rising or high-employment situation, for it is difficult to ask labor to restrain demands for hourly pay when hours may be cut or layoffs are likely because of deficiency of demand.

Let us consider then the impacts of an incomes policy adopted when employment is expanding or high in the face of inflationary pressures of cost-push or kinds other than excess demand. Assume first a program that is mandatory in character and comprehensive in application, covering wages, prices, rents and (via excess profits taxes) total profits.

Under the circumstances assumed, perhaps the most important effect, as is well known, arises from braking the extent of inflationary expectations. At the core of the inflation is a dynamic process, typically initiated by an economic shock and propagated through cost–price linkages, with amplifying power supplied by expectations concerning prices and a struggle for income shares. The cure consists, ordinarily, not in reversing the direction of price movements, but in reducing and then halting their upward movement. With assurance that the rise in costs will decelerate, 'price-makers' (viewing wages, rents and other costs as prices) can allow for less inflation in their asking prices. For example, given a high rate of inflation (say 10 per cent), with the assurance that a substantially lower ceiling will be placed on the allowable rate of future inflation (say 5 per cent), 'price-makers' can reduce by one-half the inflation allowance in their demands. Such success as the limited US experiment in price controls had from August 1971 to the end of 1972 surely was largely owing to the psychological 'shock' effect of the introduction of controls. Beyond the external developments of late 1972 which were the initiating force, the resumption of accelerating US inflation in early 1973 was additionally a product of renewed and growing inflationary expectations related mainly to those same external developments.

Mandatory price–wage–profit controls restrain the velocity of money by causing less of existing cash balances to be paid out for ordinary purchases and for accelerated purchases against anticipated inflation. As part of the same process they restrain the demands for credit in the banking system. In turn, pressure on interest rates is reduced, which leads to a host of favorable consequences. Far less pressure is placed on the central bank. Disturbances to the money and capital markets with adverse consequences for financial institutions and the general public, discussed at length earlier in this study, are reduced. The unfortunate selectivity of severe general monetary restraint can be minimized. Restraint of interest rates means smaller interest components in prices, especially significant in capital-intensive industries. Forces that may lead to increased unemployment as a result of given or accelerating rates of inflation are reduced. Increasing aggregate demand can lead to rising output (itself anti-inflationary) and is not 'wasted' on needless rises in prices. Rising output means rising real income and rising real savings. At the same time other potential savings can become realized savings (facilitating growth) rather than vanish via rising prices for all forms of goods and services. The favorable interest rate effect also facilitates growth. Additionally, the time dimension in investment decisions becomes a smaller threat because of reduced possibilities of escalating costs during construction periods.

Of course, comprehensive mandatory controls bear important disabilities. These have been and are recited regularly by opponents of controls. They include production disincentives from freezing of prices at unprofitably low levels for some firms, inducements to increase profit margins by lowering quality, shifts of productive capacity to the most profitable lines, deterrents to plant expansion when price controls inhibit profits, misinvestment caused by distortions associated with frozen prices, and slowness of administrative responses to requests for permission to raise prices. Serious disabilities in a comprehensive, mandatory incomes policy include also large administrative costs and difficulties involved in enforcement. These are real and must not be underestimated. Not only must a body of administrators be established, but additional burdens are placed on existing public agencies such as the courts and other law enforcement bodies, as well as on those being regulated. This is, in an important sense, a diversion of resources which would otherwise be available in generally productive pursuits.

The positive arguments above rest largely on the assumption that a comprehensive, mandatory incomes policy will be effective. This, of course, cannot be taken for granted, and its possible ineffectiveness is elevated into a likelihood by most opponents and constitutes one of their basic arguments against it. To be effective there are always prerequisites to be met. First there must be strong public support for such a policy – strong enough to neutralize possible opposition from the participants. Wartime offers the best conditions from this point of view, and some of the ardor of a war period is needed in a peacetime setting – not an easily met requirement. Other prerequisites have been referred to above, that excess-demand conditions should preferably be absent to deter black markets and prevent intolerable strains on the system, and that a high-employment policy should prevail. As noted earlier, if an unemployment threat is added to an inflation threat, there is little hope of obtaining labor's co-operation to ensure the effectiveness of wage controls. Higher hourly wages help to offset both inflation and reduced work time. Finally, vitally important for the effectiveness of an incomes policy is the wholehearted support of those administering the program. This was demonstrated strongly – in negative fashion – in the US experiment that began in August 1971. By the beginning of 1973, government officials were effectively dismantling the program and increasingly indicating their distaste for its continuance. By late 1973, termination dates were being announced. Under the circumstances, there were diminishing incentives to take the program seriously and increasing incentives to raise prices and/or to hold back and acquire inventories in anticipation of rising prices. There was, of course, decreasing incentive to labor to restrain its demands. In short, no incomes policy can be effective if its administrators do not believe in them.

We turn next to less stringent types of incomes policies. These may take a large variety of forms. There is the 'jaw-boning' approach used in the United States in the 1960s, when informal wage–price guidelines were highly publicized, with strong pleas for compliance by the government and adverse publicity given to non-cooperating organizations. There is the variety of voluntary approaches used in Western Europe, in which fairly elaborate, cooperative arrangements are made by labor, business and government to arrive at socially desirable wage and price changes for the forthcoming planning period. In these arrangements, tax concessions may be offered by government to obtain restraint in demands by labor. These arrangements may be viewed as a 'social contract,' as in the United Kingdom, the Netherlands and Austria.[15] Suggested devices for use in the United States include the taxation of employers who make wage settlements exceeding approved limits[16] and the requirement that price and wage changes in key industries be subject to delay while a governmental agency analyzes them and reports publicly on their reasonableness.

The usefulness of voluntary devices is a subject of inconclusive debate. If successful, they would have impacts and confer benefits much the same as cited for mandatory controls, but without the more severe costs. Much depends on the circumstances in which they are used: size of country; homogeneity of the population; socio-economic attitudes of the population and its government; character and vigor of the government; degree of centralization, strength and discipline of trade union organizations; social attitudes of business; tax structure; employment situation. It may be that Western Europe and Japan have more favorable situations than does the United States with respect to such environmental factors.[17] The sheer geographic and demographic size of the United States presents difficulties not found in other capitalist, industrialized countries. On the other hand, if full employment is part of the plan, incomes policies may have opportunities for success previously not present in the United States.[18] One should also note that claims of past ineffectiveness of such programs in the United States cannot be substantiated since one cannot say what would have happened in their absence. Participants in the pricing process may state that voluntary programs have no effect, but the heat of the protests suggests the opposite, namely that fear of public opinion does generally have a restraining effect.[19]

Voluntarism has the virtue of avoiding the real allocational, distributive and equity difficulties that can plague a system of firm controls. Undoubtedly, labor and business would refuse to adhere to government requests when their real interests were being injured significantly. At the same time the mere existence of machinery to discuss prices and wages within an incomes policy framework may, in the long run, make for 'sweeter reasonableness' of management and labor with respect to public responsibilities. It may also lead to experimentation among different forms of voluntarism with evolution toward more promising forms.

To sum up on public evaluation of incomes policies, both mandatory and voluntary, there have been a variety of experiences with such policies, beginning with World War II and continuing throughout the postwar inflationary periods in various countries. A considerable body of literature has documented and evaluated these experiences, and except with respect to wartime has tended to be unfriendly to the incomes policies pursued, especially the mandatory ones.[20] Opposition to such policies, moreover, has come not merely from business management, but also from labor, which tends to see in them distributive injustice, with relative sacrifices being made by labor on a scale far outweighing those made by the well-to-do and wealthy. Labor also often objects to being denied the right to get what it can by flexing its muscles. Academic economists, too, generally tend to oppose incomes policies, a goodly number on simple ideological grounds. Many other academic economists would oppose them in terms of theoretical and pragmatic criteria.

Despite their disabilities, indicative planning requires incomes policies for success in meeting objectives of plans, including dealing with inflation. Success of such planning requires a sharp reduction in the uncertainties facing labor and business, that is, an increase in security, if they are to be induced to perform in accordance with plans of government. Obtaining labor's support for incomes policies in turn requires some reform in the negotiating targets and in the economic environment to give such security. Security for labor means essentially reasonable certainty of an *annual* income (after taxes) sufficient to meet basic needs and a margin above it to provide amenities consistent with one's position in a socioeconomic hierarchy. Hourly wages are only a means to this end and a very imperfect one at that. Missing are the length of the work-week and the number of work-weeks per year. It is fairly evident that labor sets its demands partly in terms of uncertainties over them, adding appropriate allowances to hourly wage demands, and it is hourly wages that are critical in business costs. Were meaningful full employment reasonably assured, were government to back this up as the employer of last resort, and were bargaining to be over an *annual* wage, labor would have reason to be more modest in its demands as translated into hourly wages, in turn to support an incomes policy.

An additional element in labor's security package relates to fear of inflation. The knowledge that business was supporting an incomes policy, thus cooperating in price restraint, would presumably be of great help in reducing uncertainty over this point. Fear of unexpected inflation might be dealt with by building threshold indexing arrangements or alternative devices into labor contracts. Instead of labor's demanding immediate cash in the income package for the uncertainty of future inflation, there could be recognition of degrees of inflation, with specific future rises in income to be activated only at predetermined levels of inflation.

For business, security means minimal uncertainty with respect to costs and stability of demand at prices that provide reasonable profits. It is the prospect of such security that would give business the incentives to conform to government plans, including incomes policies. To the extent that there is a successful shift to annual income bargaining which reduces unit labor costs, and to the extent that full-employment markets spread overhead costs over a larger, more stable output, business would have a more secure, less inflation-prone environment in which to operate – in terms of both labor costs and purchases of supplies and capital goods. It, too, should then have a stake in the success of incomes policies.

With respect to the choice between voluntarism and mandatory controls in the United States, it is probably best to begin with a voluntarist approach. Escalation toward a mandatory approach should be held in reserve (with stand-by powers on hand) for use in emergencies or dangerously inflammatory cases. One might start with a combination of price guidelines and required prenotification of price rises for basic, standardized items in highly concentrated industries, with mandatory governmental analysis and reporting on rises exceeding the guidelines. Criteria for the designation 'highly concentrated industry' would obviously have to be established and made very clear. Items subject to price guidelines and reporting requirements would exclude those sold at retail, professional and personal services, rents, admissions to theaters and other public events and farm prices. Wage rises awarded to unions holding significant market power nationally or in substantial local areas would similarly be subjected to public analysis and reporting when in excess of guidelines. Although such actions may have only modest effect in the short run, if kept up year after year, a form of social responsibility may ultimately take root in management and labor in this general area. With respect to prices, since the number of items subject to voluntary restraint and reporting would generally be small for the individual affected firm, it might well be that over time such firms would become accustomed to the situation and learn to live with it just as did public utilities in the past.

Meanwhile, in the United States (and where applicable in other countries) efforts should be made to establish an environment conducive to the success of voluntary incomes policies. Government must take the lead with moral suasion, with legislative actions in some situations and by providing administrative machinery to facilitate voluntary negotiation. For example, efforts should be made to reduce the fragmentation of labor organizations by minute specialties. Centralization of unions should be encouraged generally. Modernization of the entire negotiating framework between labor and management should be stimulated, possibly to include an annual, national labor–management conference to establish guidelines for major contract settlements in the coming year. Consideration might be given to putting labor representatives on corporate boards of directors to facilitate more harmonious relations. Labor should also be encouraged to develop economic research staffs competent to give expert advice on the behavior of the economy, the significance of wage-price decisions for that behavior, and vice versa. Machinery should be developed to give the government administrative power to move flexibly to coordinate tax policy with, and thus to influence, wage decisions. Obviously, this list could be extended greatly in terms of creating a hospitable environment for the growth of successful incomes policies.

Let us add a note concerning governmental wages and prices. Governmental bodies at all levels should be subject to scrutiny and review with respect to their wage–price policies and machinery should be developed to make this possible. The government is the largest of all industries; it has grown greatly in the United States and other countries, and although not profit-motivated often behaves much like private enterprise. In the United States, too, unions have become powerful in the government sector. One should no more routinely approve a rise in teacher salaries, police salaries, military salaries, postal rates or government electric rates than a rise in telephone rates proposed by a privately owned telephone company. In short, government should be integrated into the machinery and processes of incomes policies.

5.3.5   Organization for Planning

We do not present blueprints here for the organizational apparatus of indicative planning, but suggest certain requirements. An overall planning and operating group would obviously be needed and very important would be the necessity of subordinating all other government agencies to it. Especially important in the United States would be the necessity for ending the independence of the Federal Reserve authorities, who now have virtual veto power over governmental macroeconomic policy. More generally, since it would be necessary to coordinate basic credit and monetary policies with overall plans, the numerous federal agencies in the credit and monetary fields would have to be subordinated to a centralized agency. It would be necessary also to require non-member banks to obey the monetary and credit directives of the Federal Reserve authorities.

Also very important would be the necessity of coordinating with overall government economic policy the policies of the huge array of other independent and non-independent government agencies that have economic powers. These agencies are mostly well known, but the cumulative extent of their economic powers is probably not generally appreciated. Among the major agencies are the Interstate Commerce Commission, the Federal Power Commission, the Civil Aeronautics Board, the Federal Communications Commission, the National Aeronautics and Space Administration, the Federal Highway Administration, the Federal Maritime Commission, the Army Corps of Engineers, the General Services Administration, the Postal Service, the Social Security Administration, Amtrak, the Commodity Credit Corporation and the Federal Trade Commission. Executive departments, especially defense, transportation and agriculture, would require coordination of activities where economic policy is affected. (Even without adoption of formal indicative planning, it is desirable that the vast powers of the independent and non-independent agencies not be used in independent, uncoordinated fashion.)

Much can be learned about organization for planning by examining two US periods of major economic experimentation, World War II and the 1930s. Here were organizational experiments in great variety. There were the Reconstruction Finance Corporation, the Defense Plant Corporation, the Public Works Administration, the Works Progress Administration, the Office of Price Administration, the War Labor Board and a host of others. All the ingredients for supply planning, demand planning, and wage–price stabilization may be found and their experiences examined. This is not to suggest simple emulation of wartime and Great Depression activities: it is to point out that there were agencies to extend credit to private firms engaged in government-planned activities (war-related production), agencies to build facilities and lease them to private enterprises, agencies to stockpile materials of key importance to the economy and agencies that employed great numbers of unemployed and, in the case of WPA, in effect acted as an employer of last resort. More recent large-scale government activities in the credit field (in housing, agriculture and elsewhere) would also be a useful guide.

FOOTNOTES

1. Of interest in this connection is the fact that for many years prior to 1970 Japan subordinated control of inflation to achieving rapid economic growth. See Hugh Patrick and Henry Rosovsky, 'Japan's Economic Performance: An Overview,' in Hugh Patrick and Henry Rosovsky (eds), *Asia's New Giant*, Washington, DC, Brookings Institution, 1976, p. 27.
2. Cf. Almarin Phillips, *Promoting Competition in Regulated Markets*, Washington, DC, Brookings Institution, 1975.
3. See, e.g., J. H. McArthur and B. R. Scott, *Industrial Planning in France*, Cambridge, Mass., Harvard University Press, 1969; J. S. Harlow, *French Economic Planning*, Iowa City, University of Iowa Press, 1966; Vera Lutz, *Central Planning for the Market Economy: An Analysis of the French Experience*, London, Longmans, 1969; David Liggins, 'What Can We Learn from French Planning,' *Lloyds Bank Review*, April 1976, pp. 1–12; David Liggins, *National Economic Planning in France*, Lexington, Mass., D. C. Heath, 1975; Pierre Bauchet, *Economic Planning: The French Experience*, New York, Praeger, 1964; John Hackett and Anne-Marie Hackett, *Economic Planning in France*, London, George Allen and Unwin, 1963.

   For a view of the United Kingdom's brief venture into indicative planning, see Malcolm Maclennan, Murray Forsyth and Geoffrey Denton, *Economic Planning and Policies in Britain, France and Germany*, New York, Praeger, 1968, especially Ch. 4.
4. For views of Japan's experiences, see OECD, *The Industrial Policy of Japan*, Paris, OECD, 1972; Patrick and Rosovsky (eds), op. cit.; W. V. Rapp, 'Supply Management: A Key Element in Japan's Economic Policy,' *Morgan Guaranty Survey*, September 1975, pp. 10–15.
5. See Hackett and Hackett, op. cit., pp. 69–72, 240–6, 261–71, 369–70; McArthur and Scott, op. cit., pp. 296–306; Liggins, 'What Can We Learn from French Planning,' pp. 6–9.
6. See Patrick and Rosovsky, 'Japan's Economic Performance: An Overview,' in Patrick and Rosovsky, op. cit., pp. 43–7; Gardner Ackley and Hiromitsu Ishi, 'Fiscal, Monetary and Related Policies,' in Patrick and Rosovsky, op. cit., pp. 234–43; P. H. Trezise and Yukio Suzuki, 'Politics, Government, and Economic Growth in Japan,' in Patrick and Rosovsky, op. cit., pp. 789–809; Rapp, op. cit., argues that supply management was probably the most important feature in Japanese economic planning.
7. For data on stockpiles of key imported minerals and metals, see *Morgan Guaranty Survey*, March 1974, p. 13. Under the Energy Policy and Conservation Act enacted in 1975 the United States in fact committed itself to establishing a national stockpile of oil (*Economic Report of the President*, Washington, DC, 1976, pp. 7, 8). Advocacy of a grain reserve was a theme of Mr Bob Bergland at a news conference prior to beginning his role of Secretary of Agriculture in the Carter Administration (*New York Times*, 14 January 1977, pp. D1, D11).
8. See, e. g. *Economic Report of the President*, 1976, pp. 250–1.
9. See US Congress, Congressional Budget Office, *Temporary Measures to Stimulate Employment: An Evaluation of Some Alternatives*, Washington, DC, 2 September 1975, pp. 78, 84.

10. Such a fiscal policy is embodied in the Humphrey-Hawkins Bill which was introduced in the US Congress in 1976. It proposed sufficient job creation by the government to reduce unemployment among adults aged twenty years and older to 3 per cent. (See *New York Times*, 14 March 1976, Section 1, pp. 1, 28.)

11. At year-end 1974 liabilities and capital of federally sponsored credit agencies exceeded $80 billion (*Federal Reserve Bulletin*, May 1976, p. A37). Subsidies of all categories (cash, tax benefits, credit terms and in-kind) were estimated by the staff of Congress's Joint Economic Committee to be well above $100 billion in early 1977 (*New York Times*, 20 March 1977, Section 4, p. 3).

12. *New York Times*, 10 November 1974, Section 3, p. 3.

13. *Survey of Current Business*, various issues.

14. ibid.

15. See Hannes Suppanz and Derek Robinson, *Prices and Incomes Policy: The Austrian Experience*, Paris, OECD, 1973; OECD, *Socially Responsible Wage Policies and Inflation*, Paris, OECD, 1975.

16. See H. C. Wallich, 'Alternative Strategies for Price and Wage Controls,' *Journal of Economic Issues*, December 1972, pp. 89–104, and Sidney Weintraub, 'Incomes Policy: Completing the Stabilization Triangle,' in ibid., pp. 105–22.

17. With respect to Western Europe, see A. H. Raskin, 'Europe's Labor Scene: Unions Fostering Closer Relations with Both Industry and Government,' *New York Times*, 22 July 1976, pp. 1, 4; cf. John Hein, *Aspects of Incomes Policies Abroad*, New York, The Conference Board, 1972, pp. 11, 12, 38–40; *Skandinaviska Enskilda Banken Quarterly Review*, 3, 1974, p. 95.

On the other hand, a distinguished labor economist, J. T. Dunlop, finds the US environment more conducive to wage restraint in important respects than is the case in Western Europe. For example, he finds decentralization of bargaining leading to less wage drift (i.e., local augmentation of wage decisions reached at national levels). He also finds less likelihood 'that an increase in one sector ... will ... spread semi-automatically throughout large reaches of the economy'. (See 'Inflation and Incomes Policies: The Political Economy of Recent US Experience,' in *Public Policy*, Spring 1975, pp. 159–65.)

18. Cf. Hein, op. cit., p. 8.

19. For a thoughtful defense of voluntary restraints and a design for their future use by one who had personal experience with them as chairman of the US Council of Economic Advisors, see Gardner Ackley, 'An Incomes Policy for the 1970's,' *Review of Economics and Statistics*, August 1972, pp. 218–23.

20. Besides those cited earlier, useful studies include Frank Blackaby (ed.), *An Incomes Policy for Britain*, London, Heinemann, 1972; Barry Bosworth, 'Phase II: The US Experiment with an Incomes Policy,' *Brookings Papers on Economic Activity*, Vol. 2, 1972, pp. 343–83; Ekhard Brehmer and M. R. Bradford, 'Incomes and Labor Market Policies in Sweden, 1945–70,' *Staff Papers*, March 1974, pp. 101–26; J. K. Galbraith, *A Theory of Price Control*, Cambridge, Mass., Harvard University Press, 1952; Walter Galenson (ed.), *Incomes Policy: What Can We Learn From Europe*, Ithaca, New York, Cornell University, 1973; C. D. Goodwin (ed.), *Exhortation and Control: The Search for a Wage-Price Policy 1945–1971*, Washington, DC Brookings Institution, 1975; D. T. Llewellyn, 'Incomes Policy: The Wider Issues,' *Industrial Relations*, September 1970, pp. 33–60; OECD, *Inflation: The Present Problem*, Paris, OECD, 1970; William Poole, 'Wage-Price Controls: Where Do We Go from Here,' *Brookings Papers on Economic Activity*, Vol. 1, 1973, pp. 285–99; Michael Parkin and M. T. Sumner (eds), *Incomes Policy and Inflation*, Manchester, Manchester University Press, 1972; Lloyd Ulman, 'Cost Push and Some Policy Alternatives,' *American*

Economic Review, May 1972, pp. 242–57; Lloyd Ulman and R. J. Flanagan, *Wage Restraint: A Study of Incomes Policies in Western Europe*, Berkeley, University of California Press, 1971.

6 Concluding Observations

6.1 Recapitulation

The economic record of the United States since 1966 has not been a good one. On this judgement a general consensus probably exists. Variation would be found in the marks accorded different elements in that record – unemployment, inflation, growth, allocation of resources, distributional equity, fiscal equity. The record is in part accidental, a product of chance political events such as the Vietnam War and Middle East oil politics and chance natural events such as crop failures. It is also, however, a product of the ideology of generally mainstream, post-Keynesian economists, of their prevailing methodology, and of the anti-micro-policy environment that stems partly from that methodology.

Important consequences of the prevailing ideology, the prevailing methodology and the anti-micro-policy environment have been the primacy of demand management and placement of its dials at levels presumably consistent with bringing inflation down to more acceptable levels. In this process, restrictive monetary policy has been the active tool of policy, with fiscal policy (for all levels of government combined) being something of a residual, forced to accommodate itself in considerable measure to the effects of monetary policy. Given the ideological and methodological background, the role of monetary policy has been particularly appealing to many because of its veneer of *laissez-faire*, its speed and flexibility of implementation, with no need for legislative action.

This reliance on severely restrictive monetary policy is unfortunate, for it is a defective tool to cope with the tasks of control assigned to it since 1966. In an inflation whose major forces do not come from the direction of demand and where the environment is filled with impediments to competitive forces, severe monetary restraint can succeed only by creating sufficient unemployment for sufficiently long to weaken labor severely. But even this implies that counteracting agents such as unemployment insurance will be very temporary in nature and so not act as a partial neutralizer of the monetary restraint.

Severe monetary restraint also has significant inflationary effects. In major sectors of the economy, interest is an important cost item – in housing and public utilities especially. In other sectors where there is heavy capital intensity or great durability of capital, or where for other reasons there is heavy reliance on external funds, the cost-raising effect of severe monetary restraint will be felt in a significant degree. It will be felt in public finance as states, cities and other local government units have to levy higher taxes to meet higher interest costs. In practice, it will tend to feed inflation by restricting aggregate supply far more than aggregate demand, as the latter tends to be supported by savings, unemployment compensation (public and private) and welfare.

Finally, extreme restraint stimulates the growth of monetary velocity via stimulating the development of money substitutes. This reflects dynamic interactions that tend to change existing relationships between interest rates and monetary aggregates. As a result, while lowering the rate of growth of monetary aggregates may imply higher interest rates, the higher interest rates have a feedback leading to the development of more money substitutes and new relationships between monetary aggregates and interest rates in which the latter are restrained.

Imposition of extreme monetary restraint involves mass destruction of capital values – in bonds, stocks, mortgages and in all existing capital goods whose valuation involves a capitalization of a future stream of earnings. Aggregatively, the losses have been of the order of hundreds of billions of dollars in a severe credit squeeze.

Sectorally, such losses affect the liquidity and hence the safety of financial institutions – banks, insurance companies and others. Compounding the difficulties are the adverse differentials in inflows and outflows of funds at thrift institutions generated by the interest rate disparities of 'borrowing short and lending long.' Adding further to the difficulties are the obstacles faced by debtors of financial institutions in refinancing existing debts and obtaining new credits, thus posing default threats.

The upshot of extreme monetary restriction is instability in financial markets. Depository institutions may be threatened with runs. Other financial sectors may be faced with parallel phenomena. Securities firms are subjected to threats of failure and the investment banking machinery may be injured harshly.

Outside the world of financial institutions, severe monetary restraint can perform its appointed task of restraining demand only by causing trouble for individuals, business firms and non-profit organizations. Interest rates high enough to have the inflationary impacts described are also significant elements on the cost side of income statements of business firms. At the same time, restraint on aggregate demand makes it more difficult to meet those increased costs. Liquidity problems and failures are a consequence.

At the household level, people in all walks of life are injured by falling capital values. Those saving for home purchases, children's education and other purposes may be victims. Retired persons may find assets and pensions impaired, and estates may fall seriously below the levels planned for survivors. Difficulties may be imposed on those trying to sell or buy homes. Financial defaults occur.

Non-profit organizations (educational, cultural, medical, scientific, humanitarian, etc.) are likely to be victims of extreme monetary restraint. More serious than rises in borrowing costs to them are the declines in asset values of their endowment funds, the decline in asset values of gifts in the form of securities, the lessened ability and willingness of donors to make contributions and, ultimately, the decline in earnings on assets caused by depressed levels of economic activity. Compounding their difficulties are reduced appropriations by state and local governments stemming from recession-induced falls in revenues in those many cases where public support exists.

Finally, and probably most important, is unemployment and its consequences for individuals: economic, social, psychological, physical, medical and others. Many paragraphs were spent on this point earlier, and we merely remind the reader of this familiar and unfortunate story. It is a tale that embraces hunger, malnutrition, inadequacy of clothing and shelter, recreational deprivation, lost educational opportunities, cultural deprivation, inadequate medical attention, mental illness, inadequate services by cities, states and school districts, absence of aesthetic amenities, crime, social deprivation, social unrest and social strife.

A logical question that follows from all of the above is 'were these hardships necessary' or were they simply an offering at the altar of establishment ideology and methodology? The view here is that these hardships were largely unnecessary, that restrictive monetary policy was not capable of dealing with the types of inflationary forces generally at work since 1966, that the severe restriction provoked innovative behavior in the financial world that partly offset the restraint and which will continue to offset in part future monetary restriction. Only in the period 1966–9 and for perhaps a short period in 1973 were demand-pull forces important in the inflation. For the rest of the time cost-push, political forces, scarcity forces and possibly exchange rate forces were dominant.

To sum up, it is the view here that over most of the period since 1966 substantially easier money would have been more effective in fighting the inflation. Aggregate supply would then have been substantially greater after 1969, while aggregate demand would probably have been only slightly larger, given the cushions present in the economy. Cost-push forces would probably have been reduced since there would not have been the intense pressure to get a greater portion of a shrinking pie; that is, the cost-push forces emanating from redistributional demands and those emanating from efforts to maintain real incomes in the face of a shrinking value of the dollar and falling real aggregate income would have been dulled significantly. In industries where interest is a major cost element, cost pressures would have been reduced. In government, higher aggregate economic activity would have enlarged the income of units at all levels, and in combination with lower welfare costs and reduced interest costs would have reduced deficits, thus permitting lower levels of taxation, at least at non-federal levels.

Long-term economic growth in the United States has undoubtedly suffered as a result of the persistent monetary restraint of the period beginning with 1966. In countries other than the United States, high interest rates have probably had less inhibiting effect on investment in view of the much larger public sectors and in view of the policies in some countries (e.g. Japan and France) of assuring full credit availability and moderate interest rates to private industries deemed important to economic wellbeing. In the United States, on the other hand, construction of even desperately needed electrical capacity was delayed after 1973 by virtually penal rates of interest (reflecting weakened credit standing of public utilities) and that which has taken place involves higher priced facilities to users because of the extraordinary levels of cost of capital funds. Comparable problems existed in housing, where again the private sector is dominant. Here, too, the extreme instability generated in the housing industry by repeated doses of severe monetary restraint has doubtless impaired its ability to improve efficiency. An ultimate consequence of the 'stop–go' introduced into investment generally may have been to dull the pace of technological innovation. Growth may also have been affected to the extent that very high yields on financial investment lured entrepreneurial talent away from real investment.

Public investment, too, has undoubtedly suffered as a result of a prolonged period of generally very high interest rates. Investment decisions may be linked to implied rates of return in relation to cost of funds. Budget ceilings may constrain the amount of interest that may be paid, or there may be psychological barriers to rates of interest or to proportions of budget totals that may be used for interest. On the other hand, to the extent that budgets consume greater amounts for interest, other areas may be adversely affected and growth impeded.

Finally, very high costs of funds have international repercussions. Poorer countries desperately in need of external capital may be unable to pay the price or may be required to sacrifice far too much to obtain that capital. This is true both with respect to new capital and to the refinancing of maturing debts.

6.2 Indicative Economic Planning as the Solution

Choices exist and choices must be made with respect to public policy concerning inflation and unemployment. Firmly rejected here was the choice of having 'more of the past,' modified by institutional reform to minimize adverse public and private restrictions on competition and efficiency. The outlook with a continuation of past monetary policies would include the probability of prolonged 'stagflation,' with (1) alternating periods of drift toward less high and much higher unemployment – but always high by any reasonable full employment test – and (2) alternating periods of high and very high interest rates.

To be sure, at the individual level there would be winners as well as losers in such a situation. The winners would probably include the pure rentier types – those living on secure interest (especially if tax-exempt) or quasi-interest payments without need to sell securities, other claims or real property. Other winners are possible too, but subject to offsets of various types in various combinations. For example, a manager's gains from a new money market mutual fund (stimulated by a high interest rate economy) may be offset by falls in his sales of equity mutual funds or in ordinary stock brokerage operations. Overall, however, prolonged severe monetary restraint and the recession (i.e. scarcity) created by it are likely to distribute losses of income and capital fairly generally across society leaving few real winners, mainly very wealthy persons living on tax-exempt securities and reaping vast gains. The losers encompass nearly everyone. The rich and poor share in the burden of prolonged severe monetary restraint and its resulting recession, and it may very well be that the rich pay both the highest absolute money price as well as the highest relative money price if the base for any income group is some combined valuation of income and wealth of that group at or near the start of the restraint. However, from any base related to human needs, such as incomes or resources sufficient to meet modest family needs and comforts (including education of children), the greatest real sacrifices are placed on the lower-income groups and the unemployed generally.

Most interesting from a psychological viewpoint is the willingness of key upper-income groups, particularly business executives and those with substantial security portfolios, to go to the financial slaughter of prolonged, severe monetary restraint. If proposed in a form such as taxes, such a slaughter would presumably be resisted 'to the death.' Somehow, if that tax is disguised as tight money, it becomes acceptable, even though no reasonable certainty exists that the prescription will cure the disease. One possible explanation is an excessive deference to, and reverence for, the views of central bankers. Enthronement of monetary policy since 1966 has given central bankers a degree of influence rivalled only in the 1920s. If this is the explanation, it is most unfortunate: one need only cite the disastrous performance of the Federal Reserve authorities from 1930 to 1933, when there were about 9,000 bank suspensions. One is reminded here of the 'leech theory' of medicine of many years ago, according to which it was necessary to remove body ills by attaching leeches to the body and drawing off the poisonous elements by bloodletting.

There is also perhaps a throwback to the days when periodic depression was assumed certain, that little could – or should – be done to resist it, and that positive good came from it in the form of cleansing the economic system of accumulated ills and providing a vehicle for secular change. This was part of the theory of 'healthy bankruptcy.' At the same time, current widespread acquiescence in this approach to controlling inflation by dominant elements of the business and financial world corroborates the judgement here that the really grievous burdens of such an approach are escaped by those in the upper reaches of the socioeconomic hierarchy. One also senses that those in the upper socioeconomic echelons who support such an approach see ancillary benefits for themselves over the long run, probably a more pliant labor force.

One may wonder why firm dissenters to such self-destruction among business executives and leaders seem so subdued in the debates. I suspect in part a 'country club effect' which suggests avoidance of vigorous public behavior divergent from a presumed class norm. Among less firm dissenters there are perhaps fears of alternative control approaches which would embody greater interferences by government in economic affairs. I suspect also that conservative economists in the business and financial world work hard at encouraging such fears.

On ideological grounds, too, one must wonder why a conservative business sector generally supports the monetary authorities in causing staggering declines in the market values of financial assets in an economy dedicated to a goal of market freedom. The business sector as well as government authorities would ordinarily object to price and wage controls on goods and services. They would also ordinarily object even to selective controls involving mandatory credit terms on specific categories of goods. Yet seemingly little objection is raised to causing prices of bonds and other financial assets to fall severely.

Before we leave our rejected choice – 'more of the same' – a warning is in order concerning a new rationale for the existence of substantial unemployment. This is search theory, which attempts to find the positive economic values in unemployment. Efforts are made to quantify the offsets to unemployment in the form of non-market activity (home activity and inactivity while unemployed, the utility derived from exploring the job market and looking for an improved economic situation).[1] Curiously, the economists engaged in this sort

of study make little effort to quantify the many adverse human consequences of unemployment and their feedback on economic behavior and performance of the unemployed. (Admittedly, if they
attempted it, the range of error would be enormous, as it is in efforts
to measure positive consequences.)

A second solution to the inflation–unemployment problem would
simply be to set the monetary–fiscal dials for full employment while
getting rid – as far as possible – of onerous restrictions on competition and efficiency imposed by government and private industry.
Impediments to the effectiveness of demand management would be
removed, including independence of the Federal Reserve system and
lack of fiscal coordination between federal, state and local levels of
government. A full-employment demand management approach
could also include other elements such as an incomes policy. Undoubtedly this would be a considerable advance over the situation
prevailing since 1966. However, given the inflationary forces described in Chapter 4, this would seem to leave the US economy
unnecessarily exposed to continuing inflation from existing forces,
especially those with a supply orientation, as well as to inflation
from future, random forces. Real protection against inflation, unemployment and threats to national economic welfare requires
governmental action on other fronts in addition to demand management and institutional reform. Government already intervenes in
the United States on a massive scale through tax policy, loans and
subsidies, government-owned and sponsored corporations in specific fields, regulatory agencies and authorities, laws and arbitrary
actions of a host of organs of government. Not a great deal more
would be required to harness these often diverse forces to see that
they proceed in the same direction, to see that they act in reasonably
coordinated fashion to achieve a rational set of goals with the minimizing of unsynchronized actions taken simply in response to the
pressures of private lobbying groups.

Solutions chosen should try both to maximize welfare in the short
run and reflect a longer look into the future so that they may offer
the possibility of durability. We should take a careful look at the
dominant forces in the world today and see what they tell us about
the evolving character of the capitalist economic system, especially
its apparently necessary characteristics for survival as a viable
system with dynamic properties and a capacity for meeting the
reasonable expectations for economic improvement held by hun-

dreds of millions of people throughout the world. Such an evolving capitalism is likely to be one embracing indicative planning. It is a situation in which government sets goals for the public and private sectors and takes appropriate actions to facilitate achievement of those goals with minimal direct coercion.

In this evolving capitalism, aggregate demand dials would be set for full employment and demand in the public sector would include adequate public services at all times. There would be machinery for fiscal coordination at all levels of government, thus giving assurance to lower (i.e. non-federal) levels of minimum amounts of available funds and assuring a coordinated fiscal component of demand management. The central bank would be largely passive, following instructions of the executive branch of government concerning the levels of monetary aggregates to be supplied and the related interest rate policies to be pursued to assure consistency with the overall plans. Government, finally, would be the employer of last resort, assuring all of an opportunity for constructive work.

It is often argued that meaningful full-employment aggregate demand is inflationary in terms of lack of skills by a large group of people in the labor force. However, in many of the types of public services where the United States is short-changed the most, no great skills are required. In other areas of need (e.g. teaching) skills are going unused and being allowed to deteriorate because of under-financing of education. In the final analysis, where a real public need exists and important skills are in short supply, one can use the example of World War II to redesign jobs for simplicity, dividing complicated tasks into a set of much simpler ones, thus facilitating use of unskilled labor after brief training periods. Meanwhile, full-employment markets would give industry the incentive to institute training programs of a longer-run nature to assure an adequate supply of skilled labor for the future. Likewise, individuals would have the incentives to seek, and their families more plentiful means to finance, training.

The government's role in aggregate supply under indicative planning would constitute perhaps the most distinctive change compared with the present state of affairs. The government would take all steps necessary to assure the presence of an appropriate infrastructure, assisting the private sector when necessary. It would assure reserve supplies of foods and basic raw materials to cope with natural disasters and other forms of emergencies. It would assure the presence of adequate capacity in basic industries, such as steel, petroleum refining and aluminum. All this would be financed in the varied ways now employed by the government in its *ad hoc* operations in many fields. Included would be devices such as assured credit on favorable terms, subsidies, government ownership (as in raw material stockpiling or atomic energy facilities) and government underwriting of losses.

The government would also take measures to insure that in international trade in important products, large-scale transactions involving the welfare of the people and involving quasi-monopolistic control in either buying or selling, would be subject to government supervision. Where such trading is with another government, the US government should logically become a partner in the negotiations.

Another leg of the new capitalism would consist of an incomes policy, something that seems essential and inevitable in the new approach. (Obviously, if inflationary pressures were to disappear miraculously, an incomes policy could be put on a stand-by basis.) Logically, one would initiate such a policy on a largely voluntary basis but have compulsory elements available on a stand-by basis, introducing them only in emergencies or inflammatory situations. To attract labor's support, full-employment policies would be essential, with the government as the employer of last resort, with bargaining in terms of an annual wage, and with recognition by business of the problem of distributional equity. To maximize effectiveness and minimize difficulties, it would be well to confine the policy to basic, standardized items in concentrated industries and to wage settlements involving unions with substantial market power. In such a program, changes would be desirable in current approaches to collective bargaining in the United States. A centralized system with an annual labor–management conference would be very helpful to establish guidelines for major contract settlements over the following year, thus avoiding piecemeal competitive bargaining by individual unions. With government support and even assistance through flexible tax policy, the essential ingredients of a social contract approach would be present.

A final and logical question at this point is the degree of realism involved in pinning hopes on limited economic planning. This breaks down into two separate issues: first, if adopted, what are the real potentials of indicative economic planning, and, second, how realistic is it to hope for its acceptance?

With respect to the potentials of indicative economic planning, one can extrapolate from its record in France, which has a formal planning procedure, and Japan, where the planning is less formal, and add *a priori* considerations. At the outset, it is well to recognize that it is not a utopian solution, but the reader is reminded that perfection is not attainable. More reading of newspapers in recent years would have revealed some of the difficulties encountered by France and Japan despite their efforts at planning. Still, both enjoyed high rates of growth and their economies had enviable dynamic properties. The contributions of planning in both cases, especially Japan, have been a subject of controversy, and in one sense the issue remains inconclusive since one cannot know what would have been the growth rates in the absence of the planning procedures followed.

In any event, combining fairly obvious *a priori* analysis with observations relating to France and Japan, one finds certain clear gains. For example, indicative economic planning tends to make for far greater assurance of an adequate infrastructure. It also provides the machinery for assuring the availability of needed raw materials and basic supplies (although failures may obviously still occur). It makes for a better informed business sector concerning the shape of the future. This comes about in part because government must plan its own future activities and make them known. In turn, government is in a position to inform the business sector of the most promising future choices for products and markets. This, of course, must cause business to think much more about the future, hence to plan with a longer time horizon and on a broader scale. Given, additionally, maintenance of full employment as a background condition, and given the variety of fiscal, credit and contractual incentives that planning can offer the private sector, there would be far greater likelihood of the private sector's fulfilling its widened plans in an environment of reduced economic uncertainty and increased stability. Contributing to the happier results (and desirable for its own sake) would be the coordination of the policies of a myriad of government agencies, now often at odds with each other. Government, instead of simply reacting to crises and difficulties with *ad hoc* solutions that have little future orientation, would be far more likely to anticipate them and smooth out the shocks. Finally, as a result of all the above, there would be hope for a better allocation of resources and a better socioeconomic society generally.

With respect to the likelihood of acceptance of limited economic planning, there have been new, hopeful signs on the international scene that may have some impact on the United States. Even in the United States there have been smoke signals appearing on the horizon, albeit a distant horizon. A survey of newspaper articles (*New York Times* and *Wall Street Journal*) in the period 1974–6 shows repeated reference to French and other Western European experiences, with clear evidence of greater US interest in planning approaches (including social contract devices within the scope of planning). Social contract approaches have been growing steadily in Western Europe, including, for example, Sweden, Norway, Austria, Germany and, most recently and notably, the United Kingdom. Since 1975 there has been in the United States an increasing number of newspaper articles on the subject of possible US planning, the formation of a national committee of prominent citizens to push the planning idea, the introduction of legislation (the Humphrey–Hawkins Bill) to make a start toward this goal, and formal discussion of the idea at a Democratic Party conference. Not only is the climate for change being prepared domestically at many levels, but the example of some success in other industrialized countries may pave the way for acceptance here. This is especially true in view of the increasing internationalization of large business units, bringing quick familiarity to executives and others here of innovations abroad and thus perhaps increasing their acceptability in the United States.

Realism suggests that limited economic guidance in the form of indicative economic planning must not be expected in 1977 or even 1978. It does not preclude the possibility, however, that it may arrive a little at a time over a period of several years, perhaps stripped of the inflammatory word 'planning' and repackaged in more appealing terminology. Come in some form it almost certainly will. The likely alternative – drifting while being buffeted by a host of unpleasant forces – is one that an electorate is likely to grow increasingly weary of, and finally reject.

FOOTNOTE

1. See, for example, R. J. Gordon, 'The Welfare Cost of Higher Unemployment,' *Brookings Paper on Economic Activity*, Vol. 1, 1973, pp. 133–95.

7 High Interest Rates: The Experience of the Company Sector of the United Kingdom, 1966–75

> If we play with dear money on the ground that it is 'healthy' or 'natural' then I have no doubt that the inevitable slump will ensue. We must avoid it, therefore, as we would hell-fire.[1]

It is worth bearing in mind Keynes's advice on 'How to Avoid a Slump' – advice that was not acceptable to the monetary authorities then or subsequently – when we examine certain aspects of the economic record of the United Kingdom over the decade 1966–75. It is not intended to present the financial history of the decade, except in a highly selective and episodic fashion; the government sector is neglected, the balance of payments scarcely figures, and such interesting and important areas as the innovations in the London money markets are passed over without comment. Instead it examines the consequences of sharply increased interest rates for companies that are ill-equipped to safeguard the liquidity of their balance sheet position in conditions of financial uncertainty and economic recession, paying special attention to 'The Second Great Crash'[2] of 1973 and 1974.

7.1 A Case Study of High Interest Rates

As a case study in credit restraint and associated interest movements to unprecedented peacetime levels, the period in the financial history of the United Kingdom from the end of 1965 to the end of 1975 has much to recommend it. But the experience of the past ten or eleven years demonstrates the acceleration of a trend, remarkable by historical standards, that began with the revival of Bank Rate policy in the United Kingdom in November 1951.

Arguably, the era of high interest rates in the United Kingdom commences with the 'September measures' of 1957, when Bank Rate was raised to 7 per cent and held at that level for six months. There are probably two main characteristics of this era, the first of which is the practice of sustained recourse to crisis-level Bank Rate (i.e. 7 or 8 per cent) by the UK monetary authorities. Bank Rate was maintained at crisis levels for a total of fourteen months between September 1957 and December 1965. This record indicates exceptional upward pressure on interest rates by historical standards; it is unremarkable only if we compare it with what has taken place subsequently. Bank Rate was held at crisis levels for a total of thirty-one months in the years 1966–9;[3] if we add up the periods of crisis-rate lending over the 110 years from 1797 to 1907 we arrive at virtually the same total; alternatively, thirty-one months represents almost one-half of the total period of crisis-rate last-resort lending to the UK banking system by the Bank of England between 1900 and 1970.[4] Official pressure on the structure of interest rates between the summer of 1973 and the spring of 1977 has been, in its way, of even greater severity than the experience of the late 1960s, but it is difficult to make a clear-cut comparison between these periods for two main reasons: first, 'the minimum lending rate' (MLR) of the Bank of England to the specialist banks in the discount market, which is designed to follow rather than to lead the trend in short-term market rates, replaced Bank Rate in October 1972; second, accelerating prices contributed to an escalation of money rates to new heights, so that the 'crisis level' of MLR has become variable over time, the meaning of any given level being revealed only by reference to the *contemporary* economic context. However, in practice administrative changes in MLR may still represent a 'shift in monetary policy'[5] in the fashion of traditional Bank Rate and we can offer rough justice to the facts by assuming that an MLR of 11 per cent or more represented a crisis level in the years 1973–7. On this criterion MLR was maintained at crisis levels for thirty-six months out of forty-four between July 1973 and March 1977: but, whatever the yardstick, the evidence of severe and protracted upward pressure on short-term interest rates by the UK monetary authorities is hardly in dispute.

A second outstanding feature of the era of high interest rates is largely a consequence of the first. It is the *high long-term* interest rates of the past twenty years that are startling, unprecedented and particularly damaging to the long-run growth prospects of the United Kingdom – not the short rates.[6] The market has become accustomed to 'crisis-level' Bank Rates/minimum lending rates and this expectation of rising rates has inevitably been reflected in a rising long-term yield. Again, since market forces have cut loose from what was apparently a well established secular norm in long rates (see Figure 7.4), expectations about the future trend in interest rates have been held with an even greater measure of uncertainty,[7] reflected in a much greater risk premium required by the purchaser of gilt-edged stock, raising long-term relative to short-term interest rates. At one time a 7 per cent Bank Rate was consistent with a

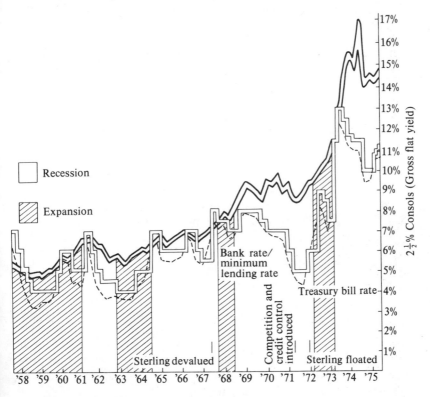

Source: *Barclays Review*, May 1976, centre spread
Figure 7.1   UK interest rates, 1957–76

secular norm of 3–3½ per cent once the overhang of long-term debt following major wars had been absorbed and private sector portfolios were in approximate long-term equilibrium once more. In the 1950s a 6 per cent long-term rate was accounted extraordinary. In the 1970s we have experienced long-term rates of interest some few per cent *above* record levels of minimum lending rate, the yield on consols (depicted in Figure 7.1) reaching a peak of 17.4 per cent in December 1974.

At this juncture the reader may be assailed by perfectly proper doubts about the legitimacy of the emphasis of the analysis so far. Were not the protracted spells of very high rates of last-resort lending to the banking system by the Bank of England a necessary method of maintaining London's competitiveness as a repository of short-term capital and of supporting the sterling exchange rate? Moreover, in an age more notable for its accelerating rate of price inflation than for the behaviour of interest rates, should we not direct our attention to real (or deflated) yields rather than to money rates of interest? An attempt to answer these points is made a little later in this chapter.

7.2   What Kind of Financial Stability?

A stable and low-risk financial environment is generally agreed to be a crucial prerequisite of sustained economic growth. The case for financial stability is part of a more general argument that, to prevent the familiar 'stop–go' pattern of postwar UK economic policy, aggregate demand should expand at a steady and predictable rate on the upswing of the business cycle, thereby eliminating the need for any subsequent financial contraction and economic downswing. Thus 'the basic remedy for the "stop" lies in the control of the "go"'.[8] It is important that the specious nature of an economic philosophy that can prescribe a 'dash for growth' (to use the phrase used to describe Treasury policy in 1972–3) be properly appreciated and that the shortcomings of the UK record in this respect made plain.

The two economists normally presumed to have had the greatest influence on the strategy of monetary management in the United

Kingdom since 1945 have emphasized the need for a stable financial climate. Both Professor Milton Friedman and the late Lord Keynes have argued that a contractionary monetary policy can contribute to, or even be a prime cause of, an economic recession;[9] both have advocated a gradualist approach to business expansion, sustaining confidence, avoiding bottlenecks and consequently price increases and balance of payments difficulties; both have recommended that the money supply be increased at a rate appropriate to the level of planned expenditure in the economy. Yet there remain important differences of emphasis between the two. Friedman has argued for a rate of growth of the money stock 'that would on the average achieve rough stability in the level of *prices* of final products',[10] i.e. steady monetary expansion at a rate designed to accommodate the growth of real output and real income over a number of years. Keynes urged that the money supply be permitted to grow at a rate that would preserve the stability of the long-term *money rate of interest* (granted, in the 1930s, a period more notable for relative price stability than the past ten years); i.e. the monetary authorities should increase the money supply to satisfy the increased demand for transactions balances associated with rising incomes and growing planned expenditure, keeping constant the supply of idle balances and hence (in a stable financial climate in which the demand for money to hold is uninfluenced by growing uncertainty or a shift in expectations) the long-term rate of interest.[11] Thus Keynes emphasized that in their role as *lenders* the banks generally hold the key to whether a new level of economic activity may be attained.[12]

A common explanation of the erratic quality of domestic financial management in the United Kingdom is that this outcome has been a consequence of balance of payments difficulties exacerbated by inadequate currency reserves and by the competitive pressures associated with London's role as a centre of international finance. That the need to correct the UK balance of payments position has regularly overridden the requirements of the domestic economy is beyond dispute. Nevertheless, two comments are relevant. First, balance of payments difficulties on current account normally result from a too-rapid expansion of demand and should therefore not arise in a properly supervised financial system;[13] financial stability is therefore self-perpetuating because its operation removes the necessity for officially sponsored policies of financial disruption which produce economic recession. Second, since UK interest rates must be competitive with US rates in particular to attract and retain short-term funds in London, it is important, as Ervin Miller has emphasized, that the United States pursues policies designed to avoid sharp fluctuations in interest rates that reach levels far out of line with historical precedent, instead of communicating instability to the United Kingdom and other financial systems by violent swings in short-term interest rates.

However, irrespective of the justification, or lack of it, for UK financial policies, it is useful to highlight certain details of recent performance and to measure the UK record against the yardsticks of financial stability first of Friedman and then of Keynes.

Notable differences emerge in certain periods between the respective rates of change of the narrow version of the UK money supply (M_1) and the broad version (M_3). For example, over the twenty-three months from January 1973 to December 1974, M_1 increased by 18 per cent, M_3 by over 60 per cent. In the third quarter of 1973 M_3, its growth swollen by arbitrage operations in certificates of deposit issued by the banks, expanded by over 35 per cent; M_1 *contracted* by almost 14 per cent, causing the Governor of the Bank of England temporarily to suspend an apparent belief in M_3 as the version of the money stock most relevant to future expenditures.[14] Nevertheless, as is evident from Figures 7.2 and 7.3, even when rates of change in M_1 and sterling M_3 are deflated to remove the influence of inflation, neither the broad nor the narrow version appears to conform to the financial stability prescription of Friedman, or indeed, to mention three distinguished British monetarists, to that of Laidler, Parkin or Walters. One must be careful not to overstate the case. As Graham Hacche's study revealed,[15] the demand for money apparently changed its character towards the end of 1972, and the growth of the interest-bearing deposit component of M_3 relative to M_1 in 1973 is consistent with this change. Again, the decline in real national disposable income in 1974 and 1975 should logically be associated with a decline in the transactions demand for money balances, suggesting a possible justification for the reduction in the real value of M_1 and M_3 sterling balances. But, this said, British monetarists have been highly critical of the course of the expansion path of the UK money supply, however defined. Professor Laidler, for example, forecast with impressive accuracy that the swift deceleration of M_3 following its over-rapid growth in 1972 and 1973, would result, *inter alia*, in a collapse of the stock market in the

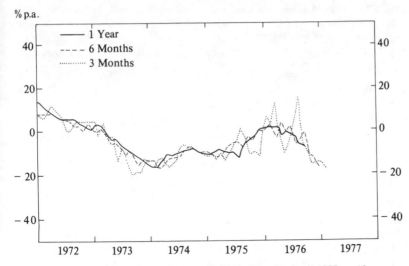

Source: W. Greenwell and Co. Monetary Bulletin No. 65, April 1977, p. 10

Figure 7.2   Rate of change in real M_1 1971–7

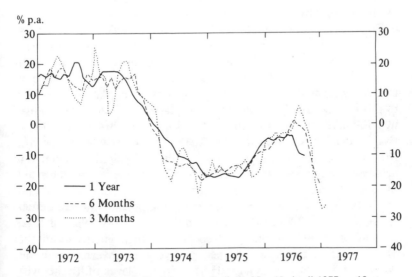

Source: W. Greenwell and Co. Monetary Bulletin No. 65, April 1977, p. 10

Figure 7.3   Rate of change in real sterling M_3 1971–7

Table 7.1   Peak Monetary Squeezes

	M_1 in real terms		M_3 in real terms	
	6-month growth	11-month growth	6-month growth	11-month growth
Current 1976/7	−17% p.a.	−10% p.a.	−18% p.a.	−9% p.a.
	6-month growth	12-month growth	6-month growth	12-month growth
1974	−17% p.a.	−17% p.a.	−18% p.a.	−17% p.a.
1969	−12% p.a.[a]	−9% p.a.	−5% p.a.[a]	−2% p.a.[a]
1965/6	−6% p.a.[a]	−7% p.a.	−3% p.a.[a]	nil[a]
1961	n.a.	−8% p.a.[b]	n.a.	n.a.
1957	n.a.	−10% p.a.	n.a.	n.a.

[a] Based on quarterly data.
[b] Based on monthly data for the current accounts of the London Clearing Banks.

Source: W. Greenwell & Co., *Monetary Bulletin* No. 65 (April 1977).

autumn of 1974. Pessimistic forecasts based on the similar monetary contraction of 1976–7 have been made in the spring of 1977. Table 7.1 indicates why.

But if a modern monetarist would be compelled to award low marks to the UK authorities' contribution to the long-term financial stability of the economy, a modern Keynesian (which is to say an economist with a proper appreciation of Keynes's own priorities) might be tempted to award the authorities no marks at all. Earlier in this chapter an effort was made to place the remarkable changes in UK interest rates since the end of 1965 in an historical perspective. Evidence from two sub-periods, the first of twenty-four months, the second of twenty-three months (truncated slightly the better to achieve a trough-to-peak trend), amply illustrates not only the extent but also the *rate of change* in the entire structure of domestic rates in these years. In the first sub-period Bank Rate was altered by stages from the 5½ per cent level in force in May 1967 to 8 per cent in May 1969, a change associated with an increase of over 40 per cent in the level of yield of five-year government bonds (from 6.4 to 9.0 per cent) and also in the level of twenty-year government bonds (from approximately 6.7 to 9.5 per cent). In the second sub-period chosen the price of the Bank's last resort lending was adjusted in several steps from a level of 5 per cent in January 1972 until a level of 13 per cent was being maintained in December 1973, a fact remarkable to those who had become accustomed in the 1960s to regard a Bank Rate of first 7 per cent, then of 8 per cent, as signifying a sterling crisis of major proportions. The yield on five-year government bonds increased by 130 per cent over the twenty-three months in question (from less than 5.5 per cent to over 11.5 per cent), the yield on twenty-year gilts by 60 per cent (from about 7.7 to 12.4 per cent). Moreover, in the following twelve months further increases saw the yield on five-year bonds rise to 13.5 per cent and that on twenty-year bonds to 17.5 per cent (i.e. an increase of a further 40 per cent in the nominal level) by December 1974. Figure 7.1 above, which depicts the similar trend of the yield on consols, reveals just how astonishing this rise in yields has been even by the standards of the postwar high-rate era. As we shall see presently, increases in interest rates that are large, rapid and incompletely anticipated tend to create special problems for both borrowers and lenders.

7.3   Real versus Nominal Interest Rates in an Era of Rising Prices

To many readers the analysis up to this point may seem to have evaded the basic issue. Let us therefore confront the approach of this chapter with the question which has been avoided up till now: if interest rates in the 1970s have generally been negative in real terms when deflated by the retail price level, so that the borrower/spender has gained at the expense of the saver/lender, how can Ervin Miller's indictment of high nominal rates as a penalty on borrowers possibly be valid? Surely sharp increases in money interest rates are simply the capital market's method of adjusting belatedly to the reality of an inflationary environment by restoring, partially at any rate, the incentive to save and to lend?

It is probably best to tackle these problems in two stages. First, what is the relationship between real and money yields? Traditional monetarist analysis suggests that the anticipated real rate of interest should be equal to the money rate of interest after correction for any change in the price level. But neither Keynes nor a modern monetarist could accept this argument without qualification.[16]

Modern economic thinking provides several reasons why nominal rates fail to adjust by the full amount of the expected rate of inflation, causing the real rate of interest to diminish as inflation accelerates. First, inflation reduces real money balances, which by itself should, in theory, eventually cause the real rate to increase by the same percentage as the money rate. It also reduces the real value of all financial deposits that are of fixed money value and offer a money yield below the current rate of inflation. Therefore the resultant decline in wealth prompts asset-holders to increase their rate of saving (reduce their rate of consumption) in an effort to restore the former level of wealth-holding, and consequently prevents the equilibrium level of the real rate of interest from increasing by the full amount of price inflation.[17] An empirical study undertaken in the Strathclyde region of Scotland by A. A. Tait and E. Burrell found evidence of a real balance effect in the period 1972–4.[18] But intuitively, the extent of the reduction in real balances in the 1970s, evident in Figures 7.2 and 7.3, has been too significant to be wholly offset or ignored in expenditure plans, even in the absence of detailed information about the *reallocative* effects of inflation over the same period which have inflicted a special burden on certain sections of the community. Table 7.2 sets out a price index of changes 1966–76 and includes quarterly data on the personal savings ratio. Although

Table 7.2   Price Index of Changes, 1966–76
Average 1970 = 100

	General index of retail prices	Percentage increase on year earlier	Personal savings* ratio
1966	83.1	3.9	9.2
1967	85.2	2.5	8.5
1968	89.2	4.7	8.0
1969	94.0	5.4	8.1
1970	100.0	6.4	9.0
1971	109.4	9.4	8.6
1972	117.2	7.1	10.2
1973	128.0	9.2	11.4
1974	148.5	16.1	14.2
1975	184.4	24.2	14.8
1976	215.0	16.5	14.2

*Personal saving as a percentage of personal disposable income.

Source: *Economic Trends*, June 1977, Tables 10 and 42.

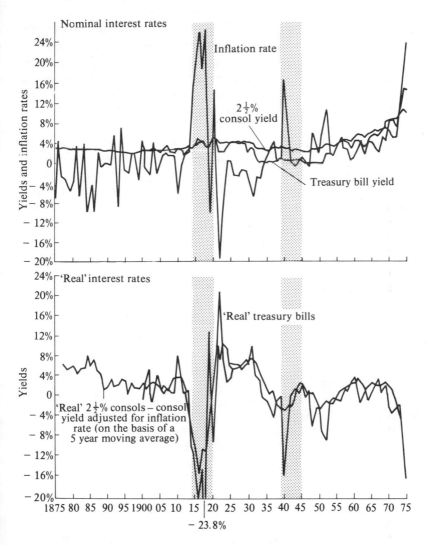

Source: *Barclays Review*, May 1976, centre spread

Figure 7.4   UK Interest rates and inflation, 1875–1975

the change in real balances (moving inversely with retail prices) has not been the only influence on the rate of personal saving, and has almost certainly not been the main reason for the shift in the propensity to save, it is evident that there is a rough similarity in the trends of the two series.

The second main reason is generally assumed to be more important and its empirical support is more solidly based. Alongside the *price-induced wealth effect* we must consider the *interest-induced wealth effect*.[19] The impetus to aggregate spending given by the inflation-induced rise in the investment demand schedule (or the 'marginal efficiency of capital schedule') as increased profits are anticipated by businessmen will be partly offset in the short term by a reduction in the rate of spending associated with the interest-induced wealth effect. If this latter effect alone is operative, the result is to delay rather than to prevent a complete adjustment of nominal rates to the expected rate of inflation; *but* the postponement may be for several years. The total effect of these two varieties of wealth effect operating together has been to reduce the real value of the wealth of the personal sector in particular by a substantial amount. The Bank of England's Economic Intelligence Department tentatively estimated that in 1974 alone the purchasing power of net assets owned by persons was reduced by very roughly 20 per cent, or some £40 thousand million – a sum well over half of personal disposable income in 1974 – by the combined effect of general inflation, the slow-down in house prices and the fall in value (rise in yields) of stocks and shares.[20] Any conclusions about data on wealth are inevitably highly tentative, but the Bank of England's study supports the view that *the value of financial assets* rather than total wealth has had a significant influence on spending since the mid-1960s when the estimates began and was responsible for a large part of the unforeseen rise in saving in 1974 and 1975. A *portfolio balance effect*, whereby households attempt not only to increase wealth in an absolute sense but also to restore the ratio of financial to total assets to its former level, will also act to curb expenditures and therefore, presumably, to contribute to the failure of real interest rates to adjust completely in the short run. From a practical point of view it matters very little whether spending is curtailed because, as the Radcliffe Report liquidity analysis would have it, the 'enabling power'[21] or 'financial strength' of household balance sheets is so drastically reduced that expenditure plans are inhibited, or whether, to apply the logic of the portfolio adjustment process, any reduction of liquid assets below the level desired for transactions and precautionary purposes causes expenditure to be cut back until the desired proportions have been re-established. In Table 7.3, which provides information on different aspects of personal saving, it can be seen that in 1973 and 1974 the propensity to hold financial assets increased much more sharply than the savings ratio.

Table 7.3   Personal Saving and the Propensity to Accumulate Financial Assets
£ million (rounded to nearest £50 million)

	Personal saving (1)	Personal sector financial surplus (S–I)[a] (2)	Personal savings ratio %[b] (3)	'Household' saving ratio %[c] (4)	Col. (2) ÷ Col. (1)[d] (5)
			%	%	%
1966	2,450	1,150	9.2	8.1	47
1967	2,350	950	8.5	7.5	39
1968	2,350	650	8.0	6.7	27
1969	2,550	800	8.1	6.8	31
1970	3,100	1,300	9.0	7.6	41
1971	3,300	800	8.6	7.1	24
1972	4,500	1,350	10.2	8.8	29
1973	5,900	2,500	11.4	9.7	42
1974	8,600	5.300	14.2	11.7	62
1975	11,000	7,100	14.8	12.0	64
1976	12,100	7,600	14.2	n.a.	63

[a] Savings minus capital expenditure plus net capital transfers by the personal sector
[b] Personal saving as a proportion of total disposable income
[c] Personal saving as a proportion of personal disposable income after allowing for stock appreciation and depreciation of capital stock (other than houses).
[d] The division is made with original rather than rounded data.

Sources: *Economic Trends*, June 1977, Table 10; *Bank of England Quarterly Bulletin*, March 1977, p. 27, Table B.

A third main reason advanced for the incomplete adjustment of nominal rates to inflationary expectations is that such expectations adapt only slowly to changes in the rate of inflation.[22] Since the expected rate of inflation is not directly observable, a useful proxy is that the expected rate is equal to a weighted average of current and past rates of inflation, where the weights decline geometrically over time. When inflation accelerates, as in the 1970s, the 'expected future rate' will therefore tend to lag behind current realities since memories of times of more stable prices will act as a slight drag on the upward adjustment of rates. Finally (and here too there may be a partial explanation of Table 7.3), many households are in practice 'locked into' contractual savings arrangements with life assurance companies or pension funds, notwithstanding any decline in the real rates of return on funds channelled to these institutions and on-lent in the capital market.

The case for increasing real rates of interest in the United Kingdom to some positive level irrespective of the rise in money rates necessary to achieve this goal has been made by Peera, Wann, Barr and others; more rigorous expositions of the argument applied to less developed countries suffering from rapid inflation have been provided by, e.g. Shaw and McKinnon.[23] Peter Wann, for example, argues that, apart from the stimulus to saving, 'there is an added incentive to the optimum use of capital with the fullest utilization of plant and machinery, a focusing of attention on areas of research which may lead to capital-saving inventions, and an inducement to liquidate speculative holdings of land or raw materials.'[24] The argument against sharp increases in rates and against sustained high levels of money rates of interest which this chapter seeks to construct is necessarily very different in character.

7.4   Rising Interest Rates and the Company Sector

An analysis of the UK company sector benefits from taking into account the *double impact* of a rise in interest rates. First, the illiquidity of company portfolio assets and liabilities rises and the vulnerability of many companies to further financial pressure is markedly increased, their expenditure plans inhibited. Second, the increased interest charges (whether they are negative in real terms matters very little in this context) may represent a substantial imposition on company outgoings if (i) indebtedness has increased to record levels in a preceding period of business expansion and refunding is necessary at the new interest level; (ii) the expected earnings out of which such payments must be made have been diminished by the onset of a business recession; (iii) the deterioration of the liquidity position of the company's balance sheet has created a portfolio disequilibrium which requires that liquid assets be built up and short-term loans repaid, i.e. that some part of operating balances be diverted to achieving a preferred structure of assets and liabilities. Thus, in a sense, A, the 'cost of borrowing effect' of increased interest rates, achieves its impact because B, the 'general liquidity effect' of the same change, has made them vulnerable to pressure from this quarter. Effect B 'sets up' the company for effect A.

The basic assumption of this chapter is that changes in liquidity influence consumption and investment spending. This premise is widely accepted. The *nature* of the connection, however, remains controversial.

The liquidity concept requires an explanation. The liquidity of a portfolio refers to the ability of the asset-holder to pay off quickly any unexpected obligation that cannot be postponed. Liquidity refers to the 'moneyness' of the portfolio. In a slightly different sense it refers to the asset-holder's 'financial strength',[25] representing his estimated command over additional real resources on the assumption that his beliefs are well founded in (i) the realizability of his financial assets and (ii) in his borrowing potential.

Let us at this stage replace 'asset-holder' with 'company', bearing in mind that certain of the arguments about liquidity may be equally relevant to the activities of households or financial institutions.

The liquidity of the balance sheet is generally assumed to refer to the current position, subjectively assessed, rather than to the company's desired portfolio structure or need for cash. It embraces both sides of the balance sheet, and is a *net* assessment, the current position being determined by 'the liquidity characteristics and money amount of assets owned relative to the maturity schedule and money amount of debts owed.'[26] However, the importance of the liquidity approach emerges most clearly in the context of cycles in economic activity and in particular at turning points in the cycle when the interaction of 'financial decisions' and 'real decisions' is often suddenly thrown into relief. For analytical purposes it is convenient to separate three interrelated components of a company balance sheet: (i) the liquidity of financial assets (neglecting physical assets such as stocks of finished goods, which possess their own liquidity attributes), (ii) the ability to borrow, and (iii) the illiquidity of company debts. The last set of reliable balance sheet data on the whole of the UK private sector takes us only up to 1966[27] and, in spite of the quality of the estimates, valuation and other conceptual problems make even the limited comparison offered below a hazardous exercise. However, if we award share capital the status of honorary debt, then company financial liabilities in 1966 were approximately double the size of company financial asset holdings, whereas in the balance sheet of the personal sector financial liabilities were only about one-fifth of the size of financial assets. From Table 7.4 and other evidence it would appear that the liquidity position of the company sector, *in a purely quantitative sense*, has subsequently deteriorated.

The principal concern of this chapter is with the impact of increases in interest rates, not only on borrowing costs – to which we turn presently – but on lending flows and on the capacity of companies to adjust their portfolios to desired positions in the conditions of uncertainty and illiquidity associated with such changes. Uncertainty and economic pessimism may, as perhaps in 1973 and 1974, be attributable to despondency at the world economic situation and to what is seen as the inconsistency of government policies in a general sense rather than to changes in interest rates specifically. Interest rates may therefore be interpreted as the occasion of, rather than the reason for, 'foul-weather' (or recessional) illiquidity, which has more profound causes and which is immediately attributable to a variety of counter-cyclical official measures. There is merit in this argument, yet because the role of interest rates is generally understated rather than overstated it is to be hoped that the acknowledged bias of this narrative will be accepted as a corrective rather than a simple-hearted failure to appreciate the role of fiscal policy, debt management and other government contributions to financial pressure.[28]

Generalization about the company sector has very limited value, but before we turn our attention directly towards the plight of small concerns in conditions of financial instability several general points may be made which have a special bearing on their balance sheet positions.

Of the three components of balance sheet liquidity identified above the ability to borrow and the illiquidity of debts are most likely to determine whether a struggling company can survive in a severe business recession. Marketable bonds and securities with fluctuating capital values were less than 20 per cent of company financial asset holdings in 1966 and the typical small company may hold none at all. The liquidity of encashable financial assets such as bank or build-

Table 7.4 UK Industrial and Commercial Companies
£ million (rounded to nearest £100 million)

	Local authority temporary debt, Treasury bills, etc.	Selected liquid assets (end-year figures of outstanding amounts)		Total identified	Less bank advances	Net total	Change on preceding year
		Deposits with building societies and finance houses	Bank deposits				
1962	1,000	200	2,200	3,500	−2,400	+1,100	
1963	1,100	200	2,600	3,900	−2,800	+1,100	0
1964	1,000	300	2,600	3,900	−3,300	+600	−500
1965	800	300	2,800	3,900	−3,800	+100	−500
1966	700	300	2,900	3,800	−4,000	−200	−300
1967	700	300	3,300	4,300	−4,200	+100	+300
1968	600	300	3,600	4,500	−4,600	−100	−200
1969	500	400	3,400	4,300	−5,100	−700	−600
1970	400	400	3,800	4,500	−5,900	−1,400	−700
1971	500	400	4,700	5,700	−6,400	−800	+600
1972	500	300	6,900	7,700	−9,700	−200	−1,200
1973	600	300	9,100	10,000	−14,400	−4,400	−2,400
1974	600	200	9,000	9,800	−18,000	−8,200	−3,800
1975	800	300	10,700	11,800	−17,700	−5,900	+3,300
1976	1000	300	12,500	13,800	−21,000	−7,200	−1,300

Sources: *Financial Statistics, Economic Trends*, various issues.

ing society deposits is unaffected by rapidly rising interest rates. On the other hand, when *errors of judgement*[29] about the prospective yield of expenditure that is wholly or partly loan-financed, or about the stability of future profits occur, the lender–borrower relationship between financial and business firms may be vital to the latter's continued existence, as indeed may the involvement of other businesses, operating through cash-flow interdependence. Stated simply, over-optimism induced by buoyant markets may cause borrowers *and* lenders to underestimate the likelihood of a sharp deterioration in the financial strength of the balance sheet of a company that accepts a greater burden of debt relative to its income than ever before, i.e. to underestimate both the risk of default and the risk of illiquidity. The successful raising of funds may depend not so much on the offer made by the borrower and *his* estimate of the potential yield of loan-financed spending, as on the *lender's* generally less sanguine estimate.[30] When lending institutions permit the company sector as a whole to accept a debt–income ratio that past experience suggests is dangerously high, their responsibility for limiting the consequences of forecasting errors made at (what subsequently proves to be) the top of the boom is plain – and here it must be conceded (again this is germane to the exceptional trauma of the economic system in 1973 and 1974) that novel and unpredictable outcomes cannot sensibly be contained in that part of a risk premium that is based on a projection of past experience.

Fortunately, the UK banking system has a traditional obligation to prevent industrial and commercial companies from suffering the full consequences of errors in their anticipation of profits and in their related capacity to tolerate rising ratios of external debt to current investment. This obligation is, at once, an aspect of the Government's stated commitment to stable economic growth, to the Bank of England's acceptance of a support function in the financial system, which is normally reassumed after exercise of the control function has caused financial disruption, and, in some measure, to the responsibility, not to mention the self-interest, that is part and parcel of the lender–borrower relationship. Unfortunately, as we shall see, in the case of the small company, lender's self-interest and company fortunes need not naturally coincide, and, as the ability to borrow is curtailed, so does the illiquidity of debts tend to become effective.

The illiquidity of debts is represented by the extent to which money owed reduces the financial strength of the asset-holder's balance sheet and results principally from the combined effect of rising borrowers' and lenders' risks[31] as a crisis in confidence – generally emanating from a powerful squeeze in the money markets and rapidly escalating interest rates – gets under way. The maturity of debts, which in a period of expansion and easy credit conditions were readily renewed by financial lenders, suddenly becomes effective. Although previously bank or other borrowing had required no matching liquid assets on the other side of the balance sheet, the outstanding loan may now become a virtual deduction from income as repayment falls due.

Borrowers under severe pressure are, by definition, trapped for the moment in a portfolio imbalance with outstanding short-term indebtedness, and indeed may be compelled to accept an even less preferred balance sheet position to avoid bankruptcy. To quote R. N. McKean, because of the increased pressure of short-term indebtedness,

debtors then have to resort to distress selling of assets, distress calling of other debts owed to them, in the general struggle to restore cash balances. . . . If financial institutions and others start selling long-term investments, the debtor corporations may not feel extra pressure, but yields will go up, and new financing by long-term, as well as by short-term, loans is more difficult to obtain. Increased illiquidity of debts implies reduced ability to borrow, whether for refinancing or for other purposes.[32]

The 'distress calling of other debts owed' by businesses under severe financial pressure may, of course, be unsuccessful (i) either if, as is likely, their trade debtors are experiencing similar pressures to the financially vulnerable creditor concerns and are unable to comply with the appeal; or (ii) if the trade debtors in question are large companies with powerful resources which use their bargaining position to improve their liquidity at the expense of smaller trading partners. A company that is a small and replaceable supplier to large businesses but which considers other large concerns to be its indispensable customers is liable to be a substantial, if most reluctant, net credit-giver. In a situation of recession illiquidity the ability of a company to pay its debts becomes more closely connected with the prompt payment of money owed to it by other companies and households. The size of an unanticipated cash requirement which can cause financial embarrassment is therefore diminished. The vulnerability of a company to higher interest charges, as well as to increased down payments or even enhanced collateral requirements, is inevitably greater in such circumstances.

Interest rates as a business cost and indeed as an element in cost-push inflation ('interest-push')[33] which should not be ignored make an important claim on our attention nowadays for three main reasons. First, the order of magnitude of interest charges in the 1970s has been quite different from 1959, when the Radcliffe Report argued that interest payments were insignificant relative to other costs and to the risks involved in everyday business operations, and the interest-induced changes in company liquidity are correspondingly more severe; no economist could today dismiss the associated effects on the availability of internal and external funds as of little account. Second, interest rate increases have taken place against a background of long-term deterioration of company sector liquidity in a quantitative sense, which does not take into account the particularly sharp *qualitative* declines in liquidity in, for example, 1969 and 1974. The net liquidity total of selected liquid assets minus bank advances is set out in Table 7.4 above. The series commences in 1962 rather than 1966 in an attempt to show how far the liquid asset position of UK companies has altered since the early 1960s.

The third reason is that interest payments have become a much more important item in company outgoings since 1966. In this, as in other aspects, the UK economic system is similar to that of the United States (see Table 1.1). As a rough guide to the growth in importance of interest payments to financial institutions columns (6) and (7) of Table 7.5 below offer two alternative ratios: the first, payments of interest etc., excluding dividends on ordinary shares, to financial institutions as a percentage of total company income from the United Kingdom and abroad; the second, with the same numerator divided by gross trading profits from UK operations minus stock appreciation. Since the receipts from sales of stocks that have increased in value are generally employed in restocking, there is a case for arguing that column (7) offers the 'truer' insight into the change in the relative importance of interest rates as a charge on available income. Column (7) shows that the ratio of interest costs (and other payments which cannot be separated from interest in company sector statistics) to gross trading profits net of stock appreciation in 1974 was more than three times the size of the same ratio in 1966. Column (8) shows a change in the ratio of total pay-

Table 7.5 The Changing Importance of Interest Payments as a Claim on the Income of UK Industrial and Commercial Companies £ million (rounded off to nearest £100 million), seasonally adjusted

	Total income from UK and abroad (1)	Gross trading profits from UK operations only after deducting stock appreciation (2)	Stock appreciation (3)	Payments of interest etc., excl. dividends on ordinary shares (4)	Payments of interest etc. to financial companies (5)	Col. (5) ÷ Col. (1)* (6)	Col. (5) ÷ Col. (2)* (7)	Col. (4) ÷ Col. (2) (8)
						%	%	%
1966	6,000	4,700	300	900	600	9.3	11.9	19.8
1967	6,000	4,900	100	900	600	9.1	11.3	19.4
1968	6,900	5,200	500	1,100	700	9.6	12.6	20.6
1969	7,200	5,200	600	1,200	800	10.5	14.5	23.4
1970	7,700	5,300	900	1,300	800	10.4	15.2	24.6
1971	8,600	6,200	800	1,300	800	9.2	12.7	21.1
1972	10,100	7,300	1,100	1,500	1,000	8.9	13.3	20.8
1973	13,600	7,800	2,500	2,400	1,800	13.3	23.1	30.3
1974	15,500	6,900	4,100	3,300	2,700	17.6	39.4	48.5
1975	15,000	7,600	4,100	3,300	2,700	17.9	35.0	43.4
1976	18,800	9,400	5,400	3,800	3,100	16.6	33.1	40.5

*The division is made with original rather than rounded data.

Source: *Economic Trends*, May 1977, Table 58.

ments of interest etc. to gross trading profits net of stock appreciation from less than 20 per cent to well over 40 per cent in 1974. By going back to 1959 even more emphatic comparisons can be made. Companies' 'income-gearing', measured by the ratio of interest payments to real pre-tax profits, increased more than sixfold between 1959 and 1974.[34] But what catches the eye, whichever of the ratios of Table 7.5 we examine, is the astonishing jump in the relative significance of interest payments between 1972 and 1974. Whether we focus on changes in interest costs or on the level of annual outgoings they now represent for the company sector, the insignificance of the incentive/disincentive effect can obviously no longer be taken for granted on the basis of the results of surveys that are twenty years old, particularly when both the liquidity position and the profitability of UK companies have suffered a massive deterioration in the interim.

We must be careful not to exaggerate the importance of this rise in the relative significance of interest costs as a deduction from company income. It is generally emphasized that the net of tax cost of fixed-interest finance is virtually half the gross cost, though, as we shall see presently, companies most in need are often unable to claim this tax benefit. Again, if we switch our attention from 'income-gearing' ratios (relating indebtedness or interest payments to company earnings) to 'capital-gearing' ratios (relating indebtedness to capital assets valued at *replacement* cost) the situation seems much less alarming.[35] For example, if company indebtedness is valued at market value rather than nominal value the level may be seen to have declined from 21.2 per cent in 1966 to 16.0 per cent in 1976, although bank advances as a proportion of total company borrowing shot up from around 38 per cent in 1966 to over 70 per cent in 1976.

However three further comments are in order. First, company earnings fluctuate, their decline tending to coincide with a rise in interest rates signifying a financial crisis and the onset of a business recession. The variability of the profits of small firms is greater than that of large,[36] but their capacity for balance sheet adjustment during a credit squeeze is much more limited. A prudent company which sets a limit to the ratio of interest payments to earnings and which was already on or close to this limit should therefore attempt to reduce its outstanding debt in the same proportion as (or, if profits are declining, in a greater proportion than) the rate of interest rises. According to this style of reasoning, small firms may be especially vulnerable in this situation. Second, if we assume that the market value of the equity of a company is a more appropriate measure of the valuation of its physical capital assets than replacement cost (this good accounting procedure is in accord with the practice of Keynes in the *Treatise*), then management's relief at contemplating their 'capital-gearing' ratio in 1974 or 1975 would presumably evaporate. Third, if we arrive at a valuation of company-retained earnings in terms of their equivalent in distributable cash (the equivalent cash distributions, or ECD, approach), by multiplying them by the ratio of the rate of return that a company is expected to earn on retentions over the rate of return on alternative financial assets, then a doubling of interest rates must, *ceteris paribus*, in effect *halve* the value of the cash equivalent in the hands of the shareholders.[37]

7.5 Illiquidity, Declining Profitability and the Plight of the Small Firm

Two important studies of the UK company sector were published in the March and June issues of the *Bank of England Quarterly Bulletin* in 1976.[38] Their findings go a long way to substantiate a belief in the influence of financial variables upon company expenditures which the Bank of England made plain as long ago as March 1967 in an earlier analysis of company sector liquidity.[39] In particular, it has been discovered that *relative* profitability (defined as the ratio of the rate of return to the cost of capital and described in column (3) of Table 7.6 as the financial valuation ratio) appears to be a very significant explanatory variable of quarterly changes in fixed investment by UK companies. Three further factors appear to have become critically important since 1973: (i) sharply reduced profits, which have diminished expectations of profit as well as the availability of much preferred internal finance; (ii) greatly increased nominal rates of interest, which have created cash-flow problems for financially vulnerable companies (see Table 7.5 above); and (iii) the inability of companies to receive the full benefit of specially designed fiscal incentives because their 'profit exhaustion' does not enable them to qualify immediately for tax relief on interest pay-

Table 7.6   The Cost of Capital, Rate of Return and Financial Valuation Ratio

	Post-tax real rate of return on capital[a] (1)	Post-tax real cost of capital[b] (2)	Valuation ratio[c] (3)
	% p.a.	% p.a. (end year)	
1960	9.7	8.8	1.08
1961	8.1	8.3	0.95
1962	7.6	6.3	1.20
1963	9.2	5.8	1.55
1964	9.3	6.5	1.36
1965	6.6	5.3	1.14
1966	5.5	5.7	0.93
1967	5.9	5.0	1.17
1968	5.3	3.9	1.33
1969	4.1	4.0	0.99
1970	3.4	4.4	0.72
1971	4.3	4.6	0.90
1972	5.3	5.1	0.99
1973	4.5	6.1	0.69
1974	2.2	6.6	0.30
1975	3.3	5.9	0.50
1976[d]	2.9	6.8	0.40

[a] Column (1) represents the tax-adjusted historic cost rate of return after revaluation of the capital stock and capital consumption but net of stock appreciation. It is a 'forward-looking' calculation which takes into account all current investment incentives. The treatment of tax relief on stocks is consistent with its treatment in the calculation of the cost of capital. See *Bank of England Quarterly Bulletin*, March 1976, pp. 41–3 and 48–50.
[b] Column (2) is a general measure of the cost of capital which incorporates both equity finance and borrowing. Details of this calculation are given in the *Bank of England Quarterly Bulletin*, June 1976, pp. 203–5.
[c] Since the rate of return is the ratio of profits to physical capital employed at replacement cost (each adjusted for tax), while the corresponding cost of capital is the ratio of the same profit figure to the financial valuation of companies, *relative profitability* is simply the ratio of the financial valuation to the tax-adjusted replacement cost of capital.
[d] Provisional estimates.

Source: *Bank of England Quarterly Bulletin*, June 1977, p. 156, Table A.

ments, thereby effectively doubling the cost of capital to the disadvantaged company.

The picture is one of growing portfolio imbalance in the company sector which became critical in 1974. A study of key financial ratios derived from the balance sheets of *large* companies[40] shows a significant decline in each ratio between 1965 and 1974; the ratio of shareholders' interest to fixed assets, for example, fell from 1.23 in 1965 to less than 1.0 in 1974. When the *average* ratio falls below the level normally described as the tolerable minimum, as occurred in this case, it is evident that a significant minority of companies must have been experiencing liquidity problems of extreme severity; bankruptcies reached record levels in 1974. The massive reduction in levels of stocks (as well as in fixed investment) and the net repayment of bank advances during 1975 are symptoms of companies' efforts to eliminate portfolio imbalance and move to a preferred, and more liquid, balance sheet position. It is also significant that financial pressure had eased sufficiently in 1975 to enable the average company to carry out this adjustment of the structure of assets and liabilities; at its most elemental a company in serious financial difficulties cannot afford to repay bank loans, which is to say it is in no position to *save*.

It is time to attempt to justify certain emphases of our earlier discussion of financial instability in which figured the somewhat improbable figure of the euphoric British businessman. Certainly many of the financial phenomena of recent years can be satisfactorily explained with the help of traditional tools of Keynes's analysis of the trade cycle. The sharp rise in liquidity preference associated with the collapse of the marginal efficiency of investment and of stock market values in 1974 is described by the precautionary motive broadly defined.[41] On the other hand, the finance demand for money,[42] which describes the financing requirement of planned expenditures, contracted and with it the demand for overdraft finance with which it is particularly associated. A sharp rise in the rate of interest, it will be remembered, was said to produce a variety of 'effects'. (i) The desire of financial institutions and other lenders to make loans to the private sector is reduced by the interest-induced decline in asset values, which at once unbalances and renders illiquid lenders' portfolios; the uncertainty about the financial and economic climate engendered by the move raises the risk premium on loans to households and companies and sharpens discrimination between preferred and less preferred customers; the former effect(s) reduces the supply of loanable funds, the latter diminishes the eligible demand for loans. (ii) At the same time the desire to borrow is inhibited by the change: in the new issue market underwriters, acting as agents for prospective borrowers and sensitive to changes in the financial climate, advise against what they believe to be a relatively expensive fixed-interest commitment;[43] alternatively, an issue of equities will raise a smaller capital sum on given future earnings. The borrower is, like the lender, afflicted by an uncertainty about economic prospects which in his case manifests itself in a desire for greater liquidity and a growing reluctance to borrow and spend which is frequently fostered by the banks and other lending institutions. In other words, the lender may *induce* pessimistic (or, in different circumstances, optimistic) expectations which shift the schedule of the demand for loanable funds, already diminished by stiffer credit standards, further to the left.[44] The demand for capital goods itself is of course reduced by the rise in the rate of interest functioning as a rate of discount because the increased discount rate diminishes the present value of the stream of prospective returns from investment. Moreover, if the rate of inflation is exceptionally high and *expected to fall*, this prospect will raise the subjective cost of long-term fixed-interest debt to the borrower far above the difference between the relevant current nominal rate of interest and the present rate of inflation.[45] Finally, in conditions of uncertainty, when borrower and lender alike are anxious to guard against increased illiquidity and the possibility of default, internal and external finance are *complements*, not substitutes,[46] and financial ratios may limit a company's propensity to increase its indebtedness. This constraint is reinforced by the fact that, as shown by King's recent study[47] and consistently with our argument about the burden of borrowers' and lenders' risk, external finance is much more expensive than internal funding. In such circumstances financial gearing ratios may become genuine barriers to expansion.

The reasons for changes in the flow of new issues by UK companies (see Table 7.7) are presumed to be fairly complex and a proper analysis would take into account changes in stocks, trends in profitability and retained earnings, changes in the availability of bank loans, fiscal incentives, etc. However, if we compare the trend in company issues with the trend in interest rates (see Figure 7.1), employing that most casual form of empiricism, visual inspection, the hypothesis that a sharp rise in interest rates will tend to be followed by a decline in new issues does seem to be more or less borne out by what actually occurred in the new issue market between 1966 and 1976. It should also be remembered that the *real* value of given sums raised by new issues declined significantly between

Table 7.7 Capital Issues by UK Companies
£ million; quarterly figures rounded to the nearest £5 million

	1st quarter	2nd	3rd	4th	Total
1966	210	100	245	85	640 (75% debt)[b]
1967	85	95	155	85	420 (82% debt)
1968	35	200	260	180	675 (46% debt)
1969	245	225	30	95	590 (67% debt)
1970	75	80	70	150	380 (82% debt)[a]
1971	115	115	180	280	695 (53% debt)
1972	200	430	185	150	970 (32% debt)
1973	65	80	35	30	200 (20% debt)
1974	0 (2.4)	30	30	95	160 (26% debt)
1975	260	475	565	280	1,580 (14% debt)
1976	410	465	180	105	1,160 (8% debt)

[a]The total is a rounded version of original figures, not a total of rounded quarterly issue figures.
[b]Total debt as a percentage of total issues.

Source: *Midland Bank Review*, February issues, 1967–77.

1966 and 1976. For example, at 1970 prices the value of new issues was £730 million in 1966 and £530 million in 1976, not £625 million and £1,160 million.

A crucial element in Keynes's thinking was the importance of re-allocative effects between and within sectors in determining the *level* as well as the distribution of economic activity[48] – though there is little scope for such effects in the consolidated macroeconomic models which commonly pass as 'Keynesian'. Households have had much greater success than companies in increasing or maintaining real income levels between 1966 and 1975 (though 1976 is believed to have witnessed a reduction in the living standards of a typical adult male worker of between 4 and 8 per cent): real personal disposable income was 28 per cent greater in 1975 than in 1966; real post-tax company earnings were 25 per cent higher but, without the help of special tax relief on stock appreciation, would have been about a quarter of the size of the 1966 figure in 1975 and virtually zero in 1974. Real national disposable income declined by almost 5 per cent in 1974, but real personal disposable income actually *increased* by over 1 per cent in that year, chiefly at the expense of companies.

Reallocative effects within the company sector in 1966–75 may have produced consequences almost as significant in their fashion for many small firms. The theory of financial instability articulated earlier most plausibly portrays the effects of financial pressure on the financially vulnerable small firm. Financial vulnerability has been defined, e.g. by Meltzer,[49] as being attributable to a firm's small size and relatively illiquid balance sheet position. This is correct in so far as small size tends to place firms in a relatively high-risk category among loan applicants; compared with large enterprises, their profitability is on average lower, the variability of their profits greater, their sales more volatile, their opportunities for diversification more limited, their failure rate higher. For these reasons small firms should, theoretically, suffer before, and suffer more than, larger concerns when credit standards are stiffened at a time of rising interest rates; as less preferred loan applicants, they should be more subject to discriminatory rationing of credit when the supply of loans to the company sector is outstripped by applications which, in the absence of a supply side constraint, would all be considered acceptable. A recent investigation revealed that small firms that most needed overdraft finance to relieve the pressure on their liquidity position apparently suffered most from heightened standards of credit-worthiness (trained presumably on their illiquid balance sheet position which prompted the request for additional finance) and from credit rationing during the years of the credit squeeze 1969–70.[50]

But financial vulnerability is based not on an illiquid balance sheet structure in a quantitative sense – the Committee of Enquiry into Small Firms (the Bolton Report)[51] found that small companies in the United Kingdom have higher-than-average liquid asset ratios – but on the tendency of the balance sheet of the financially vulnerable firm to *become* highly illiquid, in a fashion that is not readily reversible, in an economic recession. The essence of financial vulnerability is the inability of the illiquid firm to escape from its situation of portfolio imbalance by making adjustments towards a preferred structure of assets and liabilities appropriate to the altered economic climate. Such firms are unable to create a net inflow of trade credit in a credit squeeze; they may also be incapable of increasing or even maintaining their levels of bank overdraft finance, 'not least, because of the possible pre-emption by larger firms of available credit as they push up borrowing to previously under-utilized overdraft levels.'[52]

The evidence indicated that when credit was tightened in 1969–70 the smallest and most illiquid companies in the United Kingdom provided the largest increase in net trade credit, whereas the large and highly liquid companies reduced their net trade credit by the largest amount. The behaviour of financially strong UK companies therefore conformed much more closely to the theory of coercive trade credit of J. K. Galbraith than to the suggestion of the Radcliffe Report that, by tapping formerly under-utilized overdraft facilities and rechannelling the funds so obtained to small and needy businesses, large companies could effect a redistribution of funds which would soften the discriminatory impact of financial stringency.[53] In practice the large companies that possess the greatest measure of control over the structure of their assets and liabilities tend to offer credit grants only as part of a self-interested effort to promote sales after involuntary stock-building.

A study by the National Economic Development Council published in May 1975 provided further evidence, based on a much smaller sample, of the discriminatory effect of tight money and financial instability on small firms. The financial conservatism of small concerns reportedly caused many of them to limit investment plans to the availability of internal finance, which is to say that, in the declining profit situation of the 1970s, especially in the second half of 1974, when most companies felt 'highly constricted', they tended not to engage in new capital formation at all.[54] A majority of the (large and small) companies that responded declared that they had felt significantly constrained in their investment and financing decisions by their highly illiquid balance sheet position (for example a debt–equity ratio of less than 1.0) in 1973–4.[55] The principal complaint by all companies, though most heartfelt perhaps from the small companies, was that uncertainty about government policy tended to kill any desire to expand and that this factor was even more important than the cost and availability of finance (though many believed that after 1974 these factors would also be important deterrents to investment).[56] In the language of this chapter, the illiquidity not only of company balance sheets but of the economy as a whole was cited as the major barrier to expansion. The chief responsibility for the situation was attributed to the climate of financial instability resulting directly from government policies of economic management. Indeed, it is an interesting reflection on the economic management of the United Kingdom since 1966 that growing acceptance of the importance of monetary policy (defined to include changes in the cost and availability of loans as well as in the money stock itself) has been accompanied by monetary measures that have made a markedly greater contribution to an uncertain and frequently repressive financial climate than policies of the previous fifteen years when the rates of change in money supply and interest rates were widely regarded as irrelevant to the decisions of the real economic actors. Moreover, it is now Keynesian orthodoxy that over-rapid growth in the money supply is associated with higher rather than lower (as 'Keynesian' textbooks would have it) rates of interest,[57] so that such policies are doubly damned.

7.6 Conclusions

Between 1951 and 1973 the speed of the policy-promoted cyclical upswing tended to increase with successive cycles.[58] Although the virtues of a stable financial environment are well known, they probably bear repetition. A steady and predictable rate of economic expansion as the economy emerges from recession should help to restore business confidence, enhancing factor mobility, reducing unemployment and avoiding bottlenecks in production;[59] there should be greater price stability, reduced pressure on the balance of payments and, logically, higher levels of investment and greater productivity. Restoration of company profitability and planning confidence in the United Kingdom may also require other measures in areas this chapter has ignored, not to mention an acceptance of the realities of inflation-accounting; but financial stability must surely be the bedrock of any enduring revival.

FOOTNOTES

1. J. M. Keynes, 'How to Avoid a Slump,' *The Times*, 14 January 1937. Cited by D. E. Moggridge and S. K. Howson, 'Keynes on Monetary Policy, 1910–1946,' *Oxford Economic Papers*, July 1974, p. 240. At the time that Keynes's articles were published in *The Times* prices were rising at an annual rate of over 10 per cent. The reply of R. G. Hawtrey, who was the Treasury adviser on economic matters, is also of interest. He wrote, 'Cheap money is a condition of revival from depression. But once revival threatens to degenerate into inflation the reason for cheap money may vanish' (The Hawtrey Papers, Hawtrey's Treasury Memorandum on Keynes's articles in *The Times*, 'How to Avoid a Slump,' p. 9). Since a single quotation, however trenchant, may not necessarily convince readers of Keynes's abhorrence, in the interests of 'sustaining the boom,' of high interest rates, perhaps I might appropriately reproduce a footnote from an unpublished paper by G. C. Peden and the present writer.

In 'A Note on the Long-Term Rate of Interest in Relation to the Conversion Scheme,' *Economic Journal*, September 1932, p. 415, Keynes wrote, 'A reduction of the long-term rate of interest to a low level is probably the most necessary of all measures if we are to escape from the slump and secure a lasting revival of enterprise.' A survey of Keynes' written or reported ideas in *The Times* and *The Economist* reveals his unswerving advocacy in every year of the era of 'cheap money,' 1932–39, that long-term interest rates be lowered *yet further* from the (historically) exceptionally low levels which were maintained from 1932 onwards, though his main aim in 1937 was to persuade the Treasury to adopt policies which would prevent the long-term rate from rising. As *The Economist* observed, following Keynes' address to the Annual General Meeting of the National Mutual Life Assurance Society in February 1936, 'Mr Keynes has an established reputation as the prophet of low interest rates,' adding, 'Mr Keynes was as insistent as ever on the urgency of a further reduction in the long-term rate of interest. Not for the first time he strongly criticised the Treasury in this regard.' *The Economist*, February 22, 1936, p. 404. For references to Keynes' repeated argument that long-term rates be lowered see *e.g. The Economist*, July 22, 1933, p. 171, February 24, 1934, p. 394, November 24, 1934, p. 976, February 27, 1937, p. 478, February 26, 1938, p. 446, July 23, 1938, p. 159. See also *The Economist*, 'Letters to the Editor,' January 30, 1937, p. 240, February 13, 1937, March 5, 1938, pp. 499–500, July 16, 1938, p. 121. See also *The Times*, March 14, 1933, p. 16, January 13, 1937, pp. 13–14, March 11, 1939, pp. 17–18.

It is true that earlier Keynes was a self-professed 'dear money man' advocating that Bank Rate be raised as high as 10 per cent if necessary and kept at this level, perhaps for years, to check inflation (February 1920). See, e.g. Susan Howson, ' "A Dear Money Man": Keynes on Monetary Policy, 1920', *The Economic Journal*, June 1973. His belief in the efficacy of monetary policy continued; his views on the necessity for, or inevitability of 'dear money' as a counter-inflationary measure altered irrevocably. His views on the necessity for maintaining low interest rates in the 'boom' are perhaps unique. They are also unequivocal. As he wrote in his *General Theory*, 'Thus the remedy for the boom is not a higher rate of interest but a lower rate of interest. For that may enable the so-called boom to last ... A boom is a situation in which over-optimism triumphs over a rate of interest which, in a cooler light would be seen to be excessive' (*The General Theory of Employment, Interest and Money*, London, Macmillan, 1936, p. 322).

2. This appropriate description is the title of a recent book by Frances Cairncross and Hamish Macrae, London, Methuen, 1975.
3. Keynes wrote in his *General Theory* of 'the most dangerous technique for the maintenance of equilibrium which can possibly be imagined, namely the technique of bank rate coupled with a rigid parity of foreign exchanges' (ibid. p. 339).
4. For data on crisis lending rates see: B. Mitchell and P. Deane, *Abstract of British Historical Statistics and Financial Statistics, Bank of England Statistical Abstract* No. 2; *Bank of England Quarterly Bulletin*, March 1977 and, most particularly, Table 2 in Brian Reading's article 'Too High Interest Rates,' *National Westminster Bank Quarterly Review*, February 1970, p. 11.
5. From 13 October 1972 the penal rate for assistance to the discount markets was based on the market rate of discount of Treasury bills the previous week. Under its new title of 'minimum lending rate' the interest rate on 'front door' lending by the Bank of England was calculated at ½ per cent above the average discount rate on Treasury bills rate to rule till the following week. However if the Bank wished to indicate 'a shift in monetary policy', the rate would be altered by administrative decision in the old style, the operation of the minimum lending rate formula being suspended until market rates had moved into line. See the *Bank of England Quarterly Bulletin*, December 1972, p. 443.
6. See J. R. Hicks, 'The Yield on Consols,' Chapter 5 of *Critical Essays in Monetary Theory*, London, Oxford University Press, 1967 (a revised and modernized version of a paper read to the Manchester Statistical Society in March 1958 and subsequently submitted as a memorandum to the Radcliffe Committee).
7. Keynes, *General Theory*, pp. 170–1. R. F. Kahn brings out the importance of the earlier version of the precautionary motive in 'Some Notes on Liquidity Preference,' *Manchester School of Economics and Social Studies*, September 1954.
8. F. P. R. Brechling and J. N. Wolfe, 'The End of Stop–Go,' *Lloyds Bank Review*, January 1965, p. 29.
9. See e.g. Milton Friedman and Anna J. Schwartz, *A Monetary History of the United States 1867–1960*, Princeton University Press, 1963. See references to Keynes in n. 1 above, especially his writings in 1937 and 1938.
10. Milton Friedman, 'The Role of Monetary Policy,' *American Economic Review*, March 1968, p. 17.

11. J. M. Keynes; see, e.g. 'A Rejoinder' (to D. H. Robertson), *Economic Journal*, September 1931, and letters to *The Economist* in 1937 and 1938 cited in n. 1 above.

12. J. M. Keynes, 'The "Ex-Ante" Theory of the Rate of Interest,' *Economic Journal*, December 1937, pp. 667–8. As D. H. Robertson put it, 'It will be remembered that about a year after the publication of his *General Theory* Keynes suddenly re-awoke to the fact that banks sometimes lend money to entrepreneurs who are preparing to indulge in net capital outlay.' 'Some Notes on the Theory of Interest,' *Essays in Money and Interest*, Collins, 1966, p. 213.

13. F. P. R. Brechling and J. N. Wolfe, op. cit.

14. In a speech given at the Lord Mayor's dinner on 18 October 1973 the Governor of the Bank of England remarked: 'Many commentators appear to pass judgement on monetary policy almost exclusively by reference to ... M_3. This is placing more weight on a single yardstick than it is capable either in principle or in practice of bearing,' quoted in the *Bank of England Quarterly Bulletin*, December 1973, p. 476.

15. Graham Hacche, 'The Demand for Money in the United Kingdom: Experience since 1971,' *Bank of England Quarterly Bulletin*, September 1974.

16. Keynes's highly individual grounds for rejecting this argument were stated in the *General Theory*, pp. 142–3 (see also Paul Davidson, *Money and the Real World*, London, Macmillan, 1972, pp. 235–7). He offered what has become a more conventional reason in *A Tract on Monetary Reform* – see n. 22 below.

17. Modern writers such as Robert Mundell (see, 'Inflation and Real Interest,' *Journal of Political Economy*, June 1963) are correctly given credit for a clear statement of this point. However, A. C. Pigou, D. H. Robertson and J. M. Keynes, whatever their differences, were unanimous on the fundamental matter that an increase/decrease in the value of real purchasing power will generally be followed by a rise/fall in the expenditures of those who have not actually initiated the process by altering their rate of saving. Keynes's fairly sophisticated views on the relationship between real balances and real consumption/saving in inflation are set out in a letter to D. H. Robertson dated 31 May 1925, dealing with Robertson's analysis in his excellent book *Banking Policy and the Price-level*, published in 1926: see *Collected Writings of J. M. Keynes*, Vol. 13, pp. 36–9.

18. A. A. Tait and E. Burrell, 'Savings, Real Balances and Inflation: Some Empirical Evidence,' *The Manchester School*, September 1976.

19. The importance of the interest-induced wealth effect in Keynes's thinking was made plain by A. Leijonhufvud, *On Keynesian Economics and the Economics of Keynes*, London, Oxford University Press, 1968, Chapter 4, sections 1–3 and chapter 5, section 1. Burton Zwick's useful article, 'The Interest-Induced Wealth Effect and the Behaviour of Real and Nominal Interest Rates,' appeared in the *Journal of Finance*, December 1974.

20. *The Bank of England Quarterly Bulletin*, September 1975, p. 216. See also the discussion in the article, 'The Personal Saving Ratio,' prepared largely by J. C. Townend in the March 1976 *Bulletin*. In his scholarly work, *Money, Interest and Prices*, 2nd edn, pp. 71–2, 287–8, 622, New York, Harper and Row, Don Patinkin incorporates a real indebtedness effect and reveals, for example, that L. R. Klein found that liquid assets appeared to have a significant influence on consumption in the United States in a study published as long ago as 1949, though a similar investigation of the relationship in the United Kingdom by M. R. Fisher, *Bulletin of the Oxford Institute of Statistics*, August 1956, was less conclusive. Cf. n. 36 to Chapter 3 of this book.

21. The phrase is used by A. E. Jasay, The Working of the Radcliffe Monetary System,' *Oxford Economic Papers*, June 1960.

22. For a non-technical discussion by a leading monetarist see, e.g. David Laidler's article in the *National Westminster Bank Review*, November 1972. Keynes made the point that expectations were unlikely to adjust completely to the current price level in circumstances of abnormal rise or fall in prices in 'A Tract on Monetary Reform' in *The Collected Writings of John Maynard Keynes*, Volume IV, pp. 19–20, London, Macmillan, 1971.

23. Nurali Peera, 'Interest Rates: Illusion or Reality,' Peter Wann, 'Lower Interest Rates?', both in *National Westminster Quarterly Review*, February 1970; Nicholas Barr, 'Real Rates of Return to Financial Assets since the War,' *The Three Banks Review*, September 1975. The case for positive real rates of interest in less developed countries appears in E. S. Shaw, *Financial Deepening and Economic Development*, New York, Oxford University Press, 1973, especially Chapter 4; R. I. McKinnon, *Money and Capital in Economic Development*, Washington D.C., Brookings Institution, 1973 especially Chapters 2, 7 and 8 and, e.g. Un Tun Wai and Hugh T. Patrick, 'Stock and Bond Issues in Less Developed Countries,' *IMF Staff Papers*, 1973, especially pp. 281–4.

24. Peter Wann, *National Westminster Quarterly Review*, February 1970, p. 50.

25. For detailed analysis of 'financial strength' see W. T. Newlyn, *Theory of Money*, London, Oxford University Press, 1962, Chapter 10.

26. R. N. McKean, 'Liquidity and a National Balance Sheet,' *Readings in Monetary Theory*, Homewood, Illinois, Irwin, 1951, p. 70 (first published in the *Journal of Political Economy*, 1947). McKean in turn had borrowed the definition from an earlier work by C. C. Brown, *Liquidity and Instability*, New York, Columbia University Press, 1940.

27. See Jack Revell and Alan R. Roe, 'National Balance Sheets and National Accounting – a Progress Report,' *Economic Trends*, May 1971.

28. In his book *The Strategy of Financial Pressure*, London, Macmillan, 1972, A. T. K. Grant argues that financial pressure be thought of 'as operating through fiscal policy (see in government revenue-raising and spending) and monetary policy (seen in the financing facilities available to business enterprise and the spending public),' p. 16.

29. Keynes discussed the consequences of errors of business forecasts about investment briefly in *A Treatise on Money*, London, Macmillan, 1930, Vol. I, pp. 255 and 290, and in the *General Theory*, Chapter 22. Such mistakes are also discussed by A. G. Hart (who believed that Keynes neglected the disappointment of short-run expectations and that this was a 'major deficiency' in his book), 'Keynes' Analysis of Expectations and Uncertainty,' *The New Economics*, London, Dennis Dobson, 1947, Chapter 31, especially p. 419, and by A. R. Roe, 'The Case for Flow of Funds and National Balance Sheet Accounts,' Warwick Economic Research Papers, No. 29, August 1972, later published in *Economic Journal*, June 1973. References in this chapter are to the Warwick paper, pp. 13–14. F. A. Hayek distinguished between the 'justified errors' caused by the price system and 'sheer errors' about the course of external events, 'Price Expectations, Monetary Disturbances and Malinvestments,' 1933, reprinted in American Economic Association, *Readings in Business Cycle Theory*, London, Allen and Unwin, 1950. But 'errors of optimism and pessimism' have a long pedigree in financial literature from Henry Thornton onwards. The lender-borrower relationship has received special emphasis in the writings of Donald R. Hodgman, e.g. 'In Defence of the Availability Doctrine: A Comment,' *Review of Economics and Statistics*, February 1959, pp. 70–3, 'Credit Risk and Credit Rationing,' *Quarterly Journal of Economics*, May 1961, pp. 319–29, 'The Deposit Relationship and Commercial Bank Investment Behaviour,' *Review of Economics and Statistics*, August 1961, pp. 257–68.

30. See A. J. L. Catt, 'Credit Risk and Credit Rationing,' *Quarterly Journal of Economics*, August 1963 and 'Credit Rationing and the Keynesian Model,' *Economic Journal*, June 1965.
31. See e.g. the discussions of lenders' and borrowers' risk in Keynes's *General Theory*, pp. 144–5; Hicks's *Capital and Growth*, London, Oxford University Press, Chapter 23; D. R. Hodgman, 'Credit Risk and Credit Rationing', op. cit., A. Lindbeck, *The 'New' Theory of Credit Control in the United States*, Stockholm, Almqvist and Wiksell, 1962; A. J. L. Catt, op. cit.; J. M. Burns, 'The Savings–Investment Process in a Theory of Finance,' unpublished University of Chicago Ph.D. dissertation, 1967, and 'On the Effects of Financial Innovations,' *Quarterly Review of Economics and Business*, Summer 1971; J. A. Galbraith, *The Economics of Banking Operations*, Montreal, McGill University Press, 1963, Chapter 2; M. C. Gupta, 'Differential Effects of Tight Money: An Economic Rationale,' *Journal of Finance*, September 1972.
32. McKean, op. cit., p. 80.
33. John H. Hotson supports the position adopted by Ervin Miller in this book in his article 'Tight Money as a Cause of Inflation: Comment,' *Journal of Finance*, March 1971.
34. See 'The Cost of Capital, Finance and Investment,' prepared mainly by J. S. Flemming, L. D. D. Price and Mrs S. A. Byers, *Bank of England Quarterly Bulletin*, June 1976, p. 201. A 'Supplementary Note' on company profitability and the cost of capital appeared in the June 1977 Bulletin.
35. Ibid., p. 201.
36. Geoffrey Whittington, *The Prediction of Profitability and Other Studies of Company Behaviour*, London, Cambridge University Press, 1971.
37. A. J. Merrett, 'Measuring Trends in Profitability,' *Lloyds Bank Review*, October 1975, p. 20. It should be acknowledged that not all authorities accept the theoretical premise of this particular argument.
38. 'Trends in Company Profitability,' prepared mainly by J. S. Flemming, L. D. D. Price and D. H. A. Ingram, *Bank of England Quarterly Bulletin*, March 1976; 'The Cost of Capital, Finance and Investment,' *Bank of England Quarterly Bulletin*, June 1976.
39. 'Company Finance: 1952–65,' *Bank of England Quarterly Bulletin*, March 1967.
40. 'Company Financial Behaviour,' *Barclays Review*, February 1976.
41. Keynes wrote, 'The dismay and uncertainty as to the future which accompanies a collapse in the marginal efficiency of capital naturally precipitates a sharp rise in liquidity preference'; *General Theory*, p. 316.
42. See, 'Alternative Theories of the Rate of Interest,' *Economic Journal*, June 1937, 'The Ex-Ante Theory of the Rate of Interest,' *Economic Journal*, December 1937; his comment on 'Mr Keynes and Finance' by D. H. Robertson, *Economic Journal*, June 1938.
43. See D. H. Robertson, 'More Notes on the Rate of Interest,' *Essays in Money and Interest*, London, Collins, 1966, p. 232.
44. Keynes, *Treatise*, Vol. I, p. 159.
45. Flemming, Price and Byers provide a useful arithmetical example in 'The Cost of Capital, Finance and Investment,' op. cit., p. 194.
46. See Davidson, *Money and the Real World*, op. cit., p. 290.
47. M. A. King, 'Taxation and the Cost of Capital,' *Review of Economic Studies*, January 1974.
48. See, e.g. Keynes, *Treatise*, Vol. I, p. 173.
49. A. H. Meltzer, 'Mercantile Credit, Monetary Policy and Size of Firms,' *Review of Economics and Statistics*, November 1960.
50. E. W. Davis and K. A. Yeomans, *Company Finance and the Capital Market:*

a Study of the Effects of Firm Size, London, Cambridge University Press, 1974. They conducted an investigation into the balance sheets of 200 companies for the period 1966–70.

51. *The Committee of Enquiry into Small Firms*, Cmnd 4811, London, H.M.S.O., 1971.
52. Davis and Yeomans, op. cit., p. 74.
53. J. K. Galbraith, 'Market Structure and Stabilisation Policy,' *Review of Economics and Statistics*, May 1957.
54. M. S. Levitt demonstrated in his article, 'Monetary Theory and Trade Credit: An Historical Approach,' *Yorkshire Bulletin*, November 1964, that the Radcliffe Report suggestion that trade credit represented possible 'slippage' in a credit squeeze had been anticipated by economists such as J. S. Mill and F. Lavington. J. C. R. Dow, however, argued that it was probable that 'a reduction in bank credit will *provoke* a contraction of trade credit': *The Management of the British Economy, 1945–60*, London, Cambridge University Press, 1965, p. 324.
55. NEDO, *Finance for Investment*, May 1975, pp. 75, 98.
56. ibid., p. 91.
57. An article by Walter Eltis entitled 'The Failure of Keynesian Conventional Wisdom,' *Lloyds Bank Review*, October 1976, pointed out the inconsistency. Lord Kahn's retort in the April 1977 issue of the *Review* asserted that the orthodox Keynesian position accepted the association between a faster rate of growth in the money supply and rising interest rates. In the July 1977 issue Eltis welcomed this affirmation by a leading (perhaps *the* leading) Keynesian economist.
58. This point was made by Brechling and Wolfe, op. cit., p. 26, in 1965 but applies with perhaps greater force to subsequent periods of expansion in 1968 and 1972–3 (see Figure 7.1 for a rough indication of the duration of expansion).
59. Keynes laid special emphasis on the necessity for a gradual expansionary process in the *General Theory*, pp. 286–7 and pp. 300–1, passages that have suffered a curious neglect.

8 Interest Rates, the Personal Sector and the Housing Market

This chapter examines the selective impact of soaring interest rates and an altered rate structure on those individuals who were either trapped in mid-stream, as it were, in the housing market in 1973–4, or were effectively barred from entering the market, or, perhaps less seriously, found themselves immobilized in a portfolio disequilibrium by the dramatically altered circumstances in the mortgage and housing markets.

For the majority of owner-occupiers home ownership represents the largest single commitment to wealth; it is also normally associated with the largest component of household indebtedness. House and mortgage together form a familiar asset–debt package to which we should probably add the durables required to furnish the home and their financial requirement, which also figure in the portfolio. Home ownership is therefore a powerful influence in shaping the composition of portfolio assets on the one hand and the structure of debts on the other, or, more comprehensively, in determining the pattern of balance sheet holdings among real assets, financial assets and debt.

Most analyses of the housing market are founded on the argument that the demand for houses, in common with the supply, is normally extremely sensitive to changes in the availability of credit.[1] The basic argument of this type of theory is readily grasped. Rapid changes in new and second-hand house prices well out of line with retail and other important price indices have resulted from the direction by specialist institutions of a rapidly increasing (then suddenly decelerated) supply of funds towards a housing sector which is slow-growing and stock-dominated. The problems associated with the cycle in the supply of mortgage funds came sharply into focus in the 1970s because of the tremendous success of UK building societies in gathering from and on-lending back to the household sector both *old* and *new* personal savings. To make a popular but somewhat misleading comparison, since it ignores the powerful substitution effects that apparently operated via interest differentials, in 1971 the net increase in building society deposits was equal to over 60 per cent of new personal savings.

What made the 1972 peak of the mortgage cycle more significant than the earlier peaks in the flow of building society mortgage loans, e.g. in 1964, 1966 and 1968, was the new size dimension of societies as borrowers and lenders. Whereas in 1946 the assets of the building society movement represented only 16 per cent of the assets of the London clearing banks, by the end of 1972 societies had achieved parity of resources (though the comparison subsequently moved back in favour of the clearing banks as they took full advantage of the freedom afforded by the new monetary measures of October 1971), a consequence of a compound growth rate of over 10 per cent per annum between 1946 and end 1972.[2] This secular improvement in the competitive position of building societies to one of the commanding heights in the market for short-term loanable funds when interest rate differentials were moving in their favour therefore had the apparent result of conducting sums towards mortgage-borrowers whose expenditures invariably drove house prices rapidly upwards because of the low elasticity of production in the residential construction sector. Also, by inference, the very success of societies in attracting loanable funds for on-lending resulted in the redirection of funds away from borrowers whose expenditure might conceivably have drawn unemployed resources back into production but whose spending would, in almost any circumstances, have produced less partial and less inflationary consequences and been less obviously harmful to the welfare of a particularly vulnerable class of household – young families about to enter the housing market for the first time.

The next step is to make plain the role of interest rates in this explanation and to restate it in terms of, or to adapt it to, the theory of portfolio adjustment. Household demand for property may be assumed to respond to changes in the relative attractiveness of different real yields accruing from classes of asset in which the household has an interest. In economists' language, the wealth-owner may be regarded as dividing his wealth among various types of asset, including a house (or houses), with a view to maximizing the satisfaction he gains from his entire portfolio. He will achieve a desired asset structure when the expected services yielded by a house relative to its purchase price are at the margin equal to the equivalent ratios for other assets, i.e. when the marginal advantage from adding to each asset is the same for each additional pound spent or, in *General Theory* language,[3] when the own-rates of interest of the different types of asset are equal.

In practice we may and do envisage a house as a source of present and future satisfaction from its amenities (where 'amenities' encompasses a package of attributes, notably basic needs such as shelter, modern needs such as electricity and hot and cold running water, plus a desirable social setting and acceptable travel-to-work requirements). Although the annual stream of services that accrue from home ownership is implicit and non-measurable, the prospective buyer must none the less arrive at a mental estimate of such returns and transform them by applying the appropriate discount rate into a present value that should represent his maximum offer price. In other words, the prospective purchaser's valuation (he may be guided by a professional surveyor or perhaps by his lawyer or estate agent on this) should therefore be greater than or equal to his offer price plus all prospective purchasing costs. As far as the seller is concerned, the present value of his home should represent his reservation demand price, or the price at which he would 'buy back' his home at an auction, net of prospective selling costs, assuming that he was not under any special pressure to sell.

Since this chapter advances a predominantly demand-pull interpretation of the trend in UK house prices it may provoke some scepticism among American readers, for example, since building costs are believed to have been dominant in house-price inflation in the United States, with the probable (and notable) exception of California.[4] But it is difficult to see much evidence of cost-push forces at work in the UK property market. For example, the price of new properties in the United Kingdom increased at more than four times the rate of increase in house-building (wages and materials) costs between the end of December 1970 and the end of June 1972. Building costs began to rise much more steeply after June 1972 but house prices soon began to decelerate and between the end of 1973 and the close of the first quarter in 1977 the percentage increase in costs was almost three times that of new property prices.[5]

Let us construct a highly simplified portfolio adjustment model in an effort to trace the impact of changes in the level of nominal interest rates.[6] The most important aspect of this explanation is this. Because the rate structure of UK building societies is inflexible compared with the yields on marketable debt and also with the rates offered on deposits by the banks and other savings institutions, a change in the *level* of rates implies a change in the *structure* of rates and hence in the pattern of financial flows. Let us assume that changes in the general financial climate are initiated either by the monetary authorities or by market forces operating outside the mortgage and housing markets and postulate a general rise in interest rates. There will be a lag before the rate of interest on mortgages increases, but the occurrence of higher rates of interest on financial assets in general and on mortgage advances in particular should cause households to defer long-term borrowing and the purchase of long-lived assets such as houses as the opportunity cost of engaging in such activities increases. In the United Kingdom, the rates on *all* mortgage advances by building societies, first new, then (three months later) old, tend to alter in accordance with Building Society Association (BSA) recommendations. By contrast, in the United States and Canada the conventional mortgage contract has fixed a rate of interest for a period of years regardless of subsequent changes in market rates on other financial assets. Yet in California in particular, variable-rate mortgages are becoming increasingly common; under this form of contract the burden of periodic payments to the mortgage holding institutions gradually eases as (and if) interest rates fall and increases as the rate structure rises. The incentive to postpone mortgage-borrowing is, however, less powerful in the UK situation since the penal effects of high borrowing charges need not be perpetuated. But in the upper regions of nominal mortgage rates – and an 11 or even a 10 per cent mortgage almost certainly qualifies on this count – the effect of the interest and principal repayment burden in reducing discretionary income (disposable income minus contractual debt obligations) may be regarded as unacceptable by potential mortgagors who would be considered credit-worthy by building societies. The demand for mortgages by eligible applicants (which is derived from the demand for houses) will therefore tend to show some sensitivity to interest rates at high nominal levels, although the effective threshold of sensitivity will obviously alter according to circumstances. Bank overdraft lending rates, which have responded readily to pressures in the market for loanable funds since October 1971, will normally increase faster and farther than mortgage interest rates. Contingency bridging finance therefore increases in cost for transactors who are buying one property and selling another. Overdrafts will also become harder to obtain as the turnover in dwellings slows down and bridging loans cease to be liquidated more or less automatically. Additionally, the increase in building society lending rates will cause the risk of involuntary default to rise and hence, according to financial theory, credit standards to stiffen. The quantity of mortgages demanded in the upper ranges of mortgage rate levels will diminish as borrowers lose their eligibility status.

The critical constraints on house purchase are discussed a little later on. However, the demand price of the unconstrained potential purchaser who has access to the requisite amount of funds on request depends (i) upon the stream of prospective services from the house's amenities, adjusted for uncertainty and translated into a money value; and (ii) upon the rate of interest at which these anticipated returns are capitalized. If the potential house-buyer takes a market rate of interest or the newly increased mortgage rate as his rate of discount, his demand price for the house that he is contemplating buying will fall as the rate of interest rises.

Shifting our attention from the potential borrower, i.e. a household that is contemplating accepting a huge financial deficit (savings minus 'investment' by house purchase) on income account, to households with a financial surplus on income account (or residue of financial claims after all current spending), we can trace the effect on savers' pattern of preferences for short-term financial claims of a change in interest differentials among these assets. The increased yields on marketable securities will direct lenders' purchases towards such securities at the expense of the shares and deposits ('indirect debt' or 'secondary debt' fixed in money value) of building societies and other financial institutions with relatively inflexible rate structures. The reduced net inflow of funds into building societies results, in turn, in a diminished flow-supply of mortgage advances, assuming no simultaneous run-down in society liquid asset holdings. Orthodox portfolio balancing considerations therefore argue that the *supply* of available mortgage loans will be reduced at roughly the same time as the *demand* for loan-financed housing is curtailed. At the same time, in the construction industry the rising cost of finance to builders who rely heavily on overdraft finance may have contributed to a decline in new house-building activity, subsequently diminishing the menu of new properties for sale.[7] On the other hand, as the demand for houses increases in response to a fall in interest rates, so too, as an indirect result, will the flow-supply of mortgage advances. Thus as the demand for and supply of houses rise and fall *pari passu* as a result of external market forces, the flow-supply of mortgages alters more or less appropriately to satisfy, according to this reasoning, rather than to stimulate (according to the 'availability approach') the notional or desired demand for mortgages. However, supply side and demand side changes are unlikely to be perfectly synchronized or precisely matched in size. Any excess of eligible demand will provoke rationing[8] (largely by queueing), first at society then at movement[9] level, as society liquid assets are reduced to minimum tolerable levels; any surplus of funds relative to credit-worthy loan applications will cause building societies to accumulate liquid assets to levels in excess of 20 per cent of total assets if necessary.

The argument has a special plausibility in UK conditions because of the 'stickiness' of the borrowing (and lending) rates of UK building societies relative to market and to other institutional rates. Informal evidence suggests that substantial substitutions have been made in the 1970s between society shares and deposits and call money in the major London money markets as well as between savings deposits with other financial institutions. Figure 8.1a below reveals the extent of the interest differential between MLR and, by inference, rates which are closely linked to it, such as the local authority three-month deposit rate (see Figure 8.1b) and the Building Society Association (BSA) recommended level. Figure 8.2 shows the trend in the number and amount of building society mortgages between 1967 and 1975 and provides indirect evidence of how the ceiling on the rate of interest in effect imposed by the authorities between September 1973 and August 1975 ('moral suasion' exerted by the Department of the Environment supported by the Treasury) placed the movement at a substantial disadvantage in the market for short-term funds during 1973 and much of 1974, although the authorities did their best to arrest the outflow of funds from societies by placing a 9½ per cent limit on rates payable by banks on deposits of under £10,000 in November 1973.

So far the analysis has been seriously oversimplified. Building societies are not the only institutions that make mortgage advances,

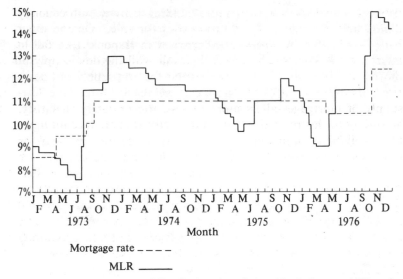

Mortgage rate _ _ _ _

MLR _____

Source: *Facts and Figures*, Building Society Association, No. 9, January 1977, p. 2

Figure 8.1a   Movements in MLR and BSA-recommended mortgage rate

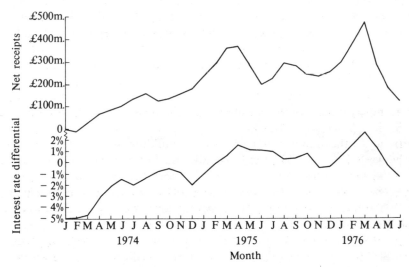

Source: *Facts and Figures*, Building Society Association, No. 7, July 1976, p. 2

*Figure 8.1b   Building society net receipts and the interest rate differential. The graph
plots the differential between the building society grossed-up share rate
and the local authority three-month deposit rate against seasonally adjusted
net receipts.*

nor are they consistently responsible for the same proportion of mortgage loans. For example, though society loans represented 92 per cent of new mortgages in 1972 and about 95 per cent in 1976, the percentages for 1973, 1974 and 1975 were 86, 81 and 85 per cent respectively, with local authorities in particular stepping up their advances (from 3 per cent of total mortgages in 1972 to 13 per cent of the total in 1974) as societies' lending flagged.[10] Again, building society finance is frequently unimportant for house purchase at the cheapest and at the most expensive ends of the

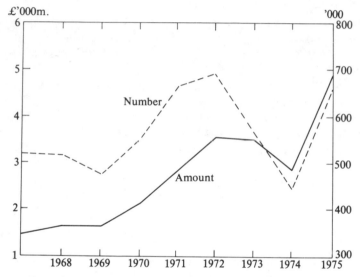

Source: *Factual Background*, Bristol and West Building Society, April 1977

Figure 8.2   Building society mortgages

spectrum of properties for sale,[11] so that for this and for other reasons, such as variations in the loan–value ratio, the demand schedules for homes and for mortgage finance may exhibit quite separate characteristics.

Space does not permit a proper analysis of the mortgage and housing markets but the following consequences of operations in the 1970s deserve a further explanation: (i) soaring house prices (a rise of roughly 120 per cent from December 1968 to December 1973, with *real* increases in average new house prices of 24.4 per cent in 1972 and 27.0 per cent in 1973), accompanied by a decline (from early 1971) in the annual rate of change of housing starts in private sector housing – total annual starts that reached a peak of 228,000 in 1972 declined to 106,000 in 1974 and had picked up to a level of only 155,000 by 1976; followed by (ii) stagnating house prices, declining in real terms by 10 per cent in 1974, by almost 15 per cent in 1975 and by about 6.5 per cent in 1976, and steeply increased mortgage rates (from 7.5 per cent in 1968 to 11 per cent in 1973), which deterred many first-time purchasers and caused those who went ahead first to effect a substantial transfer of wealth from themselves to land- and house-owners and then to suffer a decline in their real net worth at a time when the real income of many of the households concerned was actually diminishing. Any generalization about real income change probably fails to reveal the relative disadvantage of individual categories such as police constables or university professors under the UK incomes policy. But a recent estimate suggests that the real take-home pay of middle management (earning around £5000 per annum in early 1975) has been reduced by about 20 per cent between 1973 and 1977; that of top management by much more.[12] There is a parallel here with the company sector. A typical financially vulnerable household which entered the housing market in January 1974 paid a much larger percentage down payment than before, possibly incurring short-term debts in the process, bought an asset depreciating in real capital value, and was compelled to pay a mortgage rate which sharply reduced discretionary income at a time when its real income may very well have been declining.

8.1 A More Complex Approach to Interest Change and the Mortgage Market

A final stage in gauging the impact of interest changes on the market for private property is to introduce uncertainty and risk to a balance sheet analysis and to acknowledge the role of expectations as well as of changes in the availability of funds in the portfolio adjustment process.

Theoretically, a building society's loan rejection rate must rise with any increase in uncertainty either about the borrower's capacity to shoulder the burden of regular mortgage repayments, or about the society's ability to compel repayment without administrative expense and trouble. The margin of uncertainty will tend to shift against new applicants to the extent that their 'collateral' has become less acceptable. For example, when the rate of turnover in properties is low or declining and house values are rising more slowly than retail prices, then not only are real property values diminishing, but the property in question is apt to be *illiquid*, marketable only after a protracted delay or at a substantial real loss (net of all selling costs, including personal inconvenience and psychic costs). The margin will also shift against the borrower (i) if his credit rating is diminished because, independently of the liquidity of the actual or potential property-holding, the financial strength of his balance sheet has been reduced – as is almost inevitable during any period of financial disruption and economic recession – or (ii) if his real income is declining because of the inferior strength of his trade union or professional association in a period of rapid inflation. A further reason why credit standards may stiffen is that societies may revise upwards their estimate of the possible increase in mortgage rates and monthly repayments over the next two or three years when the new mortgagor is particularly vulnerable to such an increased burden. Such prospects are dynamic elements in loan appraisal which no society can afford to ignore. Of less importance but not without significance is the fact that, when the authorities fail to insulate from rate changes in other world financial centres or from a domestic financial crisis the various markets (Treasury bill, local authority and government bond markets) from which societies make up the investment package in their portfolio, and, more particularly, when they fail to safeguard the movement's competitive position in the market for short-term funds, greatly increasing the variability of societies' net inflow of funds, the resultant reduction in societies' liquidity should make them increasingly circumspect in their mortgage-lending in an effort to reduce still further the risk input in their principal form of loan. However, the critical time for building societies to draw on their experience of past cycles in financial availability and in the liquidity of the housing market is on the *upswing* of the cycle, not when the recession eventually arrives.

The premium charged to cover default risk is, or should be, a component in societies' gross margin (defined very broadly as the difference between borrowing and lending rates). In so far as societies are unable to increase the gross margin in times of economic

uncertainty when the authorities are openly hostile to increases in
the mortgage interest rate which would permit a bigger risk premium,
as is generally the case, they must protect themselves in other ways.
For example, our argument suggests that the average-advance–
average-income ratio and the proportion of house value advanced
by societies should both fall in such circumstances, and this is precisely what occurred in 1973–4: the average-advance–average-income
ratio for first-time purchasers rose from 1.96 in 1971 to 2.24 in 1973,
but declined to 2.03 in 1974 and 1.94 in 1975; the average percentage advance to first-time purchasers declined from 81.4 per cent
in 1972 to 77.3 per cent in 1973, and by the third quarter in 1974
was as low as 71.7 per cent.[13] The stiffer credit standards suggested
by these figures constitute a curb on the demand for mortgages by
new house-purchasers. However, there are good economic reasons
why higher standards of credit-worthiness should also be applied
to existing owner-occupiers who are engaged in 'trade-up', seeking
a bigger mortgage to finance the purchase of higher amenity
property. First, there are the standard arguments that the greater
the loan-financed expenditure commitment the more is the entire
wealth position endangered by any reduction in borrower's income,[14] and the lower is borrowers' tolerance to a rise in interest
rates which increases the repayment burden.[15] Second, the strain
of a highly geared portfolio position following the purchase of a
new house may compel the owner-occupier to reduce his reservation
price on his former house, sustaining a capital loss which may be
of substantial proportions and accepting a higher level of debts than
originally anticipated. The phenomenon of 'foul-weather illiquidity'
referred to elsewhere implies that the liquidity of the potential
mortgagor's assets is reduced, his prospects uncertain, his refinancing
obligations applied more strictly than heretofore, and, as a corollary,
his credit-worthiness reduced and his borrowing potential diminished. The effect on the demand for mortgages is twofold. On the
one hand, societies place additional constraints on demand by
former owner-occupiers by advancing a smaller proportion of house
value; e.g. the average percentage advance to former owner-occupiers
declined from just over 60 per cent of house value in 1972 to just
over 50 per cent in 1973 (though in practice the rise in own-payment
by the house-purchaser of over £2,000 that this represented could
generally be found from the capital appreciation of the former
property, since the average dwelling price increased by almost

£3,000 between 1972 and 1973). Since their sharp reduction in average percentage advance was associated with stability in 1972 and 1973 in UK societies' average-advance–average-income ratio to former owner-occupiers at 2.02 (falling to 1.82 in 1974 and 1.72 in 1975) the combined effect was to increase effective credit standards. Such adjustments, designed to take account of the increased risk content in various classes of loan, arise from an altered perception by societies of the financial strength of potential borrowers. The demand for mortgages and for houses must logically also be reduced because borrowers' own evaluations of their balance sheet positions alter. In other words, a borrower's notion of his prospective financial strength in the housing market is a subjective *ex ante* micro-evaluation of his potential purchasing power in this market, and, if he is realistic about any deterioration in the liquidity of his household balance sheet position, he must either seek a smaller property and a smaller mortgage or withdraw from both markets.

The essence of the preceding argument is that the eligible demand schedule for mortgages (along with the supply) will be interest-sensitive in its upper ranges. The faster the rate of change in rates, the greater will be the sensitivity. It is the nominal and not the certainty equivalent or real long-run mortgage rate that is critical, for it is the interest payments based on the nominal rate (plus any repayment of principal) that cut into household disposable income after a house has been successfully purchased. Moreover, not only does the possibility of default rise as the size of the loan and the effective interest level increases; it does so at a sharply increasing rate at levels of 10, 11 or 12 per cent. This is especially true if such high levels of nominal rates are combined with greatly enhanced down payments. To focus once more on 1973, average initial mortgage repayments were more than 60 per cent higher in 1973 than in 1972, the average down payment just under 60 per cent greater. Average initial repayments, this time measured as a percentage of average earnings (since more up-to-date figures are available on this ratio), rather than of average income, as shown in Table 8.1, jumped from about 27 per cent in 1972 to 39 per cent in 1973 and 43 per cent in 1974, though the percentage increases in the ratio for first-time buyers were quite different (20 per cent in 1972, 24 per cent in 1973, 25 per cent in 1974), largely because the typical first-time buyer bought a property well below the average price. Again, the extent of the barrier to market entry imposed by the large real increases in house prices in

Table 8.1 House Prices, Average Earnings and Retail Prices, 1968–76

Quarter	Average new house prices £	Increase	Average earnings* £	Increase	Retail prices increase	House-prices–earnings ratio	Real increase in house prices
		%		%	%		%
1968 Q.1	4,510	2.0	1,261	2.0	1.4	3.58	0.6
Q.2	4,700	4.2	1,278	1.3	2.4	3.68	1.8
Q.3	4,690	−0.2	1,306	2.2	0.6	3.59	−0.8
Q.4	4,710	0.4	1,335	2.2	1.1	3.53	−0.7
1969 Q.1	4,720	0.2	1,353	1.3	2.0	3.49	−1.8
Q.2	4,840	2.5	1,381	2.1	1.6	3.50	0.9
Q.3	4,940	2.1	1,407	1.9	0.2	3.51	1.9
Q.4	5,040	2.0	1,446	2.8	1.3	3.49	0.7
1970 Q.1	5,000	−0.8	1,491	3.1	1.8	3.35	−2.6
Q.2	5,180	3.6	1,541	3.4	2.5	3.36	1.1
Q.3	5,100	2.3	1,590	3.2	1.1	3.33	1.2
Q.4	5,230	−1.3	1,643	3.3	2.1	3.18	−3.4
1971 Q.1	5,600	7.1	1,687	2.7	2.7	3.32	4.4
Q.2	5,770	3.0	1,719	1.9	3.6	3.36	−0.6
Q.3	6,190	7.3	1,767	2.8	1.4	3.50	5.9
Q.4	6,350	2.6	1,798	1.8	1.3	3.53	1.3
1972 Q.1	6,650	4.7	1,856	3.2	1.5	3.58	3.2
Q.2	7,380	11.0	1,916	3.2	1.8	3.85	9.2
Q.3	8,680	17.6	1,982	3.4	1.7	4.38	15.9
Q.4	9,440	8.8	2,082	5.0	2.4	4.53	6.4
1973 Q.1	10,150	7.5	2,114	1.5	1.8	4.80	5.7
Q.2	10,640	4.8	2,196	3.9	3.2	4.85	1.6
Q.3	10,960	3.0	2,271	3.4	1.5	4.83	1.5
Q.4	11,240	2.6	2,346	3.3	3.4	4.79	−0.8
1974 Q.1	11,230	−0.1	2,336	−0.4	4.2	4.81	−4.3
Q.2	11,160	−0.6	2,497	6.9	5.9	4.78	−6.5
Q.3	11,450	2.6	2,723	9.1	2.5	4.20	0.1
Q.4	11,490	0.3	2,940	8.0	4.5	3.91	−4.2
1975 Q.1	11,818	2.9	3,077	4.7	6.0	3.84	−3.1
Q.2	12,401	4.9	3,202	4.1	9.4	3.87	−4.5
Q.3	12,664	2.1	3,442	7.5	4.4	3.68	−2.3
Q.4	12,746	0.6	3,580	4.0	3.5	3.56	−2.9
1976 Q.1	12,942	1.5	3,681	2.8	3.6	3.52	−2.1

* The average earnings figures are seasonally adjusted. The figures for the first two quarters of 1974 are distorted by the effects of the three-day week.

Source: *Facts and Figures*, Building Society Association, No. 7, July 1976, p. 15.

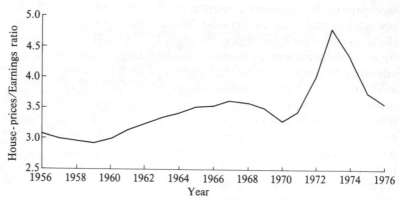

Figure 8.3   Relationship between average new house-prices and average earnings, 1956–72

Source: *Facts and Figures*, Building Society Association, No. 7, July 1976, p. 15

1972 and 1973 is demonstrated in Figure 8.3 and Table 8.1. The house-prices–earnings ratio moved from a low of 3.18 in the autumn of 1970 to a peak of 4.85 in the second quarter of 1973, the ratio slowly falling to more normal levels in the period, protracted by the standards of previous downturns in the housing market, of very moderate activity since.

8.2   The Role of Expectations in the Mortgage Cycle

It is clear from Figure 8.3 that the increase in house prices in the early 1970s was fuelled by an exceptional increase in the volume of mortgage advances by building societies taking advantage of a favourable net inflow as Bank Rate was adjusted in stages from 8 per cent in 1969 to 5 per cent in the early months of 1972. A simple but incomplete explanation of why the demand for mortgages increased alongside supply was offered on p. 210 above. Certain conventional reasons helped to explain the upsurge in the demand for properties in the early 1970s. For example, personal disposable income increased between end 1970 and end 1973 at almost double the annual rate of the previous fifteen years, council rents rose sharply and household formation increased.[16] However, a particularly important missing dimension is the role of expectations in the mortgage cycle. An entire constellation of expectations apparently operates to reinforce the demand for mortgages and property on the upswing of the cycle in housing market activity. It is anticipated by a simple projection of the volume of building society mortgage advances in recent months that mortgage finance will be readily available for first-time purchase or for moving up-market by 're-investing' the increased capital value of one's present home in a different property and taking out a larger mortgage appropriate to one's current income level. It is assumed that the real rate of interest will be negative in an inflationary environment like the 1970s – indeed, even in the period 1949–70, when the rate of inflation was supposedly at a 'tolerable' level, averaging less than 3 per cent per annum, the net real rate of interest (i.e. the average rate of interest paid to building societies on mortgage advances net of tax relief and the rate of inflation) was negative in seven of these years and only once, in 1959, above 2 per cent.[17] Again, there is a further tacit assumption that the nominal rate on mortgage advances will continue at current tolerable levels (e.g. 8 per cent for old borrowers January–November 1972) while real incomes will enjoy a secular increase. The literature of the early 1970s almost certainly boosted the demand for mortgages by publicizing the overwhelming advantage, calculated in *real terms*, of buying the most expensive property building societies were prepared to finance. Also – and this point is independent of expectations – the nominal burden of an 11 per cent mortgage rate of interest is reduced to 7.15 per cent for an individual paying the basic (35 per cent) rate of tax, and as individuals move into the upper ranges of the tax system under the impetus of inflation, they pay – again on an 11 per cent mortgage rate – 4.4 per cent at the 60 per cent tax rate and 1.87 per cent at 83 per cent.

But the critical expectation in the feverish activity in the housing market in 1972 in particular was that house prices would continue to outstrip retail prices by a substantial margin, greatly enhancing the real wealth of the owner-occupier who was mortgaged to the hilt. A long-term gain in real terms was a reasonable supposition: in the period 1956–76 house prices rose on average by 9.7 per cent per annum, average earnings by 8.6 per cent per annum and retail prices by 6.0 per cent per annum. But in the three-month period June–September 1972 house prices rose on average by 16 per cent compared with a retail price increase of less than 2 per cent, and an extensive menu of attractive properties appeared on the market, all of them holding out the prospect of large long-term capital gains and turning over very rapidly, stimulating overbidding – what economists have come to call trading at 'false', or disequilibrium, inflated prices.[18]

It is in retrospect fairly obvious from Figure 8.2 that a serious recession in the housing market was inevitable if the decline in the volume of new mortgage advances apparent in 1972 was not reversed in time to meet the annual peak demand in the months of May and June. Indeed, it is arguable that the preparations for the downturn were made as early as January 1972 when the real value of the flow-supply of building society loans began to decline. The combination of escalating house prices and rising turnover in properties required a continuously accelerating net inflow of funds to building societies which was technically impossible over the long term. The regularity of the downturn of past cycles in mortgages and in housing activity should have prepared societies for this outcome and induced them to revise their credit standards to take account of the liquidity crisis that must ensue: there is no evidence that they do so; indeed, the opposite is true: a potential high-risk situation was treated as one of exceptionally low risk simply because the housing market was temporarily very liquid.

8.3   Interdependencies in the Housing Market

Expectations are, of course, reversible, and ill-founded ones are likely to be reversed very sharply indeed. The housing market in the United Kingdom will not show a steady and sustained recovery until all the relevant financial ratios have been restored to 'normal levels' (this is currently, in May 1977, almost the case) and until the financial stability of the economic climate can be guaranteed. The reason why the housing market has remained illiquid for a much longer period than normal lies in the system of interdependencies that this chapter has attempted to describe. In closing this analysis of the impact of escalating interest rates on the UK housing market of the 1970s let us focus briefly on a category of transactor that plays a strategically important role in the housing market activity cycle, the owner-occupier mortgagor who seeks to 'trade-up' to a better-quality property. Satisfaction of a potential house-purchaser's demand for a different property depends upon his evaluation of the liquidity of his balance sheet being well-founded. This evaluation will of course be based on an assumption that any marketable financial assets that must be sold off to provide some proportion of the purchase price of the sought-after property realize their anticipated values net of all marketing costs. Second, it is presumed that his current property realizes its anticipated net value on the market without delay. Third, and critically, his assessment of his borrowing potential must be correct, including, should it be necessary, not only mortgage finance from a building society but also, as mentioned earlier, contingency overdraft finance from a bank which serves as an essential complement to his long-term borrowing requirement. If any of these assumptions, but particularly the third one, prove to be ill-founded, his notional demand cannot be made effective and a whole chain of house purchases may fail to take place. Since in 1972 and 1973 market expectations were based on mistaken assumptions about the current and prospective availability of mortgage finance, the subsequent reaction on the liquidity of the housing market and of personal sector balance sheets in general was bound to be drastic once the extent and the degree of 'false trading' became manifest. Since downward inflexibility of house prices in money terms prevents an equilibrating *short-run* price adjustment, there must be a quantity adjustment with greatly reduced turnover until, over the long term, the imbalance of household portfolios created by overtrading and the assumption of excessive debt obligations has been eliminated. As demonstrated earlier, relatively stable (or, more realistically, stagnant) house prices in an inflationary environment permit a long-run adjustment in the *real* value of different forms of household wealth. In the short term crippling adjustment costs prevent most households in this situation from contemplating any further property transactions in spite of what may be an almost intolerable debt interest and repayment commitment; they are, temporarily, without effective recourse.

8.4   Conclusions

This chapter has implicitly argued that the overactivity (1972) and subsequent protracted torpor in the UK housing market (1973–7) was largely a consequence of the authorities' practice of alternating repressive and relaxed monetary policies ('policy-on,' 'policy-off') involving substantial fluctuations in interest rates. Contemporary analyses laid much of the blame on the building societies. Societies, very much to their consternation, found themselves pilloried in the press and in bank reviews in 1972 and 1973 for contributing to an exceptional increase in house prices by 'overlending'. The above analysis suggests that the movement as a whole did lack some insight into the familiar course of the cycle in mortgage funds; yet in many ways the situation in the housing market was a novel one. Essentially, societies were guilty of a failure to perform a counter-cyclical function in the mortgage and housing markets, which was belatedly recognized as crucial, but which had never before been acknowledged to be their special responsibility. Plans for a government-sponsored stabilization fund designed to prevent a recurrence of the events in the housing market of 1972–4 were widely canvassed at one time and are by no means forgotten. The need for such a fund has been diminished by more skilful adjustments in the liquid asset holdings of society portfolios; it would disappear almost entirely if, for the very first time in the history of modern economic management in the United Kingdom, a sustained effort was made to follow Keynes's advice on the most appropriate policy for interest rates.

FOOTNOTES

1. See, e.g. J. M. Guttentag, 'The Short Cycle in Residential Construction,' *American Economic Review*, June 1971; M. J. Vipond, 'Fluctuations in Private Housebuilding in Great Britain 1950–66,' *Scottish Journal of Political Economy*, July 1969; L. B. Smith, 'A Model of Financial Intermediary Behaviour in the Post-war Canadian Mortgage Markets,' *Quarterly Journal of Economics*, August 1967; 'Mortgage Madness,' *The Economist*, 7 April 1973.
2. For an excellent analysis of the long-term role of building societies see David K.

Sheppard, *The Growth and Role of U.K. Financial Institutions 1880–1962*, London, Methuen, 1971.

3. Keynes, *General Theory*, Chapter 17, 'The Essential Properties of Interest and Money.' See also Ralph Turvey's essay, 'Does the Rate of Interest Rule the Roost?', in *The Theory of Interest Rates* (F. H. Hahn and F. P. R. Brechling, eds), London, Macmillan, 1965, Chapter 9.

4. Ervin Miller has made this point forcefully in correspondence.

5. New property prices rose by 42 per cent and building costs by 10 per cent between 31 December 1970 and 30 June 1972 and by 99 and 56 per cent respectively between end year 1970 and end year 1973. New property prices rose by only 31 per cent between end year 1973 and the end of March 1977, whereas building costs rose by 80 per cent. Although these results suggest that cost-push forces were not important in determining the house price trend they are, of course, not conclusive.

6. Similar reasoning presumably lies behind the analysis of F. Arcelus and A. H. Meltzer in their articles, 'The Markets for Housing and Housing Services,' *Journal of Money, Credit and Banking*, February 1973 and 'Credit Availability and Economic Decisions: Some Evidence From the Mortgage and Housing Markets,' *Journal of Finance*, June 1974.

7. C. M. E. Whitehead suggests that this may have been true of the last months of 1973 and subsequently: *The U.K. Housing Market: An Econometric Model*, Great Britain, Saxon House, 1974, p. 170.

8. True rationing is a supply side restriction which occurs when building societies are 'fully loaned up,' as they say; i.e. it occurs in a situation when societies' appraisal of the prospective net inflow of funds and the current liquid asset ratio suggests that they cannot meet all requests of normally acceptable quality. Rationing therefore compels discrimination among 'eligible customers'.

9. The description 'movement' is still appropriate since societies, which do not attempt to maximize profits, attempt to promote social welfare by encouraging thrift and home-ownership.

10. See Table A in *Facts and Figures*, the quarterly commentary published by the Building Societies Association, January 1977.

11. I. C. R. Byatt, A. E. Holmans and D. E. W. Laidler, 'Income and the Demand for Housing: Some Evidence for Great Britain,' *Essays in Modern Economics*, AUTE 1972, London, Longman, p. 69.

12. These calculations by A. C. L. Day (*The Observer*, 1 May 1977, p. 10) draw on the *Report of the Royal Commission on Income and Wealth*, among other sources. See also 'Supplementary note: inflation, real incomes and taxation,' *Bank of England Quarterly Bulletin*, December 1976.

13. See Table 6 in the July 1975 and July 1976 issues of *Facts and Figures*, the quarterly bulletin of the Building Societies Association. The latter ratio did, however, pick up subsequently to just under 80 per cent in 1976.

14. This argument was developed in the parallel context of the small firm by M. Kalecki, 'The Principle of Increasing Risk,' *Economica*, November 1937, p. 442.

15. See A. J. L. Catt, 'Credit Risk and Credit Rationing,' *Quarterly Journal of Economics*, August 1963 and 'Credit Rationing and the Keynesian Model,' *Economic Journal*, June 1965.

16. For a detailed discussion see Graham Ashmore, *The Owner-Occupied Housing Market*, Research Memorandum No. 41, Centre for Urban and Regional Studies, University of Birmingham, April 1975. The effect on dwelling prices is also discussed in George Hadjimatheou, *Housing and Mortgage Markets*, Great Britain, Saxon House, 1976, Chapter 3. The excellent paper by Byatt, Holmans

and Laidler (see n. 11) concentrates on the years 1967 and 1968.
17. See R. L. Harrington, 'Housing – Supply and Demand,' *National Westminster Bank Quarterly Review*, May 1972, p. 48.
18. The notion of 'false trading' owes much to the writings of J. R. Hicks and R. W. Clower, but the equilibrating mechanism that operates through *quantity* rather than price adjustments, i.e. the one especially relevant to the housing market, was explored by A. Leijonhufvud, *On Keynesian Economics and the Economics of Keynes*, London, Oxford University Press, 1966, Chapter 2.

Index